Reality Television

Reality Television

Richard M. Huff

791.456
H889r

The Praeger Television Collection
David Bianculli, Series Editor

11/06

PRAEGER

Westport, Connecticut
London

Library of Congress Cataloging-in-Publication Data

Huff, Richard M.
    Reality television / Richard M. Huff
        p. cm.—(The praeger television collection, ISSN 1549-2257)
    Includes bibliographical references and index.
    ISBN 0-275-98170-3
    1. Reality television programs—United Stateds. 1. Title. II Series.
PN1992.8.R43H84   2006
791.45'6—dc22   2006007247

British Library Cataloguing in Publication Data is available.

Library of Congress Catalog Card Number: 2006007247
ISBN: 0-275-98170-3
ISSN: 1549-2257

First published in 2006

Praeger Publishers, 88 Post Road West, Westport, CT 06881
An imprint of Greenwood Publishing Group, Inc.
www.praeger.com

Printed in the United States of America

The paper used in this book complies with the
Permanent Paper Standard issued by the National
Information Standards Organization (Z39.48-1984).

10 9 8 7 6 5 4 3 2 1

To Michelle, Ryan, Paige, and Dolly, with love.

Contents

Contents

Introduction

The introduction of reality television into the American media landscape has been nothing short of a revolution. In a mere matter of years, this newfangled genre has infiltrated virtually every corner of the television world and very quickly become a staple of every television programmer's arsenal of program choices.

No wonder: some of the most watched shows in the past six years have been reality fare, ranging from *Survivor* to *American Idol* and *Joe Millionaire*. Moreover, some reality television draws loads of family viewing and a majority of the genre appeals to younger, more elusive viewers. In many ways, the appeal of reality television has been that it could be the viewer, or the viewer's neighbor, right there on the small screen. Or at least that was the early appeal.

Back when *The Real World* first broke on to MTV's lineup in 1992, the program brought so-called real people to television in what were to be nonacting roles. Viewers of the music channel saw themselves in the seven fresh faces that made it into the first house MTV set up in New York.

By 2006, the show was still going strong. The freshness of the faces had changed, so too has the concept a bit, but the heart remains the same: seven strangers, living alone in a manufactured setting, all designed to entertain us, the viewers.

And it works. *Survivor* provided that proof years later, when it actually launched the reality revolution in the United States. With a media marketing plan designed to encourage leaks—and thereby bring more coverage—and a group of players who were brand new to a prime-time schedule that was filled with the usual TV and movie stars, *Survivor* became an instant phenomenon.

Overnight, scheming players like Richard Hatch, the loveable but cranky former military man Rudy Boesch, and the rough-around-the-edges Susan Hawk became household names. And in the course of one summer, the medium of television was changed forever.

No longer special, reality has become mainstream. Every network has dabbled in it from broadcast to cable, and with topics ranging from sports to sex. And they're hitting on all the emotions routinely manipulated in the past by scripted entertainment. There's the laughter and the real heart in a show such as *Beauty and the Geek*, where self-proclaimed geeks hang out with beautiful, if seemingly dim, women. There are the ups and downs, and the thrill of victory in a show like *The Biggest Loser*, in which folks try to lose weight. And there's the intimidation and determination of *The Apprentice*, where a group of entrepreneurs try to impress the intimidating billionaire Donald Trump.

In less than a decade, this new form of television has transformed everyday people with a hankering for attention into media stars. Many have little talent, leading to the suggestion that a willingness to make a fool of oneself is now enough to become a TV star. Other players, having seen the value in being a villain on a reality show, have milked that persona for work long beyond the run of their series.

The fact is, the prevalence of reality television has also worked its way into other forms of media. References to reality television have turned up in songs by rockers Bowling for Soup and by country singer Brad Paisley. Catch phrases from some of the shows have entered the lexicon, as well. After *The Apprentice* launched, viewers walked around repeating Donald Trump's tagline "You're fired." Trump even tried to trademark the phrase and sell t-shirts. And after *Survivor* hit big, people walked around saying "The tribe has spoken," the line delivered by host Jeff Probst as he's showing a player off the game.

For all the good stuff reality television has brought viewers, over the short time since reality programming has taken off, it's also gotten a bad rap in some circles. Actors and writers, upset they've lost work because of the push toward unscripted programming, have slammed the genre. Some critics have lambasted the form because in many shows contestants are forced to humiliate themselves for a shot at a grand prize. And others have complained about the unsavory content in some shows.

Despite the negative stabs, it is undeniable that viewers have an appetite for the format. *American Idol*, in its fifth cycle, continued to be a dominant force in early 2006, drawing nearly 30 million viewers with every episode and showing no signs of letting up. ABC's *Dancing with the Stars* proved that contestants need not eat bugs to draw big ratings. And the twelfth cycle of *Survivor* was still a huge draw for CBS, proving that a quality reality show, with producers willing to tweak the concept each time out, can last for years.

Sure, there have been a few scandals spread through reality television, which, in hindsight, were blown out of proportion. That's because somehow the media expected the "real" people on reality programs to be better than the average folks on the street. That simply did not happen.

Several years into the run of reality programming the emphasis on real people being on the show shifted to an emphasis on the situations being real, or at the very least seeming real. Average audiences don't seem to mind, based on the ratings, that some of the players may have appeared elsewhere before or, perhaps, were once actors. Now, viewers expect the same things from reality programs they expected from scripted entertainment. Is it funny? Is it dramatic? Is it good?

Just like scripted fare, reality television falls into a couple of categories, which you'll see in the pages ahead. There are competition programs, such as *American Idol*. There are twist shows, like *Joe Schmo* and *Joe Millionaire*, where the contestants are tricked into believing one thing when another is actually going on. There are workplace shows, such as *Family Plots* and *Family Bonds*.

This book also takes a look at some of the scandals that have hit reality television in its infancy. There's a peek into the casting process and what makes people go on a reality show in the first place. We delve into the rampant copycat situation in reality programming, a phenomenon that is more prevalent than in any other genre of television. And there's a look at what happens to people after they go on a reality program.

Reality programming is evolving with every new television season. What remains consistent, though, are the inspirations. Looking at a list of shows that have come as reality has grown, and it's easy to see the roots of a series. *Survivor* and the concept of throwing people together, then whittling them down through challenges and votes, all for big prizes, runs through many shows. *Who Wants to Marry a Multimillionaire* is the thread holding all reality scandals together. Over and over, the message is clear: casting is king.

The sheer number of new shows populating network lineups have dwindled a bit from the rush following the success of *Survivor*. The number of shows has leveled off a bit. The good ones survive, the bad ones fade away, and already there's a long list of failed reality shows such as *The Will*, where a family battled for the fortune of a man not yet dead, and *Wickedly Perfect*, a search for a new home guru, à la Martha Stewart.

But for all the failed shows, there are still hits. As long as viewers continue to tune in, television programmers will look for new, wacky concepts in reality. And we viewers will no doubt sit back and wonder why people would be willing to eat boiled pig rectum or put themselves on display on TV in such goofy ways.

However, while we're wondering why they're doing it, we're also laughing along with them, feeling their heartache when they lose, and, ultimately, being entertained. As viewers, we can't ask for more from television, no matter where the stars come from.

It doesn't hurt, either, if you're willing to eat live cockroaches or make a fool of yourself.

Richard Huff
Atlantic Highlands, NJ
February 26, 2006

CHAPTER 1

Survivor: The Start of It All

One by one, the *Survivor* castoffs got up and peppered Richard Hatch and Kelly Wigglesworth with questions. After 39 days on the small island of Pulau Tiga, off the coast of Borneo, it came down to this. A handful of the most recent people kicked off the strangely alluring TV reality game came back to serve as a jury—the ultimate decision makers—to decide who would become the first winner of *Survivor*.

More than 51 million people were watching at home on a hot August night. Many more, not recorded by Nielsen Media Research (the official bean counters of television viewing) were watching in bars and at parties outside of their homes, where viewership isn't counted for the record books.

But the real heat was on the televisions, where the highly anticipated finale of the first edition of *Survivor* was unfolding. The end had been filmed months earlier. The outcome, the source of speculation for much of the summer, had been successfully kept under wraps by nervous CBS executives as well as the cast and crew. At stake was $1 million, but few could have imagined that when the finale was filmed, it would change the face of television forever and become a catalyst for perhaps one of the most significant shifts in programming for decades.

On location of the show, though, around a campfire, in the darkened night, the remaining jury of seven former players came back to vote a winner between Hatch and Wigglesworth. The setting was tribal—right off of what could have been the backdrop for a Walt Disney World theme park ride.

However, this was a different kind of ride, one not created by Disney Imagineers, but rather television producers and network executives. It was a television ride that had captured its passengers—in this case, the viewers—from the first hill and continued to entertain throughout.

Hatch, a corporate trainer from Rhode Island, was best known as the openly gay player who spent much of his time on the game—and on-screen—parading around nude. Going in, he considered *Survivor* a game and played it that way. He stabbed fellow players in the back; he schemed, wheeled and dealed, made and broke alliances, and did whatever he could to manipulate his way into the finale. He did so without shame and fully focused on winning at all costs.

Wigglesworth, his only competitor at that point for the $1 million jackpot, was originally from Las Vegas, though she was working as a California river-raft guide when she was cast on the show. Wigglesworth was not the most well-liked player on *Survivor* and was almost voted off by her fellow castaways on several occasions. Yet she had made it to the key moment when she was just one vote away from a $1 million prize. And, frankly, she was presented as the most likeable between two unlikable choices for the viewers and fellow competitors.

CBS's telecast of the *Survivor* finale was one of the most anticipated programs of summer 2000. That's because the audience for *Survivor* had grown in each of the previous 13 weeks, as each installment's drama created water cooler fodder. The media, fueled in part by its own interest and the seemingly insatiable appetite of the viewers for anything *Survivor* related, had been whipped into a frenzy.

And the media attention—newspapers around the country printed special sections, weekly newsmagazines offered updates, and the Internet had sites devoted to the show—was not unfounded. Viewers held weekly parties in their homes so friends could chat about the outcome. To them this was a social event on the scale of the Super Bowl and treated accordingly.

Web sites sprang up devoted to following every word, whisper, and clue in the series. Rumors about potential winners spread all summer long, prompted partly by CBS's decision early on to not comment about any aspect of the show. "We won't confirm reports of speculation of who won *Survivor*," CBS spokesman Chris Ender told *The New York Daily News* in the weeks leading up to the finale. "We are allowing the press to run inaccurate information."

CBS's public relations strategy was brilliant. By not saying anything about the results of the game throughout, executives thereby encouraged more stories. When speculation surfaced about any of the players, real or not, it was often published, along with CBS's "no comment." Conspiracy theories were playing out in newspapers, online, and around offices all over the country. This unproven on a large scale form of television had gripped TV viewers at a point when there was no giant audience draw. Interest in the final episode capped a 10-month frenzy that developed around *Survivor*. And few could have predicted the growth of the show.

Word of the show's existence first surfaced in *USA Today* in October 1999, when the newspaper reported on CBS's radical plan to drop 16 so-called regular people on a tiny island and force them to fend for themselves. The idea was to have camera crews follow the players as they spent 39 days on Pulau Tiga, a small island near Borneo in the South China Sea. There, they would be forced to live together, compete for the right to remain in the game, and find food and shelter. And, then, every three days they would gather to vote one of the competitors off, until just one remained.

It was an odd, contrived test of sorts to see how people would live together without creature comforts. It was a test to see how they interacted with each other when at times they would have to rely on each other to survive, and yet would also have to turn on one another in the voting process. More important, it was a dramatic test whether viewers would stick with a show like *Survivor,* the likes of which had never been seen before by American audiences. "The entire winning and losing is nothing but group dynamics," producer Mark Burnett told *USA Today*. "Everything is designed to create tension in the group. It's really like a human experiment in some ways."

Burnett, a former solider in the British Army, was a producer at the time best known for the Discovery Channel's *Eco-Challenge,* a race that pitted teams of competitors against a grueling landscape. *Survivor* was different, though. Unlike *Eco-Challenge,* there was no race, no finish line to reach. The concept for *Survivor* was adapted from a show created by Charlie Parsons and had been successful in Sweden and the Netherlands. Burnett wrote in his book, *Jump In,* that he had first heard of the idea of a *Survivor*-like show in 1995 while at Fox pitching his *Eco-Challenge* race series. Parsons's version of *Survivor* had players trying to survive on a desert island while the host lived offshore on a fancy yacht. Burnett met with Parsons in 1998 and bought the North American rights to his show.

"I had a gut feeling that I could make this great concept even greater," Burnett wrote. "My *Survivor* would be bigger, more dramatic, and more epic than any nonfiction television ever seen."

The key was that *Survivor* was to be nonfiction in nature, and built around regular people, not actors, in the key roles. Before *Survivor* all but a handful of the programs on television were scripted entertainment fare, usually dramas and comedies. The only other shows on the air at the time to use nonactors as the main cast were MTV's *The Real World*, which put seven strangers under the same roof, and several other combinations of clip shows, such as *America's Funniest Home Videos*, which was built around video footage of funny moments. There were also game shows, such *as The Price Is Right?* built around regular folks. And there was Fox's long-running *Cops*, in which camera crews tracked teams of police officers as they went about their jobs.

The truth was, however, at the time *Survivor* surfaced, reality programming wasn't considered an upscale format. Moreover, the genre had been damaged in part by many clip specials airing on Fox, which tended to run the gamut from images of crooks being collared by cops to footage of animals biting people to really bad car crashes.

To that end, Fox further damaged the genre—in the minds of viewers and advertisers, who make television possible in the first place—when in early 2000 it aired *Who Wants to Marry a Multimillionaire*.

On that show, a bevy of women readied to marry a multimillionaire at the end of the two-hour program. Viewers saw Rick Rockwell select a former nurse named Darva Conger and allegedly marry her on the spot. Trouble developed early though, when they failed to connect on their honeymoon. Later it was revealed that a former Rockwell girlfriend had filed for a restraining order against him, suggesting Fox producers could have set up Conger or the other women for danger.

The fallout was so bad after *Who Wants to Marry a Multimillionaire* that Fox executives backed off the genre—a bit. "You've got to take a really hard look at these things," Fox Entertainment group chairman Sandy Grushow told reporters then. "We are all playing with fire here, and someone is going to get burned." Little did he know how badly burned the networks would be down the road, when more reality show scandals emerged, some even at Fox.

Who Wants to Marry a Multimillionaire? backlash notwithstanding, none of the previous reality shows promised to do what *Survivor* did, which was to strand folks on an island.

It wasn't an easy task for Burnett, who at the time was known just for the *Eco-Challenge* races, which garnered good critical reviews but were far from career-making programs. First Burnett needed to convince a network to buy into the concept and fund production. He pitched executives at Discovery, who said no. So did the USA Network, Fox, NBC, ABC, and CBS. The fledgling network UPN, Burnett wrote, liked the idea but couldn't afford the production.

Yet Burnett got another shot at CBS when executive Ghen Maynard said he liked the concept and got Burnett to pitch the head of the company, Leslie Moonves. Moonves said yes, launching Burnett on his way to *Survivor* fame.

Once the concept was revealed publicly and the search was on for contestants, Burnett had the media—and ultimately potential fans—hooked. The media immediately picked up on the notion and dove into the story of stranding people on an island for money. Never mind that the folks would be surrounded by camera crews and not in real danger should something terrible happen. For instance, even *Survivor*, like *Eco-Challenge*, has a trained medical team on hand. Reporters gobbled up every little detail of how the people would survive, or not, and when CBS would air the show.

More than 6,000 people filled out CBS's lengthy *Survivor* application and provided a three-minute videotape in which they explained why they should be on the show. The tapes were all over the place in terms of quality and content. Some appeared nude, or crazy. Sean Kenniff, one of those who were eventually cast on the show, in his audition tape stood in a shower sur-rounded by plastic snakes and bugs.

CBS followed up with auditions in each of the cities where it owned television stations, including the two largest media markets, New York and Los Angeles. CBS officials and Burnett decided on 16 contestants. Among them were Kenniff, a 30-year-old neurologist, a 64-year-old retired chief executive officer, a 29-year-old chemist, and a 23-year-old college student. The casting of *Survivor* was genius. Burnett & Co. picked a dis-parate bunch of players, with a wide range of ages and experiences. Rudy Boesch, a 72-year-old ex–Navy SEAL, was the grandfather of the group and brought a tough, fight-to-the-end attitude. Jenna Lewis, a 22-year-old single mom, immediately became annoying to her fellow players and view-ers at home. Colleen Haskell, a college student, was the strong, likeable, young girl. Stacey Stillman, a lawyer, bothered fellow players by constantly complaining. And, Ramona Gray, a chemist from New Jersey, earned early sympathy because she vomited the first day.

The eight men and eight women were dropped off at Pulau Tiga in March 2000, where they learned quickly to live on the nature preserve filled with snakes, rats, scorpions, sand fleas, lizards, monkeys, and mosquitoes. The 16 players were divided into two teams, or tribes, called the Tagi and the Pagong. They were given a daily ration of rice, but needed to walk for two hours to get fresh water. There were no tents, blankets, or matches. To supplement the rice, contestants began to fish with handmade spears and catch clawless lobsters with their hands. And, when fishing didn't work, they turned to rats, which they trapped and cooked. "It tastes like rat," castaway Joel Klug said when the episode aired later. "Almost like chicken, a little bit. Just use your imagination."

Burnett added to the intrigue—some critics said humiliation—by having the players compete in contests every few days. Among the early ones: eating live worms.

"Without question, getting along with each other is the hardest challenge facing them," host Jeff Probst told the *New York Daily News*. "It's 100-degree heat; there isn't much food or water. You're starving, and everybody has their own peculiar habits you have to put up with. I think there are a whole lot of times the contestants just clench their jaw and count to 10."

The early wave of media attention to the show paid off for CBS. The network sold all of the advertising time on the show to eight companies— before the first episode aired. That's an amazing feat considering no one in the United States had seen the show before and advertisers were buying on faith—and the salesmanship of Burnett—that the show would work in the all-important Nielsen department.

Despite the extensive hype leading up to the launch, network executives were loath to talk publicly about how large the audience for *Survivor* could be. CBS chairman Leslie Moonves told reporters a week before the show launched that it was less risky to put it on in the summer when viewing levels were smaller than during the traditional September to May television season. Besides the smaller audiences, competition from new shows is relatively limited in the summer, too. "I wouldn't put it on Oct. 1, but win, lose or draw, we'll make a profit on it," Moonves said.

Yet CBS launched *Survivor* in June 2000 against an episode of ABC's *Who Wants to Be a Millionaire*, a game show hosted by Regis Philbin that a summer earlier had also become a genuine television phenomenon.

Before *Millionaire*, the game show had been considered a dying genre. But, with Philbin at the helm, and little strong competition programming-wise, *Millionaire* drew millions of viewers at a time when many folks shunned prime-time television. *Millionaire* instantly became a hit and made Philbin, a longtime entertainment figure, a pop-culture icon. His tagline "Is that your final answer?" entered the lexicon and was repeatedly endlessly.

What CBS did, though, with the first outing of *Survivor* was to force viewers to choose between ABC's strongest show and the much-hyped reality. From a programming standpoint, it was daring of CBS executives to try the new show against *Millionaire*, proven hit. On the surface it seemed like a foolish move. But CBS's research to that point had indicated *Millionaire* was not appointment viewing—meaning viewers marked their calendars or rushed home to watch; rather, it was default viewing, meaning that viewers stumbled on it after searching, and failing, to find other options.

In the first head-to-head outing, *Millionaire* drew more viewers. However, the pattern changed the following week, when viewership for *Survivor* surged 17 percent from its premiere to 18.12 million viewers, according to Nielsen Media Research.

The increase in viewers for *Survivor* was just the start. It was also unusual. Typically, the audience for a new series goes down in the second week, once the hype for the launch has evaporated. But with *Survivor* the buzz was just beginning. And the show was far from usual, which helped push the word-of-mouth chatter about the show.

Newspapers covered the show as if it were a true sporting event, giving it just as much attention as a local ballgame and treating each night's episode, although taped months earlier, as if it were unfolding live that night. The main difference, of course, is that the ballgame was real, and live, whereas *Survivor* was, as Burnett has said, a "contrived" game, that had already been played out and was only being seen by America's viewing audience.

Attention to the show was pushed by CBS's media plan, which involved all of the contestants being legally silenced until they were kicked off the show, and then only speaking to the media after they appeared on CBS's *The Early Show*. CBS officials helped keep the secret of who won by threatening a $5 million lawsuit—a provision in the contestant's contract with the show—for anyone who leaked sensitive details about the outcome of *Survivor* to the media. The legal threats also extended out to the players' families. Even media members, allowed to witness insignificant events during press trips to the *Survivor* setting, were forced to sign nondisclosure agreements that threatened legal action if the reports ran before predetermined dates. CBS officials feared that newspaper stories containing any key details, such as who was (or wasn't) in a scene, could tip off viewers to the outcome of challenges or even the show. Moreover, no one got paid for appearing on the show until after the finale ended, giving all of the contestants an added incentive to keep their lips zipped.

That didn't stop others from talking about the series, though. Show fans flooded online message boards with theories of what happened on the show and why. The mix of players gave viewers of all ages someone to root for. And, over time, as the contestants were whittled down, viewers began to follow their stories, such as the relationship between Jenna Lewis and her two daughters. That attachment to the players is what helped to keep people coming back to the set.

Fans scoured every episode looking for clues either intentionally or inadvertently left in the show that helped reveal what was ahead. Some went through on-air promotions for upcoming episodes looking for clues, such as who was wearing an immunity necklace or who might have been left out of the promo. And the Internet was awash in fan sites devoted to unlocking the name of the winner of *Survivor*.

For example, in July 2000, about a month before the August finale, a cyberfan on the now-defunct Web site Survivorsucks.com claimed to have figured out that contestant Gervase Petersen won the game. The fan, in checking the computer code on images at CBS's Web site, found that all but Petersen's had a red "X," the signal the network would add later on for all kicked-off contestants. The thinking, as put forth on the site, was that his picture would never be marked with the red "X" because he won. There was also a promotional clip of a future tribal council including four people, one of them Petersen. Petersen, however, was voted off in an episode that aired on August 3. "I suspect that CBS has anticipated and been throwing us curves this whole journey," wrote a fan at Survivorsucks.com.

The fan was right. Network staffers and Burnett had been throwing curves all along, which helped drive interest in the program. CBS staffers also went to great lengths to keep the outcome of the show a secret. All footage from the final tribal council was locked up, although everyone at the taping knew who the winner was. All of those people were also legally bound to be quiet.

Leading up to the finale, there were dozens of theories, predictions, and stories about the end of the show and what it meant to the players and television in general. Reporters scoured government databases, legal documents, and the hometowns of players remaining just to get some insight into what made them go on television in the first place. For example, was someone all of a sudden buying extravagant gifts, which would have been a clue of a sudden jackpot.

"It's about 16 strangers, abandoned and forced to form their own society, voting someone out every three days," said Probst. "And here's the kicker, it's a really complicated social game. How do you navigate, how do you vote people out you're living with? There's that … sort of feeling of being lost and you combine it with being the last kid picked from a sandlot baseball game, or the last guy laid off; those are iconic, atypical moments." Whatever the draw, viewers were hooked.

Four players remained at the start of the finale. Besides Hatch and Wigglesworth, still in the game were Boesch, who, despite his age, remained tough throughout. And there was Susan Hawk, a brassy, brash Wisconsin truck driver. Hawk was the first to get the boot in the final show.

It started with a "Fallen Comrades Immunity Challenge," in which players were asked questions about the contestants previously kicked off the show. Wigglesworth won immunity, meaning she couldn't be voted off. In the first vote, there was a tie between Hatch and Hawk. Then, in a second vote, Wigglesworth voted against Hawk, sending her off with a simple "sorry."

The contestants' final day on the island started at dawn, with the three remaining players wiping mud all over their bodies in some sort of ritual, while remembering the players that had been kicked off before them. They walked over hot coals and then, for the final immunity challenge, had to place one hand on the immunity idol. The last person to remove their hand would earn immunity and a seat in the final two. After hours in the sun, Hatch moved his hand first, leaving Boesch and Wigglesworth to battle for immunity. But then, four hours and 11 minutes into the contest, Boesch moved his hand while repositioning his body. The inadvertent motion gave Wigglesworth immunity. More important, it also set her up to cast the deciding vote of whom she would be pitted against in the tribal council. She voted against Boesch.

In the last hour of the two-hour finale, Hatch and Wigglesworth appeared in the last tribal council. Each was able to make a speech to the jury, and then each of the seven members was able to ask a question of Hatch and Wigglesworth. Lewis asked each player whom he or she would pick if they could chose two other people to be sitting in the final tribal council. And Greg Buis simply asked each to pick a number between 1 and 10. Hawk, who was open and honest along the way, went into the jury process still steaming about being cut out in the end. "On this island, there are only snakes and rats," Hawk said in an emotional tirade. "In the end, let it be as Mother Nature intended: Let the snake eat the rat." She then voted for Hatch. He won by just one vote—4 to 3—over Wigglesworth. "I came to play the game," Hatch said then. "Instead of who's the better person, it's about who plays the game better."

The *Survivor* finale rivaled the end of *Seinfeld* and *M*A*S*H* in terms of attention to the outcome. However, aside from pure ratings, the finale and the whole season of *Survivor* changed the face of television—forever. In a matter of 13 weeks, CBS significantly launched the reality craze and had other producers and networks scrambling to find shows starring real people. Moreover, network executives were being flooded with pitches for reality series that ran the gamut from mundane ideas to outlandish.

Before *Survivor,* the reality genre had been considered an afterthought, driven largely by cheap clip shows of people looking stupid in home videos (*America's Funniest Home Videos),* wild police chases, or when animals do bad things to people. Even Sandy Grushow, who just months earlier backed off of the reality genre after the fallout from *Who Wants to Marry a Multimillionaire?* changed strategies. "Something happened this summer that I don't think anyone could have predicted," he told reporters in January 2001. "A little show called *Survivor* came along and turned the prime-time network landscape on its ear. Not only was the show a success, it became a cultural phenomenon. The audience has spoken and they have demonstrated that they have a huge appetite for this type of non-scripted program. So we're going to try to take advantage of that."

He was not alone. The series also created the first real wave of the new reality stars, essentially people with no celebrity credibility before appearing in a reality series, but who came out being invited to red-carpet events and landing lucrative commercial deals. Being on a reality show became a cottage industry for some. A new breed of stars was created, hopscotching from reality concept to reality concept. Where they were once regular people—although many, it turned out, were actors looking for a break—they were now stars on some level.

Thanks to *Survivor,* reality would become a true staple of television programming, finding a spot on every network's schedule. As a result, reality television changed the way programmers looked at prime-time television and how every other producer of programming would look at the medium again. The impact of *Survivor*'s success has been felt in all parts of television, from daytime dramas and sitcoms to sporting events. Having won $1 million, Hatch's life would never be the same and because of a single series—neither would television.

CHAPTER 2

Where Does This Stuff Come From?

Scan the pages of any television history book and you're likely to be able to spot some roots of the reality show genre that would develop in the mid-1990s and fully flourish after 2000.

Indeed, those roots are planted throughout television history, starting with and including some of the early shows. They weren't called reality television back then. That term wouldn't come into serious play until 2000, when CBS and producer Mark Burnett introduced American television viewers to a newfangled program called *Survivor*, in which he shipped 16 regular people off to a small island in the South China Sea where they lived for 39 days, with one getting kicked off every third day, in hopes of being the last person standing and earning a $1 million payday.

Although *Survivor* clearly gets credit for launching the reality or unscripted program craze that started in 2000, the show wasn't the first full-fledged reality program to hit American shores. No doubt, without *Survivor* the reality craze wouldn't have started in 2000 and continue well into the decade. There would be no reality scandals. The American pop culture landscape would be without such characters as Omarosa Manigault-Stallworth from *The Apprentice*, Richard Hatch from *Survivor*, Kelly Clarkson from *American Idol*, or Richard Rubin from *Beauty and the Geek*. Without *Survivor* Donald Trump's visibility may not have increased tenfold during the 2000 decade.

Although *Survivor* can serve as the touchstone for jumpstarting the reality boom in 2000, it was actually *The Real World* in 1992 that brought the concept of reality television to the American audience. The show was conceived and produced by Mary-Ellis Bunim and Jonathan Murray. Before *The Real World*, Bunim worked on such soap operas as *Santa Barbara* and *As the World Turns*. Murray worked in news and documentaries.

The executives at MTV sought out Bunim for her soap opera background. Network officials wanted her to create a scripted soap starring young people, exactly like the kind that watched the music channel. When they got the proposal, however, network officials bailed out because the costs were too high. Bunim and Murray then offered a show using real people in a similar situation, without scripts. MTV executives agreed, and agreed with the creative duo's suggestion of having the subjects live in a really nice loft.

The Real World took seven different people from around the country and had them live in a cool New York City apartment. It was no regular apartment, though. Producers and editors were sequestered in a separate room and camera crews tracked the inhabitants' every move. The residents of the first *Real World* house were in their 20s and hit squarely within MTV's audience demographics. One was a budding rap artist, Heather B; one a poet and writer, Kevin Powell; one a budding folk artist, Rebecca Blasband; and another a painter, Norman Korpi. Some were street-smart and well aware of life in a big city.

"Seven strangers, picked to live in a house, to find out what happens when people stop being polite and start getting real," said a narrator at the beginning of the show. One, a woman named Julie Oliver from Birmingham, Alabama, left her parents back home to live in the city. Her family was against the move. And, with the cameras rolling, Oliver was seen talking about her differences with her father. Her father didn't much like African-Americans, and his daughter was going to be living with two. But that was part of the appeal. The cultural conflicts and the socio-economic differences between the housemates made it seem like real life, and watchable. In some ways, the cast made it seem like it could be any college dorm or apartment complex. Watching Oliver go right into a situation of which her parents didn't approve was immensely entertaining.

In the first episode, the group was shown sitting around a table introducing themselves. Suddenly, while they were talking a beeper belonging to rapper Heather B went off. Julie then asked Heather if she sold drugs. Heather was upset, though then offered to teach Julie about African-Americans. The other housemates offered to show Julie around New York City.

The initial episode and subsequent shows were mesmerizing. Because it had never been done before, the reactions, albeit influenced by the camera crews, seemed real and realistic at the time. "We set up the situation purposefully so there would be conflict and sexual tension," Murray told the *Los Angeles Times* when the show launched. "The loft was a real pressure cooker. I mean, there are times in these episodes where people are literally in each other's face screaming at the top of their lungs."

Real World house dwellers talked to each other, moved around the city to various locations, and then talked about each other in what would become the first "confessional" segments in reality show history. In the debut episode one of the housemates complained that Eric Nies, a model from New Jersey, cared too much about his looks. And Rebecca, the budding folk singer, suggested that Eric and Julie had chemistry between them. Cast members were paid $2,600 for the three month experiment. All totaled, it cost MTV $107,000 per episode to produce.

"What *The Real World* did was come up with the idea of setting up a completely artificial family, under artificial circumstances and do *An American Family* treatment," said Professor Robert Thompson, who heads up Syracuse University's Center for Popular Television.

Before *The Real World* the closest viewers could come to seeing a real family develop before their eyes was the groundbreaking PBS series *An American Family*. The 1973 series followed the Loud Family, headed by William and Pat, going about their daily lives. Along the way viewers saw Pat ask her husband for a divorce and son Lance reveal he was gay.

The major difference between *The Real World* and *An American Family* is that the latter was a documentary, whereas the former was a created television experiment. The Louds were filmed in their home living their lives. Producers did not create situations; they happened before the cameras.

"[The purpose of] *The Real World* was not to do a reality documentary, but to create this entirely artificial, contrived world ... with rules, and then put people into that contrived world without scripts," Thompson said. "None of those people would have been in that *Real World* house otherwise."

Critics had mixed reactions to the new format, and the show, which, expectedly was compared to *An American Family*, which came nearly two decades before. "Watching *The Real World*, which fails as documentary (too phony) and as entertainment (too dull), it's hard to tell who's using who more," wrote Matt Roush in *USA Today*.

"Sure, its lightweight video-verite for the *Beverly Hills, 90210* set (how clever of MTV to schedule it right afterward). But it's also weirdly compelling. And while the experiment itself was loaded with artifice, it makes most mainstream TV series, with their wise parents and wise-cracking kids, seem so, well, artificial," wrote Phil Kloer in the *Atlanta Journal-Constitution*.

The show was a hit for MTV and made the seven housemates stars with the MTV crowd. Yet, perhaps because it was on MTV, the show didn't break out the way, say, *Survivor* would do in 2000 or *American Idol*. Surely it was a big draw with MTV's target audience, and the cast became regulars with the teen-beat set. But, it was far from family viewing—one aspect that helped drive *Survivor* and *American Idol* into the Nielsen Media Research stratosphere.

"When we first started the show, it was very experimental.... I'm not sure any of us thought there was much that would happen beyond those first 13 episodes," Murray told the *San Jose Mercury News* in 2001. (Bunim died of breast cancer in 2004.) Much did happen beyond those 13 episodes, however. In 2006, MTV aired its seventeenth version of the show, set in Key West, Florida, and was in preproduction for future editions.

The Real World was demographically aimed at MTV's core audience, which might have saved it from being ripped off repeatedly by rival networks. During the reality craze of the early 2000s, when one network had a hit with a show, rivals tried to copy it. But, for much of its early run, *The Real World* stood alone. It was copied in countries all over the world, but in America, for years, it was the only show of its kind. "Instead of network executives looking at it, they ignored it," Thompson said.

Overseas, however, *The Real World* would become the model for *Big Brother,* which was then brought back to the United States and made a regular summer offering for CBS.

Bunim and Murray would use *The Real World* as the model for *Road Rules,* another reality show that had a group of players traipsing around the country in a Winnebago and completing various tasks along the way.

The Real World and later *Road Rules* are the ground zero of the current reality wave, with Bunim and Murray being the true parents of the genre. At the time *The Real World* hit, despite the easy and obvious comparisons to *An American Family*, it was truly a revolutionary format. No matter what critics said about the concept, and some were brutal in describing the show and the newfangled way of putting people together, it was different than anything anyone had seen before. *An American Family* was a documentary; *The Real World* was anything but.

Before *The Real World* hit there were some evolutionary phases along the way, although they would occur decades before MTV launched its show. The fact is that most came during the 1950s, a period commonly referred to as the Golden Age of television. And, looking back, they were marginal steps toward today's reality shows.

The first step happened in 1948, when NBC launched *I'd Like to See*. Viewers were asked to write in what they would like to see on television or places they would like to go. Producers then presented the requests with either in-studio demonstrations or footage, or a combination of both. This was years before cross-country travel was the norm, so viewers seeing a clip of the United Nations Building or of past presidents were a big deal. Producers later added appearances by Kuda Bux, a man billed as having "X-ray vision." Viewers offered suggestions of what they'd like to see him doing while blindfolded.

I'd Like to See served as the inspiration for *You Asked for It,* a series that launched in 1950 on the Dumont Network as the *Art Baker Show.* Just as with *I'd Like to See, You Asked for It* relied on suggestions from viewers for what they would like to see. For example, viewers asked for, and got, a look into the vault at Fort Knox.

Neither show was called "reality" at the time because the term in TV land just didn't exist. Frankly, the comparison to today's reality fare is weak at best. The shows used viewer suggestions and at times showed odd or unusual nonactors doing different things. Yet, they were closer to what quiz and audience participation shows would morph into.

Lines to the realty wave of 2000 and beyond can also be drawn to *This Is Your Life.* Created in the late 1940s by Ralph Edwards for radio, the show made it to broadcast television in 1952 on NBC. Edwards would open every show by whispering to the audience and then asking them to come along as he surprised someone by walking into their office or on stage, in the case of a celebrity, and saying, "This is your life." Edwards carried a large book in his hand, which was supposed to be the story of the person's life. Then, as Edwards outlined the subjects past, people from the featured person's earlier life would walk out and talk about the person. People profiled ranged from average Americans to superstar celebrities. For instance, when he did a piece on Milton Berle, Edwards walked into the famed Brown Derby restaurant where Berle was sitting with Jerry Lewis and Dean Martin. He surprised Johnny Cash by walking on stage during the taping of Cash's television show.

In 1940 on radio, and in 1950 on television, Edwards also hosted *Truth or Consequences,* an audience participation show involving regular people. Contestants were asked trick questions that they usually got wrong. When they got them wrong, the emcee would say that since they lied, they'd have to pay the consequences. Those consequences were usually silly stunts.

In January 1948, Dumont also aired *The Original Amateur Hour* hosted by Ted Mack, an early talent show spotlighting regular folks, which would ultimately serve as the roots for *American Idol, Popstars,* and all other talent shows that came decades later.

By 1954, Art Linkletter was hosting *People Are Funny,* a show that, like Edwards's shows, used regular people in practical jokes and stunts. "Ralph Edwards and I invented reality TV," Linkletter told the *Milwaukee Journal* in 2003. Those shows were nice, Linkletter said, and didn't demean people. "We never dreamed they'd have people eating bugs on TV," he remarked.

However, although there are aspects of Edwards's and Linkletter's shows that appear in the phase of reality that came after, they were really just a few building blocks in the foundation of the format that existed after *Survivor.*

Another one of those building blocks was placed by Allen Funt, who created and hosted *Candid Camera.* Funt and his crew would place hidden cameras in a location and then pull a stunt on an unsuspecting person. The humor then came from their reactions to the situation, which they were not aware was being filmed, and then of Funt, when he stepped out of the shadows to say, "Smile, you're on *Candid Camera.*" For example, one of the stunts was a man rolling a bowling ball down the alley and having a ball without finger holes returned. Another trick involved vending machines that talked.

Another contributor to the reality foundation was Chuck Barris, the creator of *The Dating Game* in 1966 and *The Gong Show* in 1976. Gary Owens was the first host of *The Gong Show,* but Barris took over in 1977. The show was a contest of sorts among a group of amateurs who displayed their goofy and often absurd talents, such as a girl who whistled with her nose, a man who burped to music, and a guy who played the trumpet with his belly button. A gaggle of celebrities served as judges for the frivolity. And the very worst of them were literally gonged off stage during their acts.

"They all began to flit around the edges," said Thompson, "but it took *The Real World* to turn that into a programming form."

Another show during the early days of televisions that easily could have come today was *Queen for a Day,* which started out on radio and launched on television in 1951. Host Jack Bailey presided over the show as four women delivered their sob stories about how bad their lives were at the moment. The audience assessed their stories, and the winner was decided by an applause meter. The woman who told the saddest tale was crowned "Queen for a Day" and won some appliances. "It's not what they want, it's why they want it that counts with us," Bailey said.

To win the prizes, however, the women in some small way had to humiliate themselves—the sadder the story the better. "We were eternally accused of having the saddest show in all the world," Bailey once said. *Queen for the Day* could actually be the precursor of many of the reality shows that followed in the early 2000s, some of which required contestants to do something disgusting to stay viable for a prize. NBC's ratings-rich *Fear Factor*, for example, routinely included a stunt that forces contestants to eat something vile. It could be bugs, it could be internal animal parts, or it could be a mix of junk; no matter what the content, all were vomit inducing.

During the decades after the 1950s wave of game shows, much of the programming dubbed "reality" on television was really little more than documentary footage pieced together with a narrator. Fox got on the bandwagon early with a series of clip shows, piecing together dramatic car crashes or violent animals. Indeed, among the first were police chase videos that incorporated a narrator, real-life police detective John Bunnell, who got his start on a reality show. Bunnell first turned up in *American Detective*, a series that launched in 1991 and followed detectives as they investigated crimes and when they were at home, giving viewers a sense of what their family lives were.

But like *Cops*, the car crash videos were merely collections of clips of real things happening, not created scenarios for real people to react to. Also, outside of *Cops*, which has widely been considered the best of the genre, the clip shows got a horrible reaction from television critics, advertisers, and rival networks. Some of the early reality fare that drew the most criticism were those using clips of animals attacking people. CBS, for instance, had a show called *The World's Most Dangerous Animals III*, which included a clip of a cat biting a man. Fox also drew fire with a series of animals-gone-bad clip shows. In 1996, Don Ohlmeyer, then president of NBC West Coast, called one of Fox's specials "one step short of a snuff film" during a conference call with reporters.

Fox also took heat in early 2000 for airing *Who Wants to Marry a Multimillionaire?* The two-hour live special had 50 women vying in a Miss America–like pageant for a shot at instantly marrying an unseen bachelor. At the end of the show, Rick Rockwell selected and married Darva Conger. But, before their quickie honeymoon was over, it was revealed an old girlfriend had sought a restraining order against Rockwell, leading some critics to suggest he could have hurt Conger. He didn't; however, the marriage was annulled and for a short time the networks shunned reality programming.

Although the early shows hit on some aspect of what would become reality programming, none were as groundbreaking as *The Real World*.

However, for all of the innovations and revelations *The Real World* would bring to the small screen, it would be eight years before *Survivor* would really change the way reality programs impacted the TV medium. After *The Real World* hit, broadcasters abroad picked up on the concept of having real people live before the cameras. The idea of using real people thrived in Europe. The fact is, Mark Burnett, credited with jump-starting reality in the United States with *Survivor,* first heard about a show like *Survivor* in the mid-1990s. What he was hearing was a about a show created by Charlie Parsons that had been successful in Sweden and the Netherlands. Parsons's show was called *Expedition Robinson* and launched in Sweden in 1997. Players were sent to a desert island with very little to eat. They were given one personal item. They were divided into two teams and forced to build their own shelter. There were challenges, which resulted in one team having to go to an island council, where they would vote for one team member to leave the island. The host lived offshore on a yacht.

Burnett bought the North American rights to *Survivor* in 1998, and it launched on CBS in summer 2000. Launching it then gave CBS officials an out if it failed and put the show up against diminished competition elsewhere. (Summer had always been, and still is, a dumping ground for failed series and experiments.) "*Survivor* was, after all, a reality show," Burnett wrote in *Survivor II: The Field Guide.* "And reality shows had taken a big hit after *Who Wants to Marry a Multimillionaire?* aired on Fox. If *Survivor* failed it would ring the death knell for reality shows. So it was, to a great extent, an experiment."

But it worked. The show faced ABC's then-hit *Who Wants to Be a Millionaire?* a game show hosted by Regis Philbin. *Survivor* drew fewer viewers than *Millionaire* the first night out, but soon, *Survivor* was ahead and stayed ahead. It became a true water cooler show, with people talking about what happened the night before the next day at work. Some of the phrases from the show became part of the lexicon. *Survivor* had arrived.

No longer did people shy away from reality—or unscripted dramas, as Burnett called them—as they did after the *Who Wants to Marry a Multimillionaire?* debacle. *Survivor* made reality cool. CBS probably had a sense that this might occur before *Survivor* aired, however; before shooting began on *Survivor,* the network had sold out all of the available commercial time.

In addition to selling out all of the available commercial time, Burnett and his team also laid the groundwork for product integration in reality shows, a feature that has become a fixture ever since. For instance, in *Survivor,* sponsors' products became rewards for challenges. During one of the original episodes, there was a shot of a picnic table sized umbrella that bore the red and white logo of sponsor Target. And in one challenge, the winner received a full meal, including a beer, Budweiser, which was of course a series sponsor. The product placement aspect of reality television would grow dramatically in the future, too. On Burnett's *The Apprentice*, corporate sponsors are made part of the tasks, getting essentially one-hour commercials. Likewise, those sponsors have also sold products based on what the teams in the Donald Trump–fronted series develop. On another level, hairdresser Jonathan Antin continuously promotes himself, and his hair care products, on Bravo's *Blow Out*.

As happens in the television business, once someone has a hit with a program, the rivals begin to jump in with similar shows. *Survivor* had proven to the business and the advertising community that the genre was not dead and could work. More important, it was also, initially, a less expensive format than traditional sitcoms and drama. Producers didn't need to pay actors, although contestants got a small stipend. Production costs were smaller. And the turnaround time from idea to product for the airwaves was shorter.

Conversely, unlike scripted entertainment, there was very little value in reruns. Networks make money on the second telecasts of scripted series. Producers generate large revenues from the sale of reruns to stations around the country. But with reality initially there was very little viewer interest in a second telecast. CBS tried airing the first *Survivor* again right after the initial finale, though few people tuned in. But, by 2005, Fox had launched an all-reality channel, giving a home to reality reruns. Likewise, *Survivor* and other reality show reruns began airing on channels such as Outdoor Life and FX, indicating there was some secondary interest in seeing the shows again.

After *Survivor*, producers began scouring programmers abroad for new reality show ideas. *American Idol*, a powerhouse singing competition for Fox, was a hit in London (as *Pop Idol*) before being done in America. *Supernanny*, a program ABC aired about a nanny that helps families with unruly kids, also started in London. And CBS's *Big Brother*, a show about a group of people locked in a specially designed home while being covered by cameras, started out in Europe first. *Help, I'm a Celebrity, Get Me Out of Here*, which failed in an American version on ABC, was also a British import.

Virtually all of the programs that were created in the wake of *Survivor*'s success can draw a line to *Survivor* for at the very least, inspiration, if not a total concept. The competition angle of *Survivor* was copied for shows such as *Boot Camp* and even *America's Next Top Model*, which had contestants compete in challenges, had one voted off each week, and crowned a winner with a modeling contract. *Survivor* also led to the spoof show

Joe Schmo, which had actors playing the parts of the traditional reality show contestants, and only one nonactor, who wasn't in on the joke. Comedy Central took the spoof concept a step further in 2004 with *Drawn Together*, an animated reality show modeled after *Big Brother* that poked fun at all reality shows and their casts. Viewers can also see similarities to *Survivor* in a variety of shows such as Fox's troubled *Temptation Island*, and any other program that came about after *Survivor* that had people living together and competing for a prize.

And there were many. Early on after *Survivor* was a hit, broadcast and cable networks flooded their airwaves with reality fare. The low budgets combined with the ability of producers to tackle any idea in a short-run reality show made the form very popular. Early shows included *Making of the Band*, in which music producer Lou Pearlman put together an all-male pop group for ABC. The WB tried a similar concept with *Popstars*, though with women. CBS, dipping into the international idea pool, bought *Big Brother*, a reality show similar to *The Real World*, in which inhabitants never leave—unless, that is, they're voted out. Fox rolled out *Boot Camp*, with contestants going through a training camp similar to one military recruits must survive. That network also aired the dating series *Mr. Personality*, in which a group of men wearing masks attempted to win the heart of a single woman. (Former White House intern Monica Lewinsky, best known for her affair with President Clinton, was the host of *Mr. Personality*.) There were shows about restaurants, shows to find fashion designers, and some built around sports.

At one point, *Survivor* producer Mark Burnett even wanted to produce a show about a regular person going into space as part of Russia's Mir program. The show never happened because the Mir program fell apart, but if it had, the WB was ready and willing to air the series.

During the 2003–2004 television season, reality programs made up 13 percent of the prime-time landscape, up from 4 percent in 1999. In the fall of 2004, there were 21 shows on the six broadcast networks prime-time lineups.

Networks turned to reality to fill their programming gaps, and the shows brought in an audience networks wanted to reach: young adults. It was the same group that had shunned many of the comedies and dramas the same networks had offered. But, reality, with its short runs, drew in viewers who would otherwise not commit to a regular series. There was no long-term commitment required from viewers; they knew there were 6, 9, or at most 13 episodes, and the show would be done. Along with that short run came a notion that viewers had to watch; otherwise they would be short of conversation topics the following morning. The shows were also disposable.

"There's a difference between short-term popularity and long-term affection, and even the best of today's reality shows aren't likely to be repeated, much less revered, tomorrow," *New York Daily News* television critic David Bianculli wrote in January 2004.

The reality boom wasn't without problems, many problems. Contestants with shady pasts made it past rudimentary screening processes only to embarrass producers down the road and open networks to more criticism. And early on, not all shows were fully embraced by advertisers, meaning that even some of the better-rated reality couldn't draw blue-chip sponsors. Even though some shows such as *Temptation Island* or *Joe Millionaire* were drawing good or great ratings, the racy content gave advertisers the jitters. Given the ability to try anything, some producers tended to go down market. Mike Fleiss, the producer of *The Bachelor* and *Who Wants to Marry a Multimillionaire?* also produced for ABC *Are You Hot? The Search for America's Hottest People,* in which a team of judges picked apart the looks of men and women standing before them.

American audiences had appetite for the genre, although not nearly as insatiable as the appetite network executives had for the usually cheap genre that was being used willy-nilly to fill holes in schedules where traditional sitcoms or dramas failed. Some critics and television observers suggested the thirst to get more reality, more dramatic reality, often more wacky reality on television was a detriment for the medium in general. Others argued the reliance on the genre at the expense of sitcoms and dramas could have some long-term effects on the entertainment business.

"I guess I've really come around to the opinion that reality television is starting to look a lot like heroin," Dean Valentine told reporters in 2001, when he was president of UPN Entertainment. "You know, a really quick high [in the ratings] and then a really long, long low, then you need another fix again. I think the challenge for networks is to find a way of re-creating the half hour and the hour in a way that attracts that audience that's flocking so quickly to the reality shows.

"Gladiatorial combat," Valentine added, "started with a couple of macho guys beating the hell out of each other, and ended up tossing a bunch of Christians and watching lions tear them apart. "After a while, you need the kick, and the kick has to get higher and higher and higher. I don't really want to be a part of that."

Likewise, reality programming was also an easy target for watchdog groups complaining about the content of prime-time televisions. Often the reality shows, especially the dating-themed ones, had sexually laced storylines, thanks to easy accessibility to hot tubs, inhibition loosening, and readily available alcohol.

"The rising popularity of reality series, especially among young viewers, should give parents pause," wrote officials of the Parents Television Council in a report called "Reality TV: Race to the Bottom." "Even more than their scripted counterparts, reality series wallow in some of the most explicit foul language imaginable. Moreover, they frequently depict real people in real—not staged—sexual situations, turning viewers into voyeurs in a very real sense."

Writing about Fox's *Married by America,* a show that had couples being picked for marriage, *Houston Chronicle* critic Ann Hodges wrote, "Viewers will vote on who should marry whom, and they'll actually get married. Obviously, nothing's sacred in this overdone march from TV's reality mills." Fox, and the 169 stations that aired *Married by America,* were fined by the FCC for airing the show for allegedly indecent content. Each station was fined $7,000 for airing the show, which, according to the FCC documents included "scenes in which partygoers lick whipped cream from strippers' bodies in a sexually suggestive manner. Another scene features a man on all fours in his underwear as two female strippers playfully spank him." In a statement, Fox said, "We disagree with the FCC's decision and believe the content was not indecent."

And in early 2006, the FCC ruled that an episode of *The Surreal Life 2,* a show that put a group of B-level stars in a *Real World* situation for two weeks, was "patently offensive under contemporary community standards for the broadcast medium and thus apparently indecent." In the episode in question, a pool party scene included 20 pixilated views of female breasts. One of those scenes also included actor Andy Dick placing his mouth on the top portion of a woman's breast and making a sound. Making matters worse, the party was thrown by porn star Ron Jeremy, a housemate on *The Surreal Life 2.* In one bit, a female cast member suggested the partygoers play "strip truth or dare to get naked." She then said to Jeremy, "come on porn star, everyone knows about your big [bleep], though I haven't seen it."

The red hot content of many reality shows, while a big viewer draw, is the kind of stuff that made image-conscious advertisers stay away from some reality shows. Call it the *Jerry Springer* effect. Springer's ribald, circuslike show was the hottest thing on daytime talk for one stretch in 1998, even beating the queen of daytime, Oprah Winfrey, that year. However, because his show was laced with guests fighting and women occasionally lifting their shirts to reveal pixilated breasts, advertisers never supported the show on a level fitting for its ratings.

As the proliferation of reality programming continued, there was also a groundswell of concern from Hollywood actors, producers and critics concerned that the growth of this new, low-cost, no-actor product would seriously damage the scripted entertainment business. If network executives put all of the emphasis on reality, there would be no room for any other type of shows. To that end, they argued networks would no longer invest in scripted programming and instead would just order reality programs.

"It's not reality TV. It's good TV versus bad TV," Burnett said. "How many comedies have made it and dramas? Reality is going to be held to the same high standards as scripted stuff." And it was. The good stuff remained, at least most of it. Like good dramas that draw few viewers, there have been several high-quality reality shows that failed to draw a crowd. The bad stuff, well, some of it was gone in an instant, just like a bad comedy. CBS, for instance, whacked a series called *The Will* about a family trying to win the rights to a rich heir's fortune once he went toes up. It was never seen again. Fox drew fire with *Who's Your Daddy*, which revolved around an adopted woman in a game to pick from a group her real father. She found her dad; Fox officials found the show to creepy to handle. Five unseen episodes of that show remain in the network's vaults. Other programs, such as CBS's *Wickedly Perfect*, a show designed to find a new home guru similar to Martha Stewart, never caught on, either.

"I don't know what's going to happen," Kelsey Grammer told reporters just before the series finale of his sitcom *Frasier* in 2004. "I have a feeling by the nature of the audiences' cyclical nature they will want something else soon," he said. "It has gotten into a kind of narcissistic dog-eat-dog kind of programming world. When *Frasier* started on Thursday, the first thing that Fox threw against us is when animals turn on their masters. And they took a huge bite out of our programming."

"I think that has been pretty much expanded on and taken to even worse places," he added. "As long as people find that entertaining, there will be no room for sitcoms." Grammer also smartly noted that the shows appealed to an audience that grew up with video cameras in their homes, and watching themselves. "This is what's familiar to them," he said.

Oscar winner Faye Dunaway, asked why she would appear on the WB network's acting talent search *The Starlet*, admitted she never watched reality shows but that she was after the audience. "I'm not the kind of audience they target," she told reporters in 2005. "But the audience they target and they have delivered on in a very impressive way is America, is a fan base that you can't ignore, you know."

And fellow Oscar winner Sylvester Stallone cited the impact of reality television, and its ability reach viewers and change thinking, as a reason for being part of NBC's *The Contender*, a boxing competition show produced by Mark Burnett. "Reality is here to stay," Stallone said. "You are really educating and getting into people's lives [and] at this point in my life, I want to be able to influence people in a positive way."

David E. Kelley, who created such shows as *Ally McBeal* and *Boston Legal*, was one of the big-name producers who came out blasting reality programming. In fact, he had an episode of *The Practice*, his legal drama before *Boston Legal*, in which Andie MacDowell played a crazed reality television fan. He also recalled watching an episode of *Joe Millionaire* because it was going to air against *The Practice*. Kelley said his wife, actress Michelle Pfeiffer, was reading a book while he watched. He got tired of watching and was about to flip the channel. His wife stopped him. "She said, 'Wait, wait! I want to see if that bitch comes back," Kelley said, adding that at that point he knew the reality show would be a hit. Just over a year later, Kelley produced a little-watched reality show for NBC called *The Law Firm*, an *Apprentice*-like show. "I think my biggest concern is that the enemy, if we're going to call it that, was taking over the television landscape ... and most of it was god-awful," Kelley told reporters on a conference call just before the launch of *The Law Firm*, a show that had attorney Roy Black presiding over a dozen lawyers in a contest for a job. The show did so poorly in two outings on NBC that network officials moved it to cable channel Bravo for the rest of its run.

The impact of reality programming has been felt all over the television landscape. In addition to most networks getting into the arena ranging from adventure reality shows for kids on Discovery Kids, a couple of golf reality series for The Golf Channel, and auto racing reality shows for Speed TV, the genre has influenced scripted shows, too. BET has its own *Real World*–like series in *College Hill*, a show about a group of African-American college students. And a handful of series have worked in reality show storylines, or actual elements of a reality show within. Music groups INXS, Tommy Lee, and TLC have turned to reality programming to find new group members. And Martha Stewart turned to reality for career redemption following a conviction on stock trading problems.

Reality programming has been credited with putting forth more positive, and frequent, images of gays and lesbians. Bravo's decorating show *Queer Eye for the Straight Guy* became a cultural touchstone, spawning copycats, books, and other products. From the very first edition *The Real World* has been offering positive portrayals of gays and lesbians. And *Survivor*'s Richard Hatch may be the best known gay reality star so far.

The initial impact of the success of reality was a reduction in the number of sitcoms and dramas on network television as reality shows took up prime-time slots. After a couple of years, viewers tended to not care about the "real" aspects of reality. No longer did it matter as much whether the contestants were actors, or folks who just signed up because they wanted a challenge. What mattered above all was whether the show was funny or sad, or grabbed at their emotions in some way. "To me, these are our new sitcoms and our new dramas," Stuart Krasnow, the producer of *Average Joe* and other reality shows told reporters in 2004. "We have our regular written ones, and we have our written dramas. Now we have our unwritten dramas and our unwritten sitcoms. I think *Average Joe* and *Average Joe Hawaii* have elements of both drama and sitcom. But, if you can watch the television set and feel something, and feel something real, it makes you talk about it the next day." Krasnow said while waiting on line at the coffee shop he often listens to the conversations others are having. Nobody is talking about the sitcom or drama from the night before, he said. "They're talking about these shows because they can relate to them," he said.

Younger viewers, the ones who grew up with video cameras and who may be a little bit more accepting of new concepts and formats than older viewers, were drawn to shows such as MTV's *Newlyweds* starring Nick Lachey and Jessica Simpson because it was funny and endearing. It was labeled a reality show—which it was—but it drew audiences for many of the same reasons that *Seinfeld* did in its day: It was good entertainment packed with laughs. Sure, there were dramatic moments, but at the center, *Newlyweds* was a comedy. Likewise, those same audiences turned to *Survivor*, *Amazing Race*, or *The Contender* because they are as dramatic as *ER* and *CSI*.

Clearly, *The Amazing Race* and *CSI* hit their dramatic moments in different ways, but in the eyes of the open-minded viewers, they're not so dissimilar. One drama was created in the mind of a screenwriter and using actors to tell the story. The other starred nobodies and was created by a producer and a strong team of editors who could cull through hundreds of hours of raw footage to compile a compelling dramatic storyline.

The impact of reality television as a genre extends far beyond the simple introduction of new shows and concepts. Because the genre was such a draw, producers of scripted entertainment looked for ways to incorporate reality-like flairs or concepts into their programs. In 2001, Fox tried to blend reality and drama with *Murder in Small Town X*, a series that had 10 "regular people" in a contest to find the fictitious killer in a small New England town. The producers used East Port, Maine, as a location. They built some buildings and wired them with hidden cameras. They shipped in actors and had them rehearse their parts. When that was set up, the 10 players were brought. Over the course of 30 days, producers filmed the nonactors working their way through a mystery game. The Fox show never really took off in the Nielsen ranking. In fact, *Murder in Small Town X* gained more attention later in the year because the game's winner, Angel Juarbe, a New York City firefighter, was killed when the World Trade Center collapsed on Sept. 11, 2001. For winning the game, he earned $250,000 and a Jeep Liberty.

When creating *The Office*, the BBC's brilliant office-set comedy, producers Ricky Gervais and Stephen Merchant used reality television as a plot point. In the show, Gervais played an out-of-touch middle manager at a paper plant. However, the entire show was shot as if it were a reality program set in an office, right down to "confessional" moments for each of the staffers. At points, Gervais would even look into the camera, much the way a regular person would when confronted with a camera crew.

Larry David's equally brilliant series *Curb Your Enthusiasm*, which launched in 2000 on HBO, has a reality show feel to it, as did the 2005 series *Fat Actress*, an unscripted series starring Kirstie Ally, loosely based on her own struggles with being overweight in Hollywood.

Producers have also made reality shows a storyline on scripted series. In a 2004 episode of UPN's *Half & Half*, for example, one of the characters on the show worked as a talent executive at a record company that was conducting a year-long search for new stars. So, as a tie-in, the producers did a real search and invited budding singers to submit tapes. The picked five acts, which were then flown to Los Angeles to perform for a group of music video producers. A winner was selected, and that act ultimately got to sing on television.

Just after *Survivor* landed in summer 2000, the producers of the annual *Miss America Pageant* attempted to boost viewership, especially with younger viewers, by adding reality show elements, such as candid backstage features. "Move over, *Survivor*—it's every contestant for herself," producer Jeff Margolis said in a press release announcing the changes.

Elsewhere, thanks to the arrival of reality, nonfiction, film, and television garnered more of an audience, because by default it was lumped together with reality. And as more people watched "real people" play games and try to sing on television, they also turned to documentary series and films. R. J. Cutler, who earned an Academy Award nomination for his film *The War Room*, which followed Bill Clinton's campaign for president, has produced several series that have fallen into the reality genre. Among them were the series *Freshman Diaries*, which followed a group of students at The University of Austin in Texas, and Roseanne Barr's failed attempt to do a show about making a reality show.

He also produced *American Candidate* for Showtime, which was sold as "a political reality series" designed to find a political candidate. The concept was first bought by FX, and the timing was designed to find a candidate to run for president as an independent. However, when FX passed, the show moved to Showtime, although the timing wouldn't allow a real-life run for the White House. Still, though Cutler saw it as a documentary, the show was rife with reality show elements, During the 10 one-hour episodes, viewers saw candidates face each other in a series of challenges. Each week the contestants were whittled down, with the finale coming down to just two contestants. "What is referred to by the press as reality television, is, of course, a very broad genre that has very small subgenres," Cutler said at the time of *American Candidate*. "*Freshman Diaries* is really a documentary series about a group of college freshmen at the University, is thought of as a reality series," Cutler said. "But so is *Fear Factor* and *Meet My Parents* and *Big Brother*. You have these four programs and each of them couldn't be more different than the other."

That said, Cutler wasn't complaining about his work being lumped in with reality fare, because the connection to the genre was making his product more valuable. He considered the work a documentary, yet the rush for more reality helped pull his projects along. In early 2006, FX launched Cutler's *Black. White.* The series had a black family and a white family live together in California, though thanks to Hollywood makeup artists, the black family was made to look white and the white family made to look black. The idea was to have them live that way and see if they were treated differently in their Hollywood skin.

On the small screen, the format instigated a frenzy of copycatting never before seen in the television industry. A success at one network was immediately copied with a few tweaks by another. Producers pitching shows often saw their concepts picked up by networks that initially passed on their series. There were two boxing shows—one at NBC and one at Fox. There were two shows with British nannies helping families with headstrong kids—one at Fox, one at ABC. And there were two shows in which wives swapped homes for two weeks, again, one at ABC and one at Fox. The history of copycatting, though, ultimately proved that the first show tended to do better than the second one with the same idea.

Reality has had a hand in influencing big-screen films as well. After the first *American Idol*, producers rushed together *From Justin to Kelly*, a 2003 cheesy film starring winner Kelly Clarkson and top-10 finalist Justin Guarini. The campy project was roundly panned. Also out in 2003 was *The Real World: Cancun*, a film produced by Jonathan Murray and Mary-Ellis

Bunim, the creators of MTV's *The Real World*, which set out to copy the popular television show in film form, but with a whole lot more skin and bad language: Sixteen strangers were set up in a fancy hotel and followed while they frolicked during spring break. The film, however, never lived up to the standards set by the television show.

Whether they're called reality shows, or unscripted comedies and dramas, the genre will be around the television landscape for years to come. After several go-go years of the broadcast networks having a heavy appetite for reality, it died down a bit in 2005. There were 21 reality shows scheduled on the six broadcast networks' prime-time schedules in fall 2004. By fall 2005, that figure had fallen to 14. Yet, in cable, the genre was still growing strong, with networks creating shows targeted at their niche audiences. For instance, the Golf Channel had a show called *The Big Break*, in which amateur golfers competed for a prize. The network also tailed controversial golfer John Daly for a show. And Country Music Television had a reality show with a rodeo theme and one following members of the Professional Bull Riders Association. And E! Entertainment had a show called *Fight for Fame* to find new actors.

And even broad-based channels such as A&E were continuing to ramp up production of reality series. In late 2005, the network launched *Rollergirls*, following a group of professional roller derby players in Texas, and by 2006 the network had a show following a SWAT team in Texas, one following drag racer John Force (*Driving Force*) and his family, one looking at KISS band member Gene Simmons and his family (*Family Jewels*) and a show looking at a group of young men deciding between women or going into a seminary (*God or the Girl*).

Reality programming even forced the management of the annual Primetime Emmy Awards to adjust its categories in 2001 to reflect the then burgeoning genre. Yet, ABC's 2003 attempt to create a reality awards show to honor the best in unscripted programming was scratched after rival networks refused to provide clips or stars to the show. The two-hour special was to have been produced by Don Mischer.

Awards aside, the networks were still heavy on the reality trail in early 2006. Where it ends, if it ends, no one has been able to predict. At the start of 2006, viewers continued to tune in for *Survivor* and *American Idol*, while skipping by some others. "What we've learned," said Lisa Kennedy Montgomery, the host of the Fox Reality Channel's series *Reality Remix*, "is if a reality program isn't good, it's going to go by the wayside. Programmers aren't going to put reality shows on for the sake of putting on reality shows. They have to be well cast and they can't be the same old recycled ideas and challenges."

And as long as there are real people willing to eat nearly anything and do nearly anything for a shot on television, reality should be around for a while to come. Meanwhile, the show that started the reality trend, MTV's *The Real World*, continues to chug along, with the seventeenth installment of the series shot in late 2005 in Key West, Florida. The draw of the genre is the people, said Montgomery, best known as the former MTV veejay Kennedy. "There's a level of unpredictability about peoples' real lives," she said. "And it's amazing to see how someone is going to react in these situations. They're real people, not writers trying to come up with a good story arc."

CHAPTER 3

Casting: Finding the Freaks, the Geeks, and the Stars

Omarosa, Trista, Jerri, and Bob.

Before they were cast on reality shows, Omarosa Manigault-Stallworth, Trista Rhen, Jerri Manthey, and Bob Guiney were virtual unknowns going about their regular lives. Rhen was a Florida cheerleader and physical therapist. Guiney was a mortgage broker. Manthey was a small-time actor and bartender. And Manigault-Stallworth worked in the White House personnel department during the Clinton Administration. That was before they either signed up or were signed up by a friend to appear on a reality show. Soon after, they became household names.

They've also parlayed their appearance on a reality show into entertainment careers and are invited to places they've never imagined. "I never even signed myself up for *The Bachelorette*," said Guiney, who was passed over on *The Bachelorette* by Trista Rhen, only to be selected as the centerpiece for an edition of *The Bachelor*. "It was the most random happening; my two assistants signed me up for the show," he said. "I never would have signed myself up. But now all of these crazy things keep happening. It's remarkable." And for now, Guiney is part of the entertainment landscape because he was on the reality shows. The reason he got picked for the *Bachelorette* and *The Bachelor*—he's also since landed a couple of other reality jobs because of those experiences—is because producers saw a character in him that fit within their projected casting goals for their show.

In fact, ask any reality-show producer what is necessary to create a hit show and the answers are usually the same: an interesting cast and good storytelling. A portion of the storytelling, or rather the story that is told, lies in the hands of the producers. They create the show, they concoct the living situations, they find the locations, and they create some of conflict that will drive drama later in the show. The conflict comes in forms of contests, alliances, either real or imagined, and the types of people who have been selected for the show in the first place. None of those issues work well, though, without the right cast.

Take a look at the successful reality shows over the course of the short history of the genre. The most successful ones, the ones that draw the largest audience or project new faces into the so-called celebrity world, are those where the casting has been a mix of caustic, caring, and daring people. That's right, just as with a successful sitcom or drama, a lot of the draw in reality programming comes from the cast. More important, it is how that cast works together or not during the production process that can lead to success or failure of a show. For instance, Bravo's salon-set series *Blow Out* only works because Jonathan Antin, the head of the salons, is a hard-driving, outspoken boss who is willing to dress down coworkers while the cameras roll. Without that sort of headstrong personality, the show wouldn't work. And as reality programming has moved out of being a sideline business for networks and into a full-fledged genre, driving many networks, casting has become more of an art form. Early on casting reality shows was done by the seat of a producer's pants, with a feel of sorts. It's no longer such a whimsical process, but really a well-thought-out, and often, thanks to a handful of serious scandals, well-researched area of programming.

Although the whole notion of reality television is built around regular people doing extraordinary things or living in unusual situations, the people appearing on reality shows are often far from regular. In many cases, they've had some acting experience or wanted to be actors; other times they've had more outgoing careers, appeared nude, or even had criminal records. The point is that they're often not the people next door, but just playing them.

Some reality show contestants go from show to show, largely because they fit the casting needs. One example is Toni Ferrari, a buxom brunette, who became sort of a vixen/villain for hire on Fox shows. Ferrari played the part of the agitator, appearing on *Love Cruise* and later *Paradise Hotel*. On *Love Cruise* she was billed as a 27-year-old personal trainer, and as a 28-year-old bartender for *Paradise Hotel*. In an interview with the *Chicago Sun-Times*, Ferrari was asked what kind of person goes on a reality show.

"Someone who's flat-out nuts," she said. "Wacky. You've got to be stupid and desperate. I was both of those." Another example is Nick Warnock, who was among the first crop of contestants on Donald Trump's *The Apprentice*. Warnock no doubt looked familiar to at least some television viewers because two years earlier he had appeared on NBC's short-lived game show *Dog Eat Dog*.

The lessons of reality show casting stem from the early years of MTV's *The Real World*, in which over time producers tinkered with the mix to find the types of people that, when thrown together, would tend to generate television drama. Though never nearing the attention level of *Survivor*, *The Real World* was the first reality show in modern times to use regular people to create drama and conflict to entertain viewers. Back in the early 1990s, producers Mary-Ellis Bunim and Jon Murray, without the benefit of massive casting calls and the national draw of reality television, had to find six cast members for a new series targeted at MTV's 12- to 34-year-old audience.

The concept now seems very simple. Back then, however, it was anything but. Bunim and Murray wanted to take seven strangers, throw them into a house or apartment, and let them live before the cameras. Though it's the template for virtually a majority of the reality shows today, ranging from *The Biggest Loser* and *Survivor* to *Wife Swap* and *Average Joe*, it was a novel idea at the time. "We, as partners, agreed," the producers said in the introduction of the book *The Real World: The Ultimate Insider's Guide* by James Solomon and Alan Carter. "We needed diversity. We needed relatable kids from urban to suburban, financially challenged to wealthy white-yellow-black-brown and in-between, gas jockeys to disc jockeys." The group included a good-looking, street-smart tough guy from New Jersey; a sweet southern girl from Alabama who had never been to the Big City before; a gay artist; an African-American rapper; and an African-American poet who complained about noise and racism. Over time, viewers saw them play and fight together, live and learn. Viewers and producers eventually saw that original cast as a template for future casts, almost as if the were ordering off of a Chinese food menu: Just add one gay, an angry black man, a tough guy, and a sweet woman for the fish-out-of-water effect, and—voila!—it's a reality show.

Bunim and Murray, in Solomon's book, dismiss the notion of having specific slots to fill and instead say viewers tend to remember the "larger than life" characters that "shook up the households" and were not afraid to say what they were thinking. "The truth is there are no stereotypes, just interesting people and relatable stories. Each cast member is unique, they're real," the producers said. More than a decade later, though, it's easy to believe rival producers have taken the lead from *The Real World*. At times in the following seasons of *The Real World* it seemed there has been a stereotype. Since the first one there have been other angry African-American men on the cast, there have been other outspoken gay men, and in every cast there is a woman being exposed for the first time to another world on the show, much the way Julie was in the first episode.

Richard Hatch certainly filled the gay role on *Survivor,* and Colleen Haskell was the sweet girl in the big world. It's hard to believe there isn't a formula for casting shows, especially *The Real World,* given the similarities of the casts from season to season. Every outing seems to contain the fish-out-of-water aspect, some player with a hidden struggle—like an eating disorder or a fetish for self-abuse—and enough meathead male players to stir up the action.

Now, it's easy to say there are specific "roles" to fill on reality shows, but it's more likely there are specific personalities necessary to create the drama and stories necessary to make a show interesting to viewers. Watching a cast of so-called innocent people go about living on an island isn't as interesting as watching some innocents go against a few aggressive players.

"We want to get, honestly, a mix like a *Gilligan's Island* thing," *Survivor* producer Mark Burnett told *USA Today* during auditions for the first edition of the series. "I want to make sure that all of those who watch can really relate."

And when describing *Eco-Challenge,* his adventure race series, Burnett told reporters once: "It's not about the race; it's about the people's experience during the race. And the race is the backdrop." And, at another time, when talking about his plans to create a reality show to find someone to fly on a Russian spacecraft, Burnett said he was looking for "real people who are identifiable. The people who apply obviously have to be nutty about the idea that they would really, really would like to go into space," he added.

But finding the right people—the right mix of people—is what's key to making the experience one worth watching. Burnett and Donald Trump, the executive producers on *The Apprentice,* have each cited the makeup of the cast for the third edition of *The Apprentice* as the reason ratings started to slip for the NBC show. Casting for reality shows has become a cottage industry in itself. Web sites are devoted to tracking casting calls for reality shows.

Typically, finding contestants for reality shows happens in a variety of ways. First, the more well-known way, is simply holding open casting calls in major cities around the country. Second, some shows have producers and casting agencies scour the country for people fitting the needs of the show. When producers ask for *American Idol* contestants, thousands of people show up at auditions around the country. The fact is that to get a shot at being a singing sensation people will sleep outside for days in places like New York City, Houston and Los Angeles.

Casting, however, often starts with applications supplied by the producers, which usually run several pages. The *Survivor* application runs 10 pages, and also requires the reality candidate to supply a videotape audition. What's on an application?

- General rules and requirements such as age, health restrictions, and that the candidate not be running for any public office.
- Personal information about the candidate such as marriages, occupation, level of education, residences past and present, allergies, and offspring.
- Whether the contestant has been treated for any serious mental illnesses.

And then there are a series of questions designed to elicit responses that will give the producers a basic sense about the contestant. Among the questions on a *Survivor* application are the following:

- Do you have any body art (piercing, tattoo, etc)? If so please describe.
- What would be the craziest, wildest thing you would do for a million dollars?
- If you were stranded, who would you most want to be stranded with?
- What was the last outdoor experience that you had? When was it?
- Why do you believe you could be the final Survivor?

"When we cast *Survivor*, the number one thing we looked for is adventure seekers, people who don't want to go lay on Waikiki Beach for their vacations," Burnett said. "They want to go river rafting, mountaineering, jungles. Because you can't make it 39 days if you're not into adventure. And there's very few left. Everest, you know, is still a great adventure. Raft the Zambezi, the Fataleufu, go to Patagonia, the ends of the earth. And *Survivor* is up there. It's one of those things that you really get to play Robinson Crusoe."

Of course, the questions and content shift dramatically with each show and from season to season. "I've learned to trust myself," Burnett said as he was casting the second edition of *Survivor*. "You've got to know what to look for and you've got to look for people who are identifiable, *Survivor* did a good job of that…. The premise is a bunch of ordinary people attempting to do something extraordinary."

The application for *The Bachelor*, along with the requisite health and background questions, asks potential cast members whether they're "genuinely looking to get married" and "why would you truly to find your spouse on our TV show."

The application and videotapes are just the start of the casting process. Typically, as a way to drum up contestants—and media attention—producers stage open casting calls in major cities around the country. Reporters cover the potential contestants, giving the upcoming shows much-needed buzz, long before the final decisions are made. And with each season of a reality show the list of contestants grows.

Finding participants for *The Bachelor,* for example, has been done through a variety of avenues. Travis Stork, a doctor who starred in the January 2006 edition, was found walking near a casting call for female players. "Most people are nominated by their sister or their mom," executive producer Mike Fleiss told the *New York Daily News.* "The cheesy guys nominate themselves...One of my casting people saw him walking down the street and she said 'Oh, my God! That is the best-looking guy I have ever seen in my entire life,'" Fleiss added. "And she literally chased him down the street." Conversely, the show has also targeted specific professions for contestants. In early 2006, for instance, the casting team reached out to architectural firms in search of potential bachelors.

Survivor, for example, went from a few thousand the first season, to tens of thousands of applications the second time around.

At any given time, literally dozens of shows are casting, and Web sites have popped up devoted to alerting people of casting calls for the programs. Generally speaking, they tell the contestants as little as possible about the show. For example, the producers of *The WB's Superstar USA* put out a casting call looking for people think they had "what it takes to be a star." However, though the show was in search of people who believed they could be stars, what the producers really wanted were people who were not stars and could not sing. A small detail left out, that, had it been known before would have changed the entire conceit for the show.

And *Paradise Hotel*'s casting information said producers wanted were in search of people to participate in an "innovative and groundbreaking series follows 12 guests (six single men and six single women) who are given the opportunity of a lifetime—to live together in the most exclusive resort ever created. But paradise doesn't last forever.... Each week the hotel guests will vote off one of their fellow residents to make room for a new guest."

Ingrid Wiese, one of the two regular folks cast for Spike TV's *Joe Schmo 2* had no intention of being on a reality show. In fact, she was working in Washington, DC, in international relations and conflict resolution, when a producer stopped her and a friend while on the street. "It was the furthest thing from my mind," she said. "I was out with a friend who was visiting from Seattle. I don't go out that much. We walked down a popular strip in DC, and these women stopped us and asked us if we would be willing to do a two-minute video and try out for a show. She said there could be $10,000 for participating in it.

"We thought it would be a fun story to tell at lunch," she added. "They asked us about our last relationships, what our ideal man would be like. We figured we had a great story to tell."

She got a call a few days later and was soon on her way to California for an audition. She was not looking for a relationship at the time—something she said she made clear to producers—and she also figured she would never be cast. "They asked me to finish out a questionnaire," she said. "I'd written term papers that were shorter. I filled it out the night of the Oscars with my friends. I never felt I would make it."

Because of the concept of the show—she was being cast as a real person on a fake show—she was told little, but even from what she learned, she felt she wasn't right. "I never thought I would get it, because I don't think I fit the typical type of women on *The Bachelor*," she said. "I honestly didn't think I fit the part."

Producers and casting directors are often shy with details for new reality programs for a couple of reasons. On one hand, limiting public discussion of the programs helps keep the secrets of the shows away from rival producers and networks. Likewise, by eliminating key details, it makes it a bit difficult for contestants to play to the concept of the show during auditions. On the other hand, for producer of the "twist" shows, such as *Joe Schmo* or *Superstar USA*, being completely honest with contestants would ruin the concept. For instance, who would enter a show for bad singers? To that end, who would knowingly enter a show looking for average-looking men, rather than handsome men, which was the scenario for *Average Joe*.

Andrea Langi, an actress from New Jersey, went to a casting call for an NBC reality show in Philadelphia. "They said it was a reality show for NBC that was casting," she said. "They mentioned very little, they were very brief. Once I got there it was called *Adventures in Love*. I was deceived from the very, very, very moment I walked in." Langi said she realized soon after that it was for a show similar to *The Bachelor*. What it was, however, was *For Love or Money,* an NBC series that has beautiful women vie for the attention of a handsome man, with the potential for a million dollar prize depending on the outcome. If the contestants knew every detail of the game—and what changes and challenges were ahead—the reactions would not be realistic, or spontaneous.

Not all shows are populated by people from casting calls, or audition tapes, either. For example, Fox's *Joe Millionaire* was built around a group of women dating a man they've been told is a millionaire, but who is really a construction worker. Because the secret was so sensitive, producers reached out to talent and modeling agents looking for women. The women, in turn, were asked if they wanted to seek adventure and love in a foreign land, not that they would be pitted against each other for the heart of a bachelor. Producers also set up Web sites seeking potential candidates and contacted various organizations that might have members interested in specific shows.

Subscribers to the *Journal of Emergency Medicine,* a trade publication read by emergency medical technicians and paramedics recently got an e-mail that read:

> Looking for a once-in-a-lifetime experience to alter your world view—and be on TV? Here's your chance. The Learning Channel (TLC) is seeking participants for a new documentary series based on this year's BBC program "The Monastery," with a specific interest in recruiting an EMS professional. TLC has commissioned the show, along with a female version called "The Convent," for American broadcast that will follow five men and five women living in a monastery or convent for 40 days and 40 nights. The programs are not reality TV shows, so no pranksters or competition junkies.

Although the pitch might have tried to separate the series from most reality shows, there's no denying the concept is pure reality. And, by targeting specific groups, the producers may find someone meeting their casting goals.

"We were looking for girls with attitude that said, 'I am' and 'I can,'" comic Mo'Nique told reporters while discussing *Mo'Nique's Fat Chance,* a reality show for the Oxygen Network built around heavyset women. "And when those women walked into the room, their attitude said, 'Mo'Nique, I am and I can and I belong.'"

Billionaire Mark Cuban, who fronted a reality show on ABC called *The Benefactor,* in which he led a group of contestants through challenges in a quest of winning $1 million, said the producers of his show got thousands and thousands of tapes via open auditions and through the mail. "And I looked for people with different types of personalities, people who went through an interview process and came across as someone who was aggressive, able to take on a challenge, had some creativity to them and also had some diversity to them," Cuban said. "We were looking for people with different backgrounds, to make it interesting for me, and to make it a little more diverse from the show's perspective."

Not everyone applies, either. Carolyn Heinz, who participated in PBS's *Colonial House,* a reality show about people of today living in conditions of a hundred or more years past, was entered by her daughter. "My husband and I didn't really even apply, to tell you the truth," she said. "We hadn't heard of it, we hadn't even heard of [the predecessor] *Frontier House,* amazingly enough, but our daughter in New York heard about it and applied for it, and we didn't—we found out when [producer] Mary Woods was gonna call us—when we already made some kinda shortlist." Michelle Vorhees, who was on the same PBS series, simply replied to a short clip seen on the publicly funded channel looking for contestants. And Bob Guiney, the guy from the *Bachelorette* and *The Bachelor,* was signed up by two of his coworkers who thought the experience might be good for him at the time.

Casting obviously changes slightly for the kind of show and the venue. Some shows want outlandish people, to stir up the drama on air. Some want younger people, older people, couples, or siblings. "There were 5,000 people that applied," said Sallie Clement, producer of *Colonial House.* "Most of them were applying because they had very boring lives. They were looking for something that was just—different....They had things they wanted to run away from. They wanted to be famous, or they wanted to win some money. This is not a project that delivers on any of those things, on those levels, and therefore they were immediate nos," she said. Of those left, they sorted through looking for folks who were emotionally strong enough to cope with the struggle of living in a homestead for five months.

"You are only as deep as what's carved into you," she said. "And I needed people who had layers to them, because I knew this project was the most ambitious of all the house projects—and those layers were going to be peeled away. I needed people that would be introspective," she continued. "I needed people that would be eloquent. I needed an awful lot from these people."

And by far, not everyone who has been cast on a reality show is a regular person, looking for a television challenge. Reality television has become a viable option for budding actors—just those with hopes of getting acting work—to get prime face time on television. Likewise, having some acting training—no matter how minimal—can be a key reason people are cast for reality shows. Someone with acting experience can play the part producers are seeking for various slots on a reality show whether they're asked to play it or not. And, usually, once they get on the show, they also play a part similar to one they've seen before. Looking for a villain? No problem? The nice guy? No sweat. The aggressive leader? Not an issue. Actors, or some who think they're actors, often step right into those roles.

The success of reality is in the producer's ability to create drama on screen, through stunts, challenges, or putting a mix of people together and hoping they create some sparks. And with even a small idea of how reality shows work, an actor can rise above the so-called regular cast members and get prime face time.

Langi, who was cast on *For Love or Money 2* on NBC, is an actress with credits ranging from *Law & Order to Sex and the City*. Not a major player in the acting world, but she had trained enough to play any part needed. At the time, she had been going from audition to audition with not a lot of success. At the same time, she constantly faced questions from friends about trying the reality genre. "As time goes on, you wonder if that's all that's going to be on TV," she said. "There is a lot of success for people coming out of these reality shows, who haven't had aspirations and not studied [acting] for years since they were 10. I am a real person, and do have real emotions."

Langi said producers knew she was an actress going in, yet on-air she was billed as a party planner from New Jersey. "They don't want somebody who isn't comfortable in front of the camera," she said. "In the beginning, when people said, 'why don't you do reality shows,' I was like; 'I'm an actor.' They were like, wow, see the exposure?'"

Langi is not alone. Dozens of other reality show competitors have turned up with pasts that have included some professional entertainment work. Zora Andrich, the woman chosen at the end of *Joe Millionaire* by Evan Marriott, had done some local commercials in New Jersey and actually was seeking a show hosting job when producers cast her on the Fox reality show. Her main competitor at the end of the program, Sarah Kozar, had done some bondage movies before landing the reality show gig. *Survivor: Thailand* winner Brian Heidik had appeared in a couple of B-level soft core films before he got a chance on the CBS reality show. *Survivor: The Australian Outback* contestant Jerri Manthey was a low-level actress before she was picked—and ultimately became a star—on that version of the series. And Jill Nicolini, who appeared on Fox's *Married by America*, had appeared in *Playboy* and worked on local television shows in New York before getting on national television. She's since parlayed that experience into a highly visible slot on local television in New York, where she works as a traffic correspondent.

The intricacies of creating a cast for a celebrity-driven reality show are no less difficult than when using regular people. For the producers of *The Surreal Life*, a *Real World*–like program that is built around a group of severely faded celebrities living together with camera crews tagging along.

The first season of *The Surreal Life* threw together such folks as MC Hammer, Jerri Manthey, Corey Feldman, Emmanuel Lewis, and Vince Neil. The second had among its cast the former wife of fallen televangelist Jim Bakker, Tammy Faye Messner; Erik Estrada; porn star Ron Jeremy; and Trishelle Canatella, who was on the Las Vegas edition of *The Real World*.

"You can't just take a list of names and check off six and throw them in a house," said *Surreal Life* executive producer Mark Cronin. "You really have to ... cast for a lot of different things. We cast for what we call 'worlds in collision,' which is exemplified by Tammy Faye [Messner] and Ron [Jeremy]. We cast for age balance, that's why Trishelle is with us. We cast for family roles. We're looking for a father figure in the house. We're looking for a brother in the house. We're looking for a younger sister, that kind of role. And we're looking for, of course, a balance in sex—and it's a big balancing act that we do try to put the cast together, and it's not immediately obvious."

Cronin got that explosive combination in a later edition of *The Surreal Life* when he cast reality workhorses Janice Dickenson (*America's Next Top Model*) and Omarosa Manigault-Stallworth (*The Apprentice*). The two hotheads began fighting early on, and the tension grew throughout the run of the show, drawing fans and creating water cooler chatter.

When Mike Fleiss, producer of *The Bachelor* for ABC, set out to create an edition with a professional football player as the prize catch, he put the word out to teams and agents, seeking a handsome quarterback who would be willing to appear on his show. He ended up with Jesse Palmer, a third-string quarterback for the New York Giants. "The world of professional sports is as sexy as it gets," Fleiss said. "He wanted to meet girls who weren't there because he was Jesse Palmer, football guy. He said he was tired of the same old chicks that show up around the teams."

And when Mark Burnett and Jeff Probst set out to cast the All-Star version of *Survivor*, they simply grabbed a sheet of yellow legal paper and wrote down 18 names of players from the previous versions of the popular show that would compete in the ultimate *Survivor*. "It was who were the most memorable people," Probst said.

To that end, when Burnett, producer Ben Silverman and chef Rocco Dispirito were casting for the reality series *The Restaurant*, it would have been impossible to weed out actors from the list. "There are so many out-of-work actors and comedians working in the restaurant business in New York City, it's hard to tell the difference," Dispirito said. "And frankly, they really make for great waiters, because what you do in the entertainment industry is you give out ... your comedy, whatever it is you're feeling, and you give it and you give it and you give it, and that's what you have to do in the restaurant business. So it's not a bad thing, you know."

Once producers find potential candidates, they're then put through a battery of physical and mental tests, as well as extensive background checks to make sure they're fit for television. Nearly half the applicants for *Meet My Folks* and a high percentage of those for *The Bachelor* have been rejected for carrying the genital herpes virus, network executives told the *New York Daily News*.

After she was initially contacted by a producer in Washington, DC, Ingrid Wiese, who was cast on *Joe Schmo 2* was sent to California, where she went through the prescreening gauntlet. "They had us do a psychological examination, sit with a psychologist for a half-hour and talk, and a medical thing, they took some blood," said Wiese.

Depending on the show and the producers, there will also be a background check in search of legal or criminal problems in the past. Some producers hire outside companies to do the research. And there have certainly been some problems. CBS's *Big Brother* has had a handful of contestants with questionable backgrounds turn up on air—and then their histories surfaced, creating messy situations. Fox got stung with *Who Wants to Marry a Multimillionaire?*, when it was revealed that the bachelor at the center of the show, Rick Rockwell, had been slapped with a restraining order by an old girlfriend. "A couple of shows got burned, and they didn't like the publicity, so they began asking us to look into people's backgrounds," Elaine Carey, national director of investigations for the Control Risks Group told the *New York Times*.

That's just one of the hurdles potential candidates go through to actually get on a show. "I was on *Amazing Race* with my sister," said Blake Mycoskie, "We sent in a tape. We made it to the final 80 people. We were sequestered in Los Angeles for two weeks. We were given a psychological examination. Then," Mycoskie added, "we sat down with [CBS chairman] Les Moonves. And he asked us, 'Why do you want to be on our show?' That just shows the importance of casting."

Yet, despite all of the hurdles a candidate goes through just to get on the show, it's not unusual to have a contestant get on a show and be a totally different person, or turn out to be an unexpected star. "I didn't think Omarosa was going to be a great character," said *The Apprentice* star and billionaire real estate mogul, Donald Trump. "You never know who's going to be a great character until millions of people have started to see it."

And in another example, a schoolteacher who was on the only version of *The Benefactor* to air turned out to be much different than she led producers to believe. Shawn, then 29, was a teacher from California who made it onto *The Benefactor* through the auditioning process. "Shawn is a second grade teacher who, when she actually showed up and started competing on the show, her persona changed somewhat," producer Clay Newbill said. "I think it was a surprise to Mark, and to all of us."

Newbill said he and the production team were interested by Shawn's insistence that if she won she would give all of her second graders everything they asked for in an in-class writing assignment. They were also intrigued because she was divorced, remarried, and a mother and had a competitive spirit. "And we thought she was going to be a good contestant," Newbill said. "Then she got on the show … [and] you saw less and less of the sweet second grade teacher that we liked and more and more of the person that 'I've got to get this. This money is going to be mine.'"

Shawn lasted eight episodes; however, she proved, as have many other players along the way, that no amount of preshow checks can truly find out how someone will react when the cameras are turned on for real.

CHAPTER 4

Celebrities Sing, Dance, and Claw Their Way into Reality

To most people, Christopher Knight is the guy who in 1969 broke into television playing Peter Brady on the classic family sitcom *The Brady Bunch* and a few reunion shows that popped up afterward. Other than *The Brady Bunch*, Knight was an entertainment world afterthought, popping up from time to time in low-budget movies and a daytime soap. But, no matter what roles he landed, all roads—and conversations—led back to *The Brady Bunch*. So rather than become a sideshow, Knight spent much of the past couple decades growing up and becoming a successful entrepreneur. However, in 2004, Knight decided to try to relaunch his entertainment career and see what was out there. "Unfortunately for me," Knight said, "I have an audience that's sort of attached to a character that can't possibly be who I am today." Over the years he had avoided all overtures from producers to appear in reality shows that tended to thrive on having B-level stars turn up such as *Celebrity Boxing*. Yet he was intrigued when the producers of VH1's *The Surreal Life* came along.

He's not alone. Knight is one of many celebrities who have found solace, exposure, fame, and career redemption through the reality genre. Though shunned by celebrities at first, it has become a reliable venue to get exposure for celebrities in need of a boost or, like Knight, just a reentry point. They've done so through shows where they live with other celebrities such as *The Surreal Life*. They've done it by being part of competition shows such as *Rock Star INXS* or *Celebrity Fit Club*. And they've done it through a variety of series that purport to have shown the celebrities living their lives.

In Knight's case, the reality show came about as part of a plan to get back into the entertainment field after being away for so long. And, for Knight, reality provided a field for which to alter the public's perception of him. "Once one is a Brady you're expected to be angelic," he said. "This was an opportunity to recalibrate my audience." Before saying yes, though, Knight reached out to trusted friends for advice and looked at what happened to the people who have appeared on similar shows in the past.

The Surreal Life places a group of very different celebrities, usually on the downside of their careers or in desperate need of a boost, in a home to live for two weeks before the cameras. *The Surreal Life* launched on the WB Network and after two seasons moved to VH1, where it's become a cult hit, perhaps because it fits in well with the network's lineup of series such as *Behind the Music,* which highlights the foibles of fallen celebrities. "Literally, on the drive up to the door," Knight said, "I had no idea whether I made the right decision."

Getting on a reality show for any one can be a risky proposition. But the gamble is different when the person is a celebrity. Casting directors for scripted entertainment series and movies base some part of their decision on perception of a given celebrity. And considering how reality show producers take liberties in the way they present characters, celebrities are gambling they'll still be marketable when a reality show ends. Knight, having been out of the business for so long, was no different. He was looking at the reality show to rebuild and recast his image.

The television world is littered with people who have appeared on reality shows and then complained later that the way they were presented in no way reflects them in real life. But that's the harsh reality of having thousands of hours of videotape cut down to maybe 13 hours by producers trying to create a storyline. With nonactors, the damage may surface in the form of embarrassment in front of coworkers, failed relationships, and family members upset because for a short period of time their loved one looked like a goofball. The negative celebrity impact, however, could cost a career.

Knight had seen how other celebrities had benefited from appearing on reality shows, and he weighed this against the downside, which, considering where his career was at the time, didn't really matter much.

Little did he know, however, how drastically that would change and how he would be come a bigger part of the reality world.

The short history of the reality genre has already proven that marketable, recognizable reality show characters can have a life beyond their initial programs. And, just as in sitcoms and dramas, producers are always looking for interesting cast members. As the format has grown—and to some extent as the reliance on so-called real people has dwindled—celebrity reality stars are hopscotching between shows, too.

For instance, during the filming of *The Surreal Life*, Knight became romantically involved with fellow *Life* cast member Adrienne Curry, herself a reality show veteran, having won the first version of the popular UPN show *America's Next Top Model*. Indeed, the two became such a draw, producers created *My Fair Brady*, a second series to track the Curry/Knight relationship. The producers of *The Surreal Life* had done the same with a previous edition of *Life* in which Brigitte Nielsen became a goofball item with rapper Flavor Flav. Following that show, VH1 launched *Strange Love* to track the budding relationship, though the program never drew the attention of the original. Flavor Flav also got another show out of his *Surreal Life* experience. After *Strange Love* aired and went, VH1 tried to capitalize on his appeal with its viewers by creating *Flavor of Love*, a dating show where a group of women vied for the affection of the rapper, much the way women swooned for the star of *The Bachelor*. It seems that VH1 programmers were onto something. The finale of *Flavor of Love* generated the highest ratings ever in the history of the channel, roughly 6 million viewers on a Sunday night, one of the toughest nights in television.

"I don't want to become a reality junkie," Knight said. "Who's not to say that's where the industry finds itself. But I'd rather be an actor."

Besides the Curry/Knight hookup, that edition of *The Surreal Life* is also known as the one in which pint-sized actor Verne Troyer, while drunk and nude, urinated in the corner of one room. So much for celebrities risking tarnishing their precious images.

As for Knight, his feelings about the genre are not unusual.

When reality first broke big on the back of the original *Survivor*, it was an interesting novelty for celebrities, who were often asked during red carpet chats if they could ever live on bugs and rats. Most said they were fans of the show. Over time, though, as reality began to clog prime-time lineups, and thereby push scripted fare to the side, some celebrities complained about reality because it cut down on potential work for them. Thanks to a few highly successful celebrity reality experiences, the form became hip in celebrity circles.

Oddly enough, it took a reality show starring drug-addled rocker Ozzy Osbourne to convince other celebrities that the reality genre could be cool. Osbourne, who for more than two decades has been making heavy metal music, became a huge television star when he and his family—wife, Sharon;

son, Jack; and daughter Kelly—agreed to let cameras capture their home life. And what a home life it was.

Ozzy Osbourne, who rose to fame decades earlier as the bat-biting lead singer of the heavy metal band Black Sabbath, became an unlikely reality television character. In doing so, he paved the way for folks such as Paris Hilton, her mother Kathy Hilton, Donald Trump, Carmen Electra, and scores of other celebrities who have reignited or found careers through reality television.

The Osbournes gave viewers a glimpse into the life of a star family and completely played against the expected stereotypes. At the time Osbourne allowed cameras in his home, his fame had faded a bit. Sure, he sold out concert venues each summer, but outside of the core audience, few thought about Osbourne. But he was still known to older rock fans as the guy who did strange things on stage. To a younger crowd he was the headliner for a series of major rock festivals—Ozzfest—that jammed stadiums each year. That image, however, conflicted greatly with the family-like view of the Osbournes on MTV's series. Few, if anyone would have expected the Osbournes at home were, well, regular. They were, to a point.

The first episode followed the family as they adjusted to life within their new palatial home in Beverly Hills, California, where celebrities surrounded them. By episode two, Sharon was calling a dog therapist for her pets, which pooped everywhere in the house. And by the third episode, Ozzy was admitting on a radio show that he used Viagra. Welcome to the wacky world of the Osbournes, who were successful on television far beyond anyone's expectations inside MTV and out.

Some of that success may have stemmed from the fact that it appeared, at least to viewers, that the family wasn't playing to the cameras, but rather were being themselves. It was an image few could have expected, yet one what was fascinating to watch. Ozzy, who limped around his home struggling to work a newfangled remote control, chided his children for using drugs at home. Everyone swore like sailors—mom, dad, and children.

Son Jack and daughter Kelly became stars. And the family matriarch, Sharon, the financial brains behind Ozzy's fortune, was seen tossing a turkey over the fence at her neighbor, Pat Boone—yes, that Pat Boone. But in the end, they were an apparently stable family. Or so viewers thought. Soon after the second season aired, son Jack went into rehab and later Kelly did, too.

"We all really love each other and we're like any other family," Ozzy Osbourne told Reuters in October 2004. "We have our problems, and we try with the grace of God to get through them." Still, *The Osbournes* launched a television moment and a trend.

Because Ozzy was well known to radio disk jockeys, his reality show became fodder for morning talk. And suddenly, the family was everywhere. *The Osbournes* generated some of the largest Nielsen Media Research ratings in the history of MTV. More important, the Osbournes made it respectable for celebrities to dabble in reality television—and not be ashamed of doing so. Soon, celebrities everywhere believed their home life should be fodder for reality show treatment. MTV, which launched *The Osbournes* immediately signed development deals with big-name stars such as Frankie Muniz (*Malcolm in the Middle*), Hilary Duff (*Lizzie McGuire*), and Cameron Diaz. Most of the development deals for reality shows went nowhere. However, it was important for producers and MTV to get out in front of their rivals and at least sign agreements with top stars.

Even record and fashion mogul Sean (Diddy) Combs got involved, first as the star of *Making of the Band*, a reality series to create a pop group, and later as a producer of multiple reality programs, including *Run's House*, built around rapper Rev. Run (Joe Simmons) of Run DMC.

Take Nick Lachey and Jessica Simpson as an example. Before summer 2003, Lachey was best known as one of the four members of pop group 98 Degrees and Simpson was another blonde, good-looking singer. Separately, they were both successful, but not quite as successful as other stars in their genre. Then they got married. And then, their lives changed forever when they agreed to have the first year of their marriage filmed for an MTV reality show. *Newlyweds: Nick & Jessica* launched on MTV in August 2003, and immediately the couple became media darlings and the subject of much water cooler talk.

How could they not? The show, done in the vein of *The Osbournes*, was another attempt at showing viewers a different side of celebrity life. In the first episode, viewers saw the young couple going through typical life rituals. Sure, they were insanely beautiful, but they also struggled at home like most people. The roles were flipped a bit, but they seemed real. Simpson, a performer since she was a child, was used to having someone clean up for her. Lachey was a neat freak. Their differences made for fun television, and in a matter of weeks, the pop duo had completely entered the world of celebrity reality television.

"God, there's so many underwear," Simpson said in the opening episode, while sorting clothes to wash. "It's amazing all you find when you do your laundry. It's fun putting it in [the washing machine], but afterward you have to fold it."

"Do you know if there are, like, maids for celebrities?" she asked a friend. "I'm not good at this housewife thing."

Lachey, meanwhile, looked on as a good husband trying to deal with his inexperienced wife. Before the episode was over, Lachey and Simpson had a moment that will live in reality television infamy. While sitting on the couch watching television, Simpson picked at some Chicken of the Sea brand tuna. "Is this chicken, what I have, or is it fish?" she asked.

Lachey briefly looked flustered and then explained to his loving wife what she was eating was fish not chicken, despite the name of the product.

It certainly wasn't a celebrity moment, rather one in a series of moments during the run of *Newlyweds* that indicated they couple really were human. Maybe a little too human. Later on in the series, Simpson dropped $750 on undergarments and didn't realize how much she spent until it was too late. Simpson's dim-bulb demeanor and Lachey's sturdy husband approach made the show a hit and made people talk—and joke about the couple. "I think when we went into it, we realized we were going to be opening up ourselves to a lot of criticism," Lachey said. "I think if we had anything to be ashamed of, we wouldn't have done it."

Simpson and Lachey agreed to do the show following the huge success of *The Osbournes*. "The good thing about [*Newlyweds*]," said producer Rod Aissa, "even what my friends responded to, is that [they] have the same fundamental issues we all deal with.... It's real people, with real themes, that have touched all of our lives."

Newlyweds ultimately led to *The Ashlee Simpson Show*, a reality series starring Jessica Simpson's younger sister, also a singer, and a solo effort for Nick Lachey. *The Nick Lachey Project* was designed to track Lachey as he made a solo record, his second, and not focus on his home life. *Newlyweds* propelled the Lachey/Simpson relationship to such levels that every twist in their life had become tabloid fodder.

Talk of reality shows and celebrities mixing surfaced almost immediately after *Survivor* hit big on CBS. Indeed, as ratings continued to surge for the adventure series, celebrities would routinely say they wanted to appear on *Survivor*. There was even talk of doing an abridged version of *Survivor* with celebrity participants. Yet, despite all of the talk, the celebrity rush didn't occur until after Osbournes gave people a glimpse behind the scenes.

Before *The Osbournes* celebrities popped up on a couple episodes of The Learning Channel's *Trading Spaces*, as renovating participants, but those were safe shows. Celebrities wouldn't be embarrassed by appearing there, or made to eat bugs. Indeed, with the exception of *Survivor*, most early reality shows weren't well respected. The general sense, some of which continues today, is that reality shows catered in humiliation and degrading the contestants in the name of entertainment. Advertisers, the companies that spend money to have their commercials appear during the shows, were leery of the genre, largely because of the humiliation aspect—and often the strong sexual overtones. Over time, though, advertisers warmed to the genre as the content got better and it appeared there was no end in sight. That celebrities were interested in reality programming should come as no surprise.

Anyone in entertainment could see how well reality shows were doing overall, and more specifically, they were attracting huge audiences of younger viewers, a crowd that is hard to get to the set. The genre had captured the imagination of young audiences, which advertisers, and therefore television executives, crave. Likewise, reality shows were making stars of some sort out of the contestants. The first wave of reality contestants became celebrities without really doing anything other than appearing on an unscripted series. They were invited on talk shows, to movie premieres, and accorded in some cases, the kind of attention earned by folks making movies and television shows for years. In the case of Lachey and Simpson, they each had new albums in the works at the time of filming, so the show helped spread the word of their new music. If it could work for noncelebrities, there was no reason reality shows couldn't drive attention for real-life celebrities as well.

The Osbourne family's huge success after the MTV series proved that over and over. Sharon Osbourne, based on the appeal of the reality show, landed a daytime talk show deal. (The program, however, was nowhere near as successful as the reality program and was cancelled.) It held true for Lachey and Simpson. "Within three weeks of us putting it on the air, everybody wanted to be in [business] with the *Newlyweds*," said Brian Graden, who heads up programming for MTV. In fact, Lachey and Simpson's work on *Newlyweds* led to each being cast for series in development at the broadcast networks. Neither star's series was picked up, but Lachey got several guest starring roles from his work, including stints on *Charmed* and *Hope & Faith*. Likewise, together they starred in series of variety specials for ABC that had them serving as a *Sonny & Cher* for the younger generation. "I think overall it just brought us to a place we hadn't been before," Lachey said before the end of the second season. "It made people much more aware of our talent." The couple's reality life ended when their real-life relationship ended in 2006.

For every success on the celebrity reality front there have been many more failures. ABC's February 2003 series *I'm a Celebrity! Get Me out of Here*, while technically the first on the air with a celebrity version of *Survivor*, couldn't hold a candle to the original. So strong were the comparisons between ABC's series and CBS's reality granddaddy that CBS sued to stop ABC, but ultimately lost in what was the first of many copyright-related reality battles to come. ABC's series was an American version of a British show in which 10 celebrities are stranded in the Australian Outback.

The location and the premise drew immediate comparisons to *Survivor,* but the show was far from equal. Among the celebrities in ABC's show were former MTV star "Downtown" Julie Brown, Playboy model Nikki Ziering. Robin Leach, Alana Stewart, best known as Rod Stewart's ex-wife and Stuttering John Melendez, at the time a staff member of radio jock Howard Stern's morning show. "I think people may be surprised at who we really are, as opposed to what are images say we are," Stewart said. The 15-night series had a viewer component, too. Audience members could call in and vote for which celebrity faced a dare each night. One of those dares, for example, was having a bikini-clad Ziering risk life and limb, by fetching items in a crocodile-infested pond. Ultimately, viewers decided who won the game, too. ABC officials said before the show launched that the British version was a big hit and there was no reason it wouldn't work in the United States. They also said it could be done twice a year during the important ratings sweeps periods. Trouble is, viewers never caught on. The show was critically lambasted. It never grabbed audience's attention and lasted just one run.

Nevertheless, the show proved that celebrities would go on a reality show—no matter what the game, the outcome, or the risk at embarrassment. Celebrities have been willing to look silly on such series as *Fear Factor,* which requires participants to eat stuff normally not eaten on American plates and to complete creepy stunts such as lying in a coffin-shaped box while rats are poured on top. "Celebrities are more entertaining by nature because of what they do for a living," *Fear Factor* executive producer Matt Kunitz told the *New York Daily News* in November 2001, as he was preparing the first celebrity versions of the hit NBC reality series. Actress Kelly Preston, who told the producers she wanted to try her hand on the show, spawned the notion of celebrity versions of *Fear Factor.* Others soon followed, and the first celebrity version had such folks as Preston, rapper Coolio, Donny Osmond, Brooke Burns, and David Hasselhoff trying their hand at oddball stunts.

The level of celebrity involved in reality has varied, though, has yet to crack the very top box-office draws. The stars that have played on ABC's celebrity versions of *The Mole*—a reality show that has a group of people living together and participating in challenges all designed to find out who is the "mole"—were largely one-time television stars who hadn't had a hit in a while such as Corbin Bernson, Tracy Gold, and Mark Curry. Kathy Griffin, who appeared on an edition of *Celebrity Mole,* parlayed that experience into appearances on *The Surreal World* and celebrity poker shows. She also landed a reality show of her own with Bravo looking at celebrity life on the *D-List.*

In many cases, the term *celebrity* is loosely applied to the players on the so-called celebrity editions of reality shows. Several previous reality show starts have turned up in other shows as celebrities. Jerri Manthey, who was in the Africa version of *Survivor,* appeared in *The Surreal Life* as commentator on the Game Show Network's *Extreme Dodgeball* series.

As the form has grown, and become a staple, the level of stars has grown, too. Sylvester Stallone, of *Rocky* fame, was a producer and appeared on camera in *The Contender,* a critically acclaimed, though little-watched boxing reality show from Mark Burnett. Film star Gina Gershon starred in a short-lived reality series documenting a concert tour, all designed to promote a tie-in movie. And in 2006 Producer Steven Spielberg teamed with Burnett for a new flim reality show. The good thing is, however, it appears the level of stars doesn't make or break a reality show; rather like all shows, the concept does.

Take *The Surreal Life,* for example. The show is a takeoff on the *Real World,* where a group of celebrities, usually has-beens, live together before the cameras for the sake of entertainment. The first version, which launched in January 2003 to good critical reviews, was built around such stars as MC Hammer, a one-time huge rapper who lost his fortune; Emmanuel Lewis, a pint-sized television star; Corey Feldman; former *Survivor* star Manthey; Playboy Playmate Brande Roderick; and fading rock star Vince Neil. Stars for the second season were no less famous, with porn actor Ron Jeremy living in a home with *Baywatch* star Traci Bingham, one-time hitmaker Vanilla Ice, and *Real World Las Vegas* player Trishelle Canatella. The reasons behind a celebrity's jump into reality range from purely being out of work to being drawn to the genre.

The fact is that many celebrities have watched from the sidelines as networks have committed more resources to reality programs than scripted entertainment. And a quick glance of the Nielsen charts for recent seasons indicates that reality was drawing a lion's share of the available audience. Likewise, many of the stars participating in reality shows are not also vying for the big-time scripted fare. More likely, those stars are players in the low-budget television movie fare or syndicated series, which tend not to pay or draw as much attention as network or cable prime-time programming. In other cases, the reality show stars are coming from other fields such as music, where they're simply attempting to expand their reach or build interest in their recorded work.

Take Ashley Parker Angel. Angel was a member of the boy band O-Town, which was created through the ABC reality show *Making of the Band.* For three cycles, viewers watched as producer Lou Pearlman, the force behind The

Backstreet Boys, auditioned and handpicked band members. Viewers also saw the group become real pop stars. But Angel's fame faded, along with his bankbook. He struggled to survive in Los Angeles while finding a producer for his work and getting his girlfriend pregnant. Like a washed-up sitcom star, there wasn't much of a market for a former member of a manufactured-for-TV singer. Angel's music landed in the hands of MTV's Rod Aissa, who saw a *Rocky*-like story in the former O-Town band member. Soon they were shooting *There & Back*, a reality show that followed Angel as he attempted a comeback. "It's important that on the solo album people see me as the real deal," Angel said, discussing his reasons for doing the show. "One of the things that Rod said was, 'What better way to show that I've changed.' I feel I have a real opportunity to show people who I am. With me, personally the only reason to do this show was to really get a chance to show people I do have talent," Angel added. "I'm hoping people will see me for me this time around." Angel also appeared on NBC's *Celebrity Cooking Showdown*

Still, it's a big leap from liking reality shows and actually being on one.

"I saw the first [season of *The Surreal Life*]. I really liked it," Canatella told television writers in January 2004. "And I identified with a couple of people on there. Actually, I hated Corey Feldman.... I hate him, but that's why I wanted to watch because I disliked him so much I wanted to see what he was going to do next."

Ironically, that turns out to be much of the appeal of celebrity reality shows as well. Viewers want to see people they've come to know in other genres either make a fool of themselves, or prove otherwise, just as Ozzy Osbourne did. "As for me," Canatella said, "I just did it because—I mean, I've done *The Real World* before, and it's basically the same thing. But I don't have a problem. I have nothing to hide.... I'm not here to make myself look better on TV. I think we're all here just for entertainment value." Canatella has gone from *The Real World* to the *Surreal Life* to a Bravo show *Battle of the Network Reality Stars* to E! Entertainment's *Kill Reality*, a show that had a group of reality castoffs filming a movie, and she continues find work in reality. She also landed a spread in *Playboy* thanks to her TV exposure.

Erik Estrada, best known as a costar on the 1970s hit series *CHiPs*, went into *The Surreal Life* as a way to show younger viewers he was still viable. "The reason I did it was for personal reasons and also because my wife said, 'Get out there. People don't know anything about you, about who you really, really are. They have this concept of what they read in the *Enquirer*.... And I was a centerfold for the *Enquirer* for such a long time." Earlier in his career, Estrada took on the entertainment industry to get a bigger share of the profits from *CHiPs*, a move he said got him blackballed by the business. So for Estrada, a reality show was another way to get back in the game.

Generally, though, the celebrities who have warmed to the genre tend to be younger and more aware of the format. The others, such as Donald Trump, the star of *The Apprentice*, or Sylvester Stallone of NBC's *The Contender* understand the appeal with younger audiences and the potential financial upside.

Though he's never been a television star, Trump's television career is similar to those celebrities who have dabbled in reality television. He's always been in the media, but before NBC's series *The Apprentice* began, he was just a major New York City celebrity who has had financial ups and downs. On *The Apprentice*, a gaggle of business-world wannabes fight for a position within Trump's massive business organization. However, when the show shot to the ratings top, Trump's image did as well, making him a hit all over again. The series helped spawn a line of *Apprentice* licensed products, such as a Donald Trump doll; resulted in the re-release of a Trump board game; and made "You're Fired!" part of the American lexicon.

Thanks to the draw of the show, he was pulling in 40,000 people for public speaking events. The Learning Annex, a company that puts on seminars, signed Trump to the tune of $1.5 million an hour. And, in 2005, NBC announced a sixth and seventh cycle of the series. Trump was the first billionaire businessman to get involved in reality but not the only one. Richard Branson, the brains behind the Virgin Airlines and music fame, had a reality show on Fox that fared poorly. Mark Cuban, a billionaire businessman and the owner of the NBA's Dallas Mavericks also had a show that failed, and home guru Martha Stewart hosted a version of *The Apprentice* on NBC that died, too. "We learned one thing," Trump said "nobody else can do it. Not because of Martha. Tommy Hilfiger didn't work. [Richard] Branson didn't work. [Mark] Cuban didn't work. There have been 14 copies of the *Apprentice* that have failed. There's only one Trump." Ironically, Trump joked now that if he had known the high odds of television failure—about 70 percent of all shows fail the first season—he never would have done it.

Janice Dickinson is another example of a celebrity who got a career boost because of reality television and has milked the genre for several projects. Dickinson rose to prominence as a model in the 70s and 80s, and claims to have coined the phrase "supermodel" in 1979. But after her modeling days were over, she faded into the celebrity fringe, turning up from time to time in tabloid stories but never being at the forefront of the celebrity world. But then Tyra Banks, who was producing a new show called *America's Next Top Model* for UPN, cast Dickinson as judge on the show. Dickinson's wild antics on screen and willingness to say anything made her stick out on *America's*

Next Top Model. Eventually, Dickinson and Banks had a falling out, but that didn't matter. Dickinson was back in the public eye, and that was enough for her to be cast on *The Surreal Life,* where she frequently battled with former *Apprentice* villain Omarosa Manigault-Stallworth. Cable's Oxygen network thought enough of Dickinson to cast her in her own reality show, produced by Stuart Krasnow, the force behind *Average Joe* and others. The show was to follow Dickinson as she started her own modeling agency. As with every-thing else, Dickinson isn't shy about discussing the reasons she's done real-ity shows. "Good grief," she said when her Oxygen show was announced. "It's enabled me to help with my children's education, just by putting it in the bank for my kids—money."

Wayne Newton, a legendary Las Vegas performer, agreed to front *The Entertainer* for E!, in which he presided over a competition to find a new per-former. "I believe this show will fill a much need void in the training ground of on stage performers that no longer exists," Newton said when the show was announced.

"It's a case by case situation," Lachey said. "If you feel comfortable having everything on television, great. It's not for everybody. Friends and people in the business tell me they couldn't do it." Reality producers, however, are always on the prowl for interesting, if not outlandish, celebrity subjects for new shows.

Paris Hilton, the heir to part of the Hilton Hotel fortune, became an unlikely reality television star with *The Simple Life* on Fox, in which she and pal Nicole Richie spent a month with a family of Arkansas farmers. Mary-Ellis Bunim and Jonathan Murray, the minds behind *The Real World,* produced *The Simple Life.* Before the show, Hilton was known as a party girl who often made the gossip columns, but to most seemingly did nothing but go to major events in barely there outfits. Initially, her sister Nicky was to be on the show, but Richie stepped in instead.

"I thought it would be fun and interesting," Hilton told reporters in July 2003. "It's like an experience I'll never get to do and Bunim/Murray are just great producers. I love *The Real World* and I just thought it would be fun to show everyone like myself and how I am and, I don't know, sometimes it was gross, but we got into it."

And she sure did. Hilton earned laughs—and played on her heiress ste-reotype by spending time working in a fast-food restaurant. During one episode she asked the family what a Wal-Mart was. "What is Wal-Mart? Is that where they sell, like, wall stuff?" she asked. Later on she vowed she knew what Wal-Mart did, but was just playing for the cameras. Nevertheless, the scene did a lot to forward her image as being out of touch with regu-lar people. "I was just playing a part," she told *USA Today.* "If I knew what everything was, it wouldn't be funny." No matter, people watched and talked. The first season worked so well, Fox commissioned two more seasons of the rich girls' adventures in America. After the third season, though, the friends had a falling out, and the show fizzled. Cable's E! Entertainment picked up the concept and developed a strategy where the two women would appear on *The Simple Life* but never together, at least as long as their public feud continued.

Hilton's mother, seeing the success her daughter had on the small screen, also signed on for a reality show. Incidentally, Kathy Hilton didn't want her daughter to appear in a reality show in the first place. "I never thought *The Simple Life* would be the like the *Simple Life*," she said. "It was certainly not something I wanted Paris to be involved in. I tried to talk her out of it."

But, because of Paris Hilton's draw on *The Simple Life*, Hilton considered pitches from producers; ultimately choosing a concept called *The Good Life* for NBC. In the show, Hilton would oversee a contest of sorts for a grand prize of the good life, including an apartment and job. Along the way, Hilton would share knowledge of upscale living, etiquette, and being rich. "I never thought I would be doing something like this," she said. "There were eight of us sitting in a meeting and I thought, 'this sounds great.'"

Motley Crue drummer Tommy Lee, known as much for his music as his off-stage antics and marriages to Pamela Anderson and Heather Locklear, is one of those music stars who jumped to reality television. Lee spent the fall of 2004 attending classes at the University of Nebraska-Lincoln campus for *Tommy Lee Goes to College*, an NBC reality show. "This is a total fish out of water experience for me," Lee told reporters at a press conference. "I didn't have the opportunity to go to college. I was busy touring since the age of 17. So this is completely strange and bizarre, but a lot of fun and a lot of work."

Lee took classes in chemistry, American literature, and horticulture. He also performed with the school's marching band. Just participating in the show generated early interest in Lee—it also helped that he had a book out at the time—and the university. Despite the attention, though, Lee said the work was serious. "It's the real deal," he said. "I'm playing catch up since we jumped in in the middle of the semester. I'm studying my ass off trying to keep up and take the tests. It's been a while since I've studied, since high school. It's a lot of work, a lot of work."

As with any reality show, there were initial concerns that the university would come off looking silly in the series, but Lee assured all that if anything looked bad, it would be him. "If anybody's going to look ridiculous here, it's me, okay?" he said.

Lee got so much out of the reality television experience that he went back for more in 2006 on CBS's second version of *Rock Star*. Lee teamed with Mark Burnett to find a new lead singer for a band he put together with Jason Newsted from Metallica and Gilby Clarke from Guns N' Roses, which was set to launch on CBS in the summer of 2006. As with *Rock Star: INXS*, the lead singer selected would record an album with Lee's group, called Supernova, and go on a tour. "Starting a new band with old friends on worldwide television is going to be a blast, and we're going to pull out all the stops to find the most charismatic and musically talented lead singer to front Supernova," Lee said when announcing the show. "I love breaking the rules."

Lee is not alone in the world of music stars jumping to reality. Besides Sean Combs, who took over the second season of *Making of the Band*, a talent search on MTV, giving the fading series a much-needed dose of star power, reality has proven a fertile ground for music stars looking to move into—or get exposure—on television. Rapper Missy Elliott starred in a UPN talent search series *The Road to Stardom with Missy Elliott*, in which she and a panel of music insiders led 13 wannabe vocalists on a coast-to-coast tour in a contest to be the next hip-hop star. Reality television was much different from her music work, she said. "This was a whole different ball game, coming off the road and then going to television and having cameras on you constantly," she told reporters in July 2004. "I'm used to cameras, but not to that degree.... It was a lot of fun though, so it was cool. It's easier than just doing, like, a television show or a movie. So it was cool."

Fading performers Vitamin C and Tone Loc, two music stars who hadn't had a hit in years, turned up as judges on the WB's spoof of *American Idol*, *Superstar USA*, in which truly bad singers were convinced they were good.

Elsewhere, the band INXS, which had been without a lead singer since Michael Hutchence committed suicide in 1997, did what any respectable band would do—they turned their search into a reality show with help from Burnett. To that end, R&B stars T-Boz and Chilli, the remaining two members of the group TLC after the death of singer Lisa (Left Eye) Lopes, also turned to television for help in finding a new group member. "We have been blessed with great success and this is a chance for our fans to join us as we give someone a chance of a lifetime opportunity to fulfill their dream," the duo said in a statement. Incidentally, neither the INXS nor TLC shows ended up being big ratings draws.

Travis Barker of the group Blink 182 and his wife Shanna Moakler agreed to bring their unconventional life to MTV in *Meet the Barkers*. "Having the cameras in our home has been a wild experience," Moakler said at the time.

"We really wanted this to be a true documentation of our lives. We wanted to show that you can be young and successful and still balance a home and family.... We wanted to break your typical stereotypes." A second season followed the couple as they prepared for the birth of their second child. "I'm not going to benefit in any way," Barker said. "It's just showing what I do. I think it can be an inspiration to some people. I think some people who might thinking playing in a band you can't have a family or you can't be smart enough to start your own business or start your own record label. You can do that. I'm a good example. I have a high school education. I was on my own since I was 16. I'm in three bands, and I have two businesses that do very well for me. I have a beautiful wife and a family."

Gene Simmons, the bass player for the rock group KISS, has used his music fame to become a reality TV producer and star. In 2005, Simmons was the star of a VH1 reality show called *Rock School*, in which he was charged with turning a group of high-brow, young, British private school musicians into a rock group. And, he was the producer of a couple of other reality shows, including one, *Mr. Romance*, designed to find a new cover model for a romance novel book company. "People want to follow me around," he said. "I publish magazines, and I have a bizarre lifestyle. I can be up on stage and wear more makeup and high heels than your mommy did. And off stage I wear suits." With a couple of shows under his belt, Simmons eventually agreed to let cameras follow his own family life for *Gene Simmons Family Jewels*, a show scheduled to launch on the A&E Network in 2006. Simmons has been living with former Playboy Playmate Shannon Tweed for 22 years, and the couple have two children together. A&E's press materials for the show said it "will reveal a side of Gene that he has kept hidden until now, and shows how the most non-traditional, traditional family in America manages to make it work under the oddest of circumstances."

Star Trek legend William Shatner starred in a short-run reality show for Spike TV in which he duped the entire population of a small Iowa town he was there to make a film only in the end to tell them they had been fooled. Comedian Andy Dick, who, like Lee, is known as much for his off-stage troubles as he is for his humor, was the host of an *Apprentice*-like series on MTV in search of a personal assistant.

One-time Guess Jeans model and Playboy Playmate Anna Nicole Smith landed a reality show on E!, which followed her unusual life. In the show, roundly panned by the critics, Smith seemed loopy, often flaunted her sexual habits, and cried. "I saw a piece of the show and thought, omigod, I look completely stoned and drunk out of my mind," Smith told the *Daily News*. "I have a Southern drawl that makes me sound drunk all the time, but it's not from drugs or alcohol. It's just the way I talk." Early on the show took off as viewers tuned into the television train wreck.

"The show might be cut so that I look like a dumb blonde," Smith said. "But if people are going to love me, they'll love me. If they're going to hate me, they'll hate me. I just want people to know that I'm not a bitch, I want people to think I'm a good person." Whatever viewers thought about Smith, the ratings were big enough for E! officials to order a second season. The second time around, however, Smith's draw was diminished. Still, the exposure was enough for her to land a contract with a weight-loss company.

Career renewal, or regeneration, might have been what Bobby Brown and his wife Whitney Houston were after in 2005 with their Bravo Reality show *Being Bobby Brown*, but it didn't take long for viewers—and critics—to realize the two might still need some career help. The video, shot by a crew hired by Brown and his wife, captured such gems as their personal talks of life and bodily functions. "I'm not a bad guy," Brown says at one point discussing his checkered past in an early episode. "I don't rob anybody. I don't carry any guns. I like guns—call me a collector."

Later, after Brown beats his latest run-in with the courts, he and the family head out for lunch, where Houston talked about her intestines. "They gave me a 35-minute lecture on what our foods do to our system," Houston tells her group. "There are these little bugs, on the walls of your stomach.... There's a booger in there, he's got two fangs." In terms of revealing too much, Brown and Houston went overboard; yet, it wasn't enough to make the show a ratings hit—or make them commercial pitchmen like so many other stars have become after a reality-show success.

Model Rachel Hunter, who was once married to Rod Stewart, and Nicole Eggert, a former star on *Baywatch* who never quite reached the same level of fame in the years after, both agreed to appear in TBS's *The Real Gilligan's Island*, a show that used the concept of the 1960s sitcom *Gilligan's Island* as the basis of a reality show. The comedy had a group of people stranded on an island after their charter boat got stuck in a storm. In the reality version, two teams of people all from the genre in the series—a captain, a professor, and a movie star—were left to live and fight amongst each other much the way players do on *Survivor*. Hunter and Eggert played the movie star roles.

Hunter later appeared in ABC's summer 2005 hit *Dancing with the Stars*, in which she was paired with a professional dancer in a ballroom competition against teams of other stars and real dancers.

Farrah Fawcett, who in the 1970s made men's hearts beat faster as a star on *Charlie's Angels* and 20 years later made headlines for an incoherent appearance on CBS's *Late Show with David Letterman*, agreed in late 2004 to allow cameras from TV Land to follow her around for a series *Chasing Farrah*. "So many of our perceptions of Farrah Fawcett are through the tabloids, quick sound bite on the news and her roles in film and television," said Larry Jones, president of TV Land and Nick at Nite in announcing the show. "TV Land wants to take our viewers into the life of Farrah Fawcett to see what she's really about, since so few of us know what it's like to be a recognized Hollywood icon for your entire adult life."

Fawcett said she wanted to do the show to correct some of the myths about her life. "I actually thought, 'Good. Let people finally see what really is going on.' I think that it will dispel a lot of, you know, perceptions that people have about me." Fawcett told *Access Hollywood* host Nancy O'Dell before the show launched.

Wild rocker Ted Nugent fronted a series for VH1 in which he put a group of men and women through a series of outdoors stunts. That show then moved to the Outdoor Life Network.

Rev. Al Sharpton, a 2004 Democratic hopeful for the White House, was the host of a Spike TV reality show called *I Hate My Job*. In the series, Sharpton oversaw eight men as they tried to shed their current jobs in return for a shot at their dream careers. Among the job-change wannabes were a guy who dealt with cow waste and a Las Vegas card dealer. Before taking the job, Sharpton wanted to make sure the show content and goals were similar with his own ambitions. "I was very concerned it not be something bizarre or something that did not have a message to it," Sharpton said.

Other stars who have dabbled in reality include Jerry Hall, who hosted VH1's *Kept;* Faye Dunaway, who was a judge in the WB's *The Starlet;* and Ben Affleck and Matt Damon, who produced and occasionally appeared on *Project Greenlight*, a series designed to find new directing and writing film talent that started out on HBO and moved in later seasons to Bravo.

Celebrity reality shows aren't limited to entertainment stars, either. Tennis superstars Venus and Serena Williams allowed cameras to follow them for an ABC Family Channel show in 2005. The sisters said the show would be a good way to provide an insight into their relationship as well as being a good role model for working women.

Dave Navarro and Carmen Electra let MTV record the planning of their wedding *for 'Til Death Do Us Part,* a reality show that culminated in a wedding between a tattooed rocker and a former Playboy Playmate and *Baywatch* beauty. "It took us a long time to finally make the decision to do the show on MTV," Electra said. "We went back and forth for a long time. Getting married is such a personal thing. Being in the public eye is really hard. We're really proud of our relationship. We live a great lifestyle. We're in love. Why not share that with the world?" It also helped that they had a previous reality experience with MTV, a one-time show, "A Love Story," about their relationship.

'Til Death Do Us Part was different from Newlyweds and The Osbournes in that rather than recording the couple's life at all hours, MTV cameras were only there for the preparations for their wedding. Still, what viewers saw was a glimpse inside a not-so-typical celebrity world. For instance, for their wedding invitations, each was made to look dead, and then photographed, nude, on an embalming table. Along the way, viewers saw their bachelor and bachelorette parties, the groomsmen being fitted for tuxedos and Electra getting fitted for her bridal gown. "I would describe it as a cute show with an edge," Navarro said before the series launched. "It's certainly a love story. There's romance involved. Given who we are as people it can't help but be a little left of center. At the same time, it's not full of conflicts. It's not a reality show that's 24/7 into our lives." Navarro has also used his experience on MTV to become a cohost on CBS's Rock Star.

Unlike a scripted show—which is also a lot of work—agreeing to do a reality program is in a way agreeing to turn parts of your life over to a producer. In many cases, there's no down time, which is a big turn-off for many celebrity reality show participants. When cameras are on all the time, it's possible for participants to forget they're being filmed, leading to embarrassing situations later on. There's also a risk that the reality show can overshadow the star's regular career. In the case of Lachey and Simpson, the attention they got for their reality show far outweighed any of their musical work for the duration of the show. One could argue that the attention the collapse of their marriage generated in tabloid magazines was far greater than it would have been had they not been on TV.

Going in, Travis Barker said he wasn't concerned about the MTV show overshadowing his work. "If I didn't have an established career already, I might trip on it," he told reporters, "but I'm not going solo anytime soon, and I'm in three bands so ... I look to continue to make music for the rest of my life with them, so I'm not really worried about something thinking of me more as a father or a husband. I mean, that's my least fear in life for someone to say, 'I know Travis because he's a rad father, I know Travis because he's a rad husband or whatever else. It's just what I already do. They're just kind of like documenting everything I'm doing, so no one will know me for anything different." His wife, however, was looking for a little more out of the show.

"It's a dangerous thing to put yourself on television 24/7 and expose yourself in that way and put yourself into the hands of producers who can edit you and edit your conversations into just about anything we want," *Surreal Life* producer Mark Cronin told reporters in January 2003. "And I have to say that these guys are all, really, really, really brave."

According to Lachey, producers would film for about four months for each season of *Newlyweds*, starting at about 10 in the morning through midnight. "It's a pretty involved process," he said. "They get as much as they can." And for the most part, nothing is off limits except the bathroom. In the case of *Newlyweds* the bedroom was off-limits, too. "The more you do it, the harder it gets," Lachey said of letting cameras in. "With every season, it becomes a little more painful. It's more intrusive. When you start out, your tolerance is a little more forgiving."

"You can always retreat to the upstairs, where the cameras aren't allowed," he added. "We do that more frequently. But this is kind of a chapter in our lives, it's important to see it through."

For the Osbourne family, being on camera for MTV meant letting viewers into see wife Sharon learn she had cancer and going through treatments, as well as seeing Ozzy moments after a near-fatal all terrain vehicle accident. The experience—and benefits—of being the star of MTV's *The Osbournes* also led to MTV tapping the rocker for another reality series called *Battle for Ozzfest*, in which Ozzy lead a group of budding headbangers through a series of challenges in the hopes of winning a shot on stage during one of his Ozzfest concert stops. No surprise, in one episode one the contestants must bite the head of a bat, just as Ozzy did so many years before. However, not all off the stunts were as glamorous. Other stunts included working as Ozzy's security and as part of the Ozzfest cleanup crew. "It's just to let people know that we're not *The Osbournes* and I'm still active in my work as I have been for the last 37 years," Osbourne told Reuters before the show launched. "Sharon's still very active in the managerial side. We're not just sitting in the house."

Meanwhile, the fourth season of *The Osbournes* was scheduled to start airing on MTV in early 2004. But, as the Osbourne family moved ahead, Ozzy said they would be doing it without cameras. After four rounds of filming at home and on the road, life with the television show that helped reinvigorate his career had gotten to be too much. He said in November 2004 that the show was done. "When you watch a 25-minute episode, I've been filming all day," Osbourne said. "At the end of it, I didn't like having cameras around the house all the time."

Even his wife, the business mind in the house, who also rode the reality success to a talk show of her own, said it was time to go. "Now everybody's doing [reality shows]," she said. "He's done it, he's been there, he's got to do something else." Perhaps fittingly, *The Osbournes* went public with the end of the show to reporters backstage at the *MTV Europe Music Awards*.

For every *Osbournes*, *Newlyweds* or celebrity show that works, a handful of others fail or simply perplex critics and the viewers. In early 2005, Britney Spears and her husband Kevin Federline agreed to sell their home movies to UPN to be made into *Britney and Kevin: Chaotic*, a short-run reality series that followed their then-budding romance. "This fun, uniquely personal series gives viewers a rare glimpse inside the pair's relationship and life together," is the way UPN's press materials described the show. Some might say the show was a little bit too intimate. *Chaotic* was shot using the couple's own personal hand-held video cameras. In the tapes, the couple often talked about their sexual exploits and how much they loved each other, though the content had something of an ick factor.

Conversely, consider the success of *Dancing with the Stars*, which showed that stars can attempt feats few believed they could attack—and draw huge ratings—without losing their marketability elsewhere. The visibility of Kelly Monaco, the daytime star and Playboy Playmate who won the inaugural *Dancing*, went up significantly after that series. She got so popular that *Playboy* reprinted her pictures and there was talk she might join ABC's series *Desperate Housewives*. And a further indication that celebrities, at least some, were willing to jump into the genre without fear, came in late 2005 when VH1 launched *But Can They Sing*, which pitted such stars as Joe Pantoliano, Larry Holmes, and Morgan Fairchild in a singing contest.

Also in the vein of safe celebrity reality shows was NBC's *Celebrity Cooking Showdown*, a series from the prolific reality producer Ben Silverman and Sean Combs that launched on the network in April 2006. The show had a group of celebrities who, after being trained by professional chefs, were put through a series of competitions leading for a giant cook-off. The comparisons to *Dancing with the Stars* were endless. *Cooking Showdown*, like *Dancing with the Stars*, featured trained professionals teaching celebrities and leading them into competition.

Among the stars participating in the initial season were Naomi Campbell, Allison Sweeney, Tom Arnold, and Gabrielle Reese. The show also had a couple of reality show veterans. Football star Tony Gonzales had appeared in Spike TV's *Super Agent*, a show in which his real-life agent tried to groom new agents. Also on *Cooking Showdown* was Ashley Parker Angel, who broke into the entertainment world on ABC's *Making of the Band* and later had his own show on MTV called *There & Back*. "People love seeing celebrities under pressure—and with this show, if you can't stand the heat, you better get out of the kitchen," Combs, himself a reality veteran (having produced and appeared in *Making of the Band*), said in a statement.

Spike TV's *Pros vs. Joes* was also in the relatively safe celebrity category. The show had real-life sports stars facing nonathletes in sporting challenges. "I think when I finish playing there's always a part of you that wants—that always wants to keep playing," football great Bill Romanowski told TV writers in January 2006. "And when I finished, I did 'The Longest Yard,' so that kind of fueled my next year and the first year after my retirement. So this was my second year after retirement, and it was time to put the pads on again."

"There's a lot of guys that bring a briefcase to work," he added. "Well, for 16 years in the NFL I put on a helmet and shoulder pads. And I miss putting on the helmet and shoulder pads. [*Pros vs. Joes*] gave me another chance to put it on and put some licks on people."

Moreover, Roseanne Barr, one of the biggest comics and television stars of the 1980s with her sitcom *Roseanne*, tried to make a television comeback with an oddball combination of a reality show watching her as she tried to make a cooking show. The reality program was designed to air on ABC, and the cooking show was headed for ABC Family. The reality arm of the show followed Barr as she went about her daily life and as she prepared for the cooking show. Viewers watched on the reality show as she went about looking for an executive producer for her cooking show, which included her showing tapes to rabbis she regularly consulted. And the cast of characters on the show included her first ex-husband, who is married to her personal assistant.

"I have one more in me and that's it," she said in the first episode of *The Real Roseanne Show*, the reality program. "If it don't go, I'm done." The show was met with dismal reviews and even worse ratings. Then, as she was beset by health issues, the show was canceled. *Domestic Goddess*, the cooking show, never made it on the air, providing that even the biggest stars can be failures in the reality genre.

One of the scariest, perhaps frankest, celebrity reality efforts aired on VH1 in late 2005 and was built around former *Partridge Family* cast member Danny Bonaduce and his wife. Bonaduce has admitted he's struggled with drugs for nearly two decades and his police record and history of weird incidents proves he's had some problems. In *Breaking Bonaduce*, viewers saw him shoot steroids, cut his wrists, and live on the edge of violence and emotions. In one episode, he was shown seething as a marriage councilor probed him and his wife Gretchen about their struggles. In another, he's shown walking on stage during his wife's concert.

During filming of the show, his wife threatened to divorce him because he had cheated on her. Even VH1 officials were concerned when the raw footage was turned in. "When VH1 said, 'We think you're probably going to die, and we don't want to film you dying,'" Bonaduce told the *New York Daily News*, "I said, 'What kind of a TV show quits when the lead is going to die?' I thought the death of a B-lister on tape would be pretty cool."

Bonaduce said what was on the show was real, albeit altered by a mix of drugs and alcohol. "Lots of people will try to convince you that their reality show is real," he told the paper. "If I could convince you this show is a fake, I would. If I could convince you that I'm not that much of a jerk and a drunk and an ass, I would."

Former MTV veejay Lisa Kennedy Montgomery, who is the host of Fox Reality's *Reality Remix* series, said she was fascinated by Bonaduce's show. "I was disturbed by it, I was amazed it made it on TV," she said. "It was so raw, so disturbing. You can make this s——up. His marriage was dissolving." In the end, she said, *Breaking Bonaduce* set the bar very high for future celebrity shows. But it in no way will prevent other stars from trying the genre, provided young viewers continue to be drawn to reality programming.

CHAPTER 5

Altered Reality: The Makeover Craze

Delisa Stiles was at one point a 32- year-old psychologist and captain in the U.S. Army Reserves. The Army Reserves gave her a false confidence, she said. And, her relationship with her husband was on and off. Her body and her lack of self-confidence helped push her husband away, she said. They grew distant. Then she found *The Swan*, Fox's makeover reality contest, created by former Telemundo television executive Nely Galan. "I was at a crossroads in my life, my military career, my health, my job, it just presented itself," Stiles said of "*The Swan*." "It seemed like fate." Fate or not, viewers watched Stiles undergo a massive transformation and ultimately be crowned *The Swan* in season two of the Fox makeover series. The series took women who are "stuck in a rut" and overhauled their lives through surgery and mental health help. Stiles fit right in.

Stiles's average looks were dramatically changed with the help of a massive amount of plastic surgery. On her way to becoming *The Swan*, Stiles got a brow lift, lower eye lift, mid-face lift, a fat transfer to her lips and cheek folds, a tummy tuck, a breast lift, liposuction on her inner thighs, and some dental work. "To me, it was the ultimate challenge," Stiles said afterward, "to see if I was really committed to this." Besides transforming the women physically, *The Swan* has the women parade in a contest—a beauty pageant of sorts—with one being crowned *The Swan*. The crown goes to the woman who had the most remarkable transformation, and the one who showed the most dedication to the process, internally and externally, or so we're told. Stiles earned the crown in 2004, but along the way viewers saw her struggle with the collapse of her marriage while she was getting her breasts lifted. Stiles is just one of hundreds of people who have had a makeover, either physically, mentally, or in some other aspect in life because of a reality show.

In fact, makeovers are a major subcategory within the reality genre, offering fixes from everything to saggy breasts to saggy roofs. Need a personality makeover to get more dates? No problem. Want help looking better before a big wedding? No sweat, there's a show for that. Think your boyfriend is a prince hidden in a schlub's body? Well, there's a show that promises to fix those problems as well.

The makeover craze isn't just limited to the human body, either. The concept of television delivering makeovers has been extended to relationships, homes, cars, and more. Indeed, reality shows in many ways have picked up where the talk shows of early TV have—offering advice, often serious, sometimes in a humorous way—for people in desperate need of guidance.

The Swan was the brainchild of Galan, a television executive, who was going through a bad stretch of luck in her own life. Luckily for Galan, the trouble in her personal life hit just as the reality genre wave was taking off. "It really came from my own life," Galan said of *The Swan*. "I've been a producer and an executive for many years. Like most women, I hit road blocks along the way."

At 35 she found out she was pregnant, and the father of her child was not the marrying kind. So, as a single mother she was reevaluating her own life—one that on the surface had seemed fairly successful. "Like many other women, I had a baby," she recalled. "I thought, maybe I'll have a boob lift." She didn't get the lift then but, through researching the surgery, figured there might be a way to make a show out of the process of transforming a woman from an ugly duckling into a beautiful swan. Ultimately, after the success of the first two seasons of the show, Galan underwent the knife and had her breasts altered.

At the time she came up with *The Swan*, ABC was having success with *Extreme Makeover*, a similar show that offered participants extensive, life changing, plastic surgery. Galan wanted to take it a step further; rather than just offer the surgery, she required participants to undergo extensive life coaching with a variety of trainers. She pitched it as giving the women the inside job to go with the outside overhaul they were getting. The concept, she said, was that women sit back and say they would be like Oprah Winfrey, if they had Winfrey's wealth and could afford a chef to prepare healthy meals and a trainer to help run the pounds off. *The Swan* was designed to offer that and more.

Moreover, *The Swan* is far from alone in offering people makeovers as a way to create entertainment for viewers. Fact is, television has always been a fantasy medium for viewers. For many, watching a drama or comedy provides a way for them to transport themselves from their everyday lives into the worlds of others. It's a fictionalized world, of course, and one filled with commercials. Nonetheless, television has been a passive escape medium for viewers since the day the first signal was transmitted to the few sets available 50 years ago.

Changing lives, albeit in much smaller ways, has been a part of the television in the past. The 1950s game show *Queen for a Day*, a precursor to many of the humiliation-laced reality shows of today, rewarded a housewife with a horrible life story with a new appliance. She lowered herself to spill her guts on television, and she was crowned a queen, and awarded more dish detergent. None of the early dream giveaways, however, offered up hundreds of thousands of dollars in plastic surgery to players willing to share their life stories on television. "We all know people who at some point in their lives get stuck in a bad spot," Cecile Frot-Coutaz, Fremantle Media chief executive officer said when *The Swan* was announced. "They have a goal and think, 'if only I could change what I don't like about myself, I would be able to fulfill my dreams.

"With *The Swan* we're offering the kind of dream makeover that's normally available only to the rich and famous," Frot-Coutaz said. "This is a positive show where we want to see how these women can make their dreams come true once they have what they want."

Generally speaking, makeover shows tend to offer things people couldn't have in their normal lives if it were not for the reality shows. What the reality makeovers often failed to show, however, was the extreme pain the subjects went through to get their pearly whites and tightened faces. Instead, viewers got a compressed look at the process that skipped over the long, painful recovery periods most plastic surgery patients undergo.

Pain aside, the makeovers are also not limited to women. Among the men who have undergone makeovers on ABC was Ray Krone, who had 20 procedures done on his face. He got the makeover after spending a decade in an Arizona jail for a murder it turned out he didn't commit. He now lectures others on the importance of DNA testing.

Krone was known as the snaggle-toothed killer because of his off-kilter teeth. So, when given the chance to get them fixed, he jumped at it. The makeover was one way he tried to get away from his past. "I'm trying to educated people," he told the *New York Daily News,* "and I want them focusing on what I have to say, not what I look like."

Amy Rosenblum, executive producer of the short-lived series *Home Delivery* said her show would "change lives every day." Topics ranged from a man wanting to be reunited with his sister to a young boy getting a prosthetic ear.

And there are several common threads for the viewers, and the participants. Among them are the transformation of a person from someone who may not be attractive by current standards into someone better to look at. The emotional appeal is watching someone reach their goals, even if they may be superficial, like having a whiter smile. And, there's the little-talked-about jeopardy aspect of all makeovers, which either revolves around the risk the participant takes to be on the show, how they assimilate back into the real world afterward, or the risk the designers take in creating something the participants ultimately hate.

In the case of *The Swan* or *Extreme Makeover,* they're getting a huge amount of surgery at once that the average person couldn't afford. With shows like *Queer Eye for the Straight Guy,* they're getting expert advice from a group of stylists who will transform their look, attitudes and spending habits. The concept was also expanded to *Queer Eye for the Straight Girl,* though the female version wasn't as successful.

Not all aspects of physical makeovers, are about the patients, either. E! Entertainment launched *Dr. 90210,* a series centering on Beverly Hills, California, plastic surgeon Dr. Robert Rey. The behind-the-scenes show lets viewers into the office and see Rey talking to clients about the shape of their bodies and the size of their breasts. One episode included images of a woman who had four previous bad breast jobs. And a frequent visitor is porn star Tabitha Stevens, who was seen in a couple episodes getting botox shots.

And when Rey was not seen in the office, cameras followed his home life, or lack of it, with a beautiful wife and children. Viewers see Rey try to maintain a family, compete in martial arts tournaments, and keep his practice going. "Last year, I really struggled with the balance between career and family, and I think that's normal for somebody who's trying to make it, but this year I think I've seen the light," Rey said in one episode, "and I'm trying to spend more time with the family."

Bravo, also got into the plastic surgery reality game, with a short-run series called *Miami Slice,* which looked at the lives of six surgeons. "What we do is the height of arrogance," said Dr. Howell Tiller, when the show was revealed. "To make people better than God intended!" Viewers never caught on to *Miami Slice;* it lasted a season, whereas *Dr. 90210* continues on.

Makeovers are not new. There had been surgery shows, some specifically about plastic surgery, on cable channels in the 1990s. But those programs focused more on the doctors and the medical marvels of the surgery, and not on the struggles of the patients that led them to get the surgery. Moreover, they were shot more like documentaries, aired as such, and generated little interest beyond those who reveled in surgical procedures.

The trend of giving people major makeovers of any sort as an entertainment vehicle didn't happen until 2002, when ABC quietly rounded up people for a special called *Extreme Makeover*. The show took three people who were not happy with their looks and offered them a battery of surgical procedures as a way to turn their lives around. People who lined up for potential transformations were given the usual reality show background checks and met with psychologists to make sure they could handle the stress, strain and pain involved with being pinched, pulled, broken and twisted into a new person. "We were looking for strong, confident people who were dealt a bad deck of cards in the looks department," executive producer Howard Schultz told the *New York Daily News* before the show aired. "We wanted people for whom surgery would change their life and those who couldn't afford it otherwise."

Schultz, who created the concept of *Extreme Makeover*, and his team of producers and surgeons combed through more than 1,000 applicants to settle on three people for the first special. Among them were Stacey Hoffman, then a 31-year-old medical aide, who wanted facial surgery; Luke Seewoster, a 29-year-old personal trainer, who had a nose job and liposuction; and Stephanie Woodside, a 24-year-old single mother who was uncomfortable with a bump on her nose.

"This is definitely my chance and I'm going for it," Woodside said on the show. "There's no stopping me now." The male voiceover on the show said as a young girl, Woodside knew she looked different and the kids in school told her why. "I was in third grade and one of the other little third graders was curious and he just decided to ask if I had a broken nose, or what was wrong with my nose," Woodside said then. "And first, I was kind of in shock and I just told him, you know, that's just the way I am. That's just the way I was born."

Woodside got the nose fixed and more on *Extreme Makeover*, where she received six surgeries. In fact, all the participants got more surgeries than they expected. Viewers, however, didn't care. More than 13 million people tuned into the December 11, 2002 special, which changed the lives of the three participants. The special also altered the form of reality television—yet another type of show to do so—and offered hope for people with concerns about their looks and without the wherewithal to effect a change.

Like the dozens of talk shows that came before, makeover reality shows depended on a cast of characters willing to spill all on television. Talk shows depended on on-air confrontations about topics most people would be loath to discuss in public such as troubles with their marriages, lovers or life in general. Some of those same shows, however, as a way to possibly offset all of the fussing and fighting, did a handful of makeover shows each year, in which a rundown mother of 20 would get new clothes, a different hairstyle, and makeup tips before being sent back out to reality.

It was from there that shows like *Extreme Makeover* and *The Swan* came about. They, in turn led to shows like MTV's *I Want a Famous Face,* in which people who wanted surgeons to makeover their looks to resemble stars such as Brad Pitt were profiled.

After the first successful airing, ABC immediately scheduled a rerun of *Extreme Makeover* and ordered more episodes to make the show a series. But, the notion of *Extreme Makeover* wasn't universally accepted. Some within the plastic surgery community complained that the show encouraged extensive surgeries—far beyond what normal folks would have in one sitting. There were also some complaints that the show downplayed the pain and suffering a person goes through after such operations, showing, instead a glamorized vision of something that can be difficult to go through.

"It was very, very painful," Hoffman told *Good Morning America*'s Robin Roberts the day after the first *Extreme Makeover* aired. "I had draining tubes coming out from my head from having the eyebrow lift. But I think the most pain that I experienced was the chin being stretched out, and added on. That was the most pain."

None of that, of course, was included in the programs. But no matter, ratings were big and viewers indicated they were willing to watch along as people underwent life-changing surgery.

The makeover craze also extended beyond the realm of plastic surgery. Perhaps taking a page from the daytime talk show playbook, producers began to expand on the notion of offering people makeovers in other areas, such as fashion and their lives. And as with a lot of other reality programming, some of the concepts were imported from abroad.

The BBC in Britain had a nice hit with *What Not to Wear,* a series in which friends of a person in need of a fashion and image makeover nominate their pals for help on the show. The Learning Channel, which hit big with *Trading Spaces,* an American version of the BBC series *Changing Rooms,* again tried to duplicate the success of a coproduction with the BBC and remade *What Not to Wear* for the states.

The American version of *What Not to Wear* hit the airwaves in March 2003, with fashion experts Stacy London and Wayne Scot Lukas dolling out knowledge to the fashion-challenged victims. On *What Not to Wear*, the subjects were met in public places with Lucas and London poking fun at their style and dangling a $5,000 shopping spree as an enticement to play along. "You look like a majorette in a really haunted marching band," Lukas told the first subject in the series premiere, Boston resident Eileen Malveski. Lukas also attacked Malveski for her the way she kept her eyebrows.

Unlike *Extreme Makeover* or *The Swan*, the folks on *What Not to Wear* do not address the participant's body shape or size, rather they try to teach the subject how to best dress what they have. "I looked in the mirror and I didn't know who I was looking at," Malveski said at the end of the first episode, after getting her eyebrows plucked and her hair shortened. "I definitely feel sexier.

"The world can be a torture chamber," she added. "You might as well look your best when you're going through it. It was very difficult," she said of the experience, which includes some humiliation in that friends have nominated the person because they didn't dress well. "I wouldn't wish it on my own worst enemy. But now I'm glad I did it because I know where I need to work and where I need to enhance."

Television programmers have used the success of shows like *What Not to Wear* and *Extreme Makeover* to increase their own offerings. The Learning Channel has created a franchise of people ranging from *A Makeover Story* to *Buff Brides*. In *A Makeover Story* two friends are made over in preparation for a big event, while their friends and family offer up examples of when the two may have had a few fashion faux pas. *Buff Brides*, which aired on the Discovery Health Channel in the fall of 2003, followed a group of brides as they attempted to work out, trim down and shape up for their upcoming weddings.

Besides *Queen for a Day*, which launched on TV in 1956 and gave the contestant with the best sob story a gift of appliances, the makeover wing of the reality genre can actually be tracked decades back to the launch of *This Old House* on PBS. To that end, the home makeover genre has been one of the fastest growing areas of reality television, with shows ranging from simple makeovers, to major overhauls, and tips on selling.

This Old House is the granddaddy of the home makeover shows. It launched on PBS stations in 1979 with host Bob Vila and carpenter Norm Abrams leading a homeowner through a major renovation. Over the course of the season, viewers saw the home owner deal with architects, budgets, demolition, and all other aspects of the remodel. Soon, home owners were writing to the series producers to get their show featured. The hook? The homeowners needed to have the cash for the original remodel, although the show dramatically supplemented the project with donations of major new technology. Virtually every home makeover show today can draw a line to *This Old House*.

One of early reality home successes was The Learning Channel's *Trading Spaces*, which took two families, had them swap homes for a weekend, and spend no more than $1,000 remaking a room. The show launched with Alex McLeod as the host, a couple of designers and a carpenter named Ty Pennington. After a season, McLeod left and was replaced by actress Paige Davis. *Trading Spaces* hit at the right time. As home prices soared, Americans looked for ways to repair and update their own homes, rather than buying others. *Trading Spaces* took advantage of the craze and soon became a water cooler-talk generating show. Ratings rose, and in the usual television pattern, producers looked for similar shows.

Trading Spaces also spread beyond television, generating a series of spin-off books and DVDS. The show also served as a farm team for talent for future shows. Alex McLeod, after working on *Trading Spaces* went on to be the host for the first season of *Joe Millionaire*. Ty Pennington is now the host of *Extreme Makeover: Home Edition*, an ABC spin-off of *Extreme Makeover*. Designer Genevieve Gorder went on to host "Town Haul," a TLC series where she remade parts of towns. And Doug Wilson, a fellow designer, has hosted a couple of shows for TLC.

Although *Trading Spaces* was a big hit for TLC, its audience numbers and popularity were far outstripped by ABC's *Extreme Makeover: Home Edition*. The show started as a one-time special in 2003, hosted by Pennington, who led a team of contractors and designers in a project to rebuild a family's home in a week. The homes are usually demolished and rebuilt from the ground up. They're then stocked with all new appliances, fixtures and electronic equipment; thanks in part to show sponsor Sears. At the end of the episode, the family returns to marvel at their new homes. There are usually paid-up mortgages, cars, and occasionally college educations for the children.

Families were chosen based on need. Typically there's a medical situation in the house, forcing the family to focus their money and energy on the sick family member. In one case, a husband died suddenly, leaving a farm behind that needed tending. In one of the most memorable, the show rebuilt a home for a woman named Sweet Alice Harris, who ran a group-home shelter in a tough Los Angeles neighborhood. "I had [seen the program] twice, but I had no idea to ever ask them to come to Watts, because I didn't think they would come to Watts," Harris told reporters in July 2004.

Thousands of people write to the show each month seeking help from the show. Harris was actually nominated by someone else, who realized she needed help. At the start of each episode, Pennington introduces the family to the audience and talks about their struggle. Then, they're seen being sent on vacation. Moments after they leave, a team of movers gets in and packs all of the families belongings, which are then sent to a storage warehouse. Some stuff, however, is held out to add a personal touch to the new house.

Unlike *This Old House*, in which families must have the financial where-withal to cover the improvements, families are given the improvements for free. And, when the homes are done, they're usually worth much more than when the project started. Homeowners get around paying taxes on the cost of the improvements because the producers rent the home to the production for 14 days. Under current tax rules, television producers can rent homes for that long and any home improvements done during that period are exempt from state and federal taxes.

"It really is quite gratifying," Pennington said. "I mean, I've been involved in lots of home improvement projects, but I've never walked away from projects feeling the kind of gratification you do, and it really is amazing how it spreads like—its pay-forward type, and just communities, neighbors, volunteers…. It's such a positive energy that we're putting into the families' lives and it's really remarkable."

And that connection remains afterward. Producer Tom Forman gets letters and cards from each of the families involved with the show, as do the designers. A common theme is their desire to help others. So for the 2005 holiday season, Forman and the designers teamed up with previous *Extreme Makeover* families to help others. And in 2006, the crew headed to the South to help areas ravaged by Hurricane Katrina. Forman likes to say they show simply provides the family with a house. However, it's much more; it's a change of life.

The home makeover genre includes a variety of sublevels. Using the *Trading Spaces* model, The Learning Channel then launched *While You Were Out*, a show in which a team of designers and carpenters remade a room in a house while the owner was away. VH1 aired a similar version in which a celebrity remade a room for a fan. And, of course, the Home & Garden Network (HGTV) has a handful of shows in the same vein.

Turner Broadcasting's TBS, for instance, aired a show called *The Mansion*. Each week, the teams were charged with remaking a room. While they worked together, they were also working for their own benefits, because viewers had a vote on the winner, who would ultimately get the house. Michele Massato and her husband Jay were fans of the home makeover genre when she signed up for *The Mansion*. "It certainly was an experience," she said. "Once you get a taste of that, I can't say I wouldn't like a little more."

A&E also got into the home-building reality show business with *House of Dreams*. In this 2004 series, couples competed together to design and build a house, with one couple winning it in the end. George Wendt of *Cheers* fame was the host. It lasted one cycle.

One of the latest twists includes helping home owners get their homes ready for sale, among them is *Sell This House*. "How-to shows are always going to be around in one way or another," said *Sell this House* host Tanya Memme. "People are learning you don't need a professional designer.

"For the longest time, I thought, when is this fad going to end," Memme added. "But it's what people want to see. If the ratings drop, then you'll see them drop off. There are going to be specific design shows that stay and are around for a while. And then there will be the ones that go away."

The makeover genre has also spread beyond homes and faces, to cars. The Learning Channel airs *Overhaulin'*, a weekly show in which an unsuspecting person's car is taken to a secret shop and given a makeover. MTV has its own version, *Pimp My Ride*, in which a rundown car is updated to include such features as DVD players and video games. And Country Music Television has a version where the crew fixes someone's truck. The Learning Channel also tried to extend the makeover concept to small business owners in *Taking Care of Business*, a short-lived reality show. Like other makeover series, *Taking Care of Business* had a team of experts go into struggling businesses and perform a makeover. In each of the 13 episodes, viewers saw the team go into a business and perform such tasks as moving display racks, implementing sales systems, and giving owners tips on customer service.

One could argue that series such as *Supernanny*, in which a professionally nanny goes into a home with unruly kids or, say, *Wife Swap* have makeover elements as well. Though not as easy to spot, the techniques are there. For instance, in *Supernanny*, nanny Jo Frost teaches families how to deal with their children. Nick Powell, producer of *Supernanny*, said there's "take away" information in the series to help viewers.

Likewise, at the end of every *Wife Swap*, ABC's series in which the wife of a family swaps with another for two weeks, the couple share what they've learned about each other and their own lives. For instance, in one episode featuring a couple from Montclair, New Jersey, the husband Jacques [Moose] Bramhall runs a tight ship, right down to having three different sponges to do the dishes. During the episode, viewers saw him say his life is so well planned that on vacation he and his wife even planned when they'd be intimate. His experience of having a television "wife" for two weeks who was more of a free spirit changed, in some ways, his own life afterward. "After we got back, we decided we were going to be the new fun us," said Elaine Bramhall, who spent two weeks in another home. "We were down the Jersey shore, we decided to go out, we went to a nudie bar, and then we ran out of ideas."

NBC's *The Biggest Loser,* with a group of overweight contestants looking to lose weight, and VH1's *Celebrity Fit Club,* a similar concept but with celebrities, are also makeover shows of a different type.

One thing for certain, producers have yet to exhaust the potential for makeover show ideas. Casting web sites are filled with casting requests for make over shows. For instance, one post in late 2005 was searching for wives to nominate their husbands for a show called *Fix My Husband,* asking: "Has your husband become so comfortable in the marriage that he no longer looks like the man you married? If so, we want to meet him." The pitch went on to say, "Over the course of just one week, selected husbands will learn priceless pointers that will enhance their marriage, and more importantly, keep their wives happy."

To that end, as long as producers continue to drum up ideas, there will also be an endless line of people willing to take a chance at a free makeover before millions of Americans TV viewers. Just as Delisa Stiles, who said she would do it again. "In a heartbeat," she said. "I would absolutely do it again, this has given me a clean slate and a jump start."

CHAPTER 6

All Is Not What It Seems: Reversed Reality

Matt Kennedy Gould was a just an average guy when producers for a new series called *Joe Schmo* found him in Pittsburgh. He was delivering pizzas. He had just dropped out of law school. And, when they found him he was playing basketball. Gould acted a bit in college, but never really attempted to become an actor. "I think I could have been an actor," he said. "I just never wanted to be a starving actor." Gould was plucked out of obscurity to be thrust into a new reality show that was being shot for the Spike TV network, a cable channel aimed at young men.

He would be the first of many potential reality show cast members who have been put into a new subgenre of reality, perhaps best called "twists," in which the player signs on for one contest but at some point finds out that he or she has been cast in a different show. Oftentimes, the result is that the contestant is made to look silly or is the focus of the joke.

At the time he was found by producers, Gould was 34 years old and believed he was being cast for a new show called *Lap of Luxury*, in which the contestants lived in a mansion, did really cool stuff, and in the end there was a grand prize. However, the joke was on him. The entire show was about fooling him.

The scenario was similar for Joseph Halling, a Minneapolis shoe salesman. Halling was with friends at a karaoke bar when producers for a new series called *The WB's Superstar USA* encouraged him to attend an upcoming audition for singers. "I sang 'I'm too sexy,'" Halling recalled. "One of the field producers was there. She was like, 'You rock, you have to audition.'"

He was told the show was just like *American Idol*. And believing he could sing—and having an outgoing personality—Halling jumped at the chance for fame and fortune, or at the very least a little bit of attention via a prime-time reality show. The problem was that *The WB's Superstar USA* was like *American Idol* in some ways, but not a lot like the popular Fox talent search program in many more ways. Halling had never auditioned for a show before, but figured he'd give it a try. He stopped by the audition site and when he was done headed to his shoe-selling job.

What neither Gould nor Halling knew when they signed up for the new shows was that they would be part of a growing trend in reality television, in which the person at the forefront of the show is being bamboozled. They're called "twist" shows because somewhere along the way someone has been misled, usually the central character, big-time. Typically, the viewers are in on the joke—much like a *Colombo* mystery where those watching at home know the answer but must sit and watch the aging detective solve the case.

Often, though not always, the concept is built around humiliating the person who is not in on the joke for the enjoyment of those at home. And part of the appeal is watching to see if the fooled player ever figures out the joke—or at least before the show ends. Likewise, the beauty of the twist show is that there's the prime moment right at the end when the player is finally let in on the joke. This moment creates drama, no doubt, as viewers and the producers wonder, "How will they react? Will they be brokenhearted or okay with the scam?" Those answers, of course, won't be known for weeks after the series launch, but that's often enough to keep viewers glued to their television sets.

The concept for *Joe Schmo* was simple. Gould was the only regular person on the show, and the rest of the people were actors playing the parts of stereotypical reality show contestants. Every game, every challenge, every conversation was about tweaking Gould, who claimed later to have no clue he was being fooled. "I knew it was weird," he said after the show ended. "I didn't know why it was so weird until they told me."

Joe Schmo was the brainchild of two producers Rhett Reese, a writer on the big-screen film *Monsters Inc.* and Paul Wernick, who had been a producer on *Big Brother 2*, CBS's reality series built around people living together while cameras watch. Like many, Reese and Wernick had felt the reality format had become stale. That's because three years after the success of *Survivor*, most programs had attempted to copy the format of the popular CBS series. Many tried to mix cast members of different backgrounds, there were challenges to decide who was better than the rest, and in the end someone got kicked off. Some, such as Fox's *Temptation Island* were so brazen in their duplication of *Survivor* that they aped such aspects as holding eviction ceremonies at night under torchlight and used similar music. Similar complaints were made about dating shows, when others tried to copy ABC's *The Bachelor*. Indeed, television has long been considered a medium where success begets copycats, and the reality television craze was no different.

But some producers and network programmers were looking for ways to tweak the format in a way to put new life into the relatively new and still growing genre. From there sprouted the twist genre, where producers altered the tried and true formats with a bit of duplicity to create a different from of reality programming. The first entry into this new world was Fox's *Joe Millionaire*, which used the basic format of *The Bachelor* and turned it upside down.

Midway through 2002, Fox executives and reality show producers at Rocket Science Productions secretly hatched the concept of a new, albeit familiar in general, dating show.

Producers shipped 20 women to France where they lived in a chateau, while bidding for the affections of a man they thought was a multimillionaire, though he was really a construction worker. It wasn't an easy task, no doubt, especially in a world in which Web sites track casting calls—often blowing the concept of a show. More importantly, producers on all reality shows go out of their way to not let candidates know much about the program they're trying out for in the first place. They do so because they don't want contestants for new shows to audition with the concept in mind. Moreover, the concept is usually far from the show description anyway.

Still, to avoid the standard casting and publicity routines, producers for *Joe Millionaire* went outside the usual channels every step of the way. Rather than hold casting calls, which generate tons of candidates and potentially could have exposed the format, they searched modeling and talent agencies for potential bachelorettes. Contestant Zora Andrich, who had done some modeling before being cast on *Joe Millionaire*, said another agent suggested her to producers. "I never expected it for myself," she recalled. "When I got the call, they asked if I was single, yes. Adventurous? Yes. And are you open to finding love in a foreign land?" The concept sounded appealing to Andrich. "It was not like I was looking to get on any of these shows," she said. "For me, I had been single for quite some time, and looked at it as just an adventure in a foreign land. I'm a big believer in anything is possible."

Andrich was one of the women selected and shipped to France for the taping of *Joe Millionaire*. Evan Marriott, a construction worker who claimed to have made just $19,000 working part time in the previous year, in this case, played the bachelor. But rather than have him play himself, Marriott took on the role of a millionaire. He was coached how to act, what to say, and how to pretend to have a lot of money.

In the first episode, viewers saw each of the contestants learn that Marriott had just inherited $50 million. He was paired with a real butler, Paul Hogan, who helped him navigate the upper crust world and know how to hold a wine glass. "I've never seen so many glasses on a table in my life," Marriott said at one point.

Early on, the women gasped when they saw the chateau where they would live during the taping of the show. They stood by as host Alex McLeod said they would meet Evan Wallace, an heir to a fortune of $50 million. Marriott, playing the role of Evan Wallace, rode up on a horse, though it was clear he wasn't so good at that. After introducing himself, he rode off, but not before slipping in the stirrup and banging his chin on the saddle. "As I rode off, I realized I had just started the biggest lie of my life," he said on the show.

The women, however, wouldn't learn about his lack of cash until only one remained. "In a way, we're ripping off the mask of the people [who sign up for shows like *The Bachelor*], Fox reality programming executive Mike Darnell told *Daily Variety* when the show was announced. "We find out whether they're really doing this for love."

Immediately, the show was billed as the ditch digger versus the gold diggers, and each of the women were slammed publicly for being more interested in cash than love. Adding the to the gold digger tone of the show were some of the situations the producers put the women in. Early on, the 20 women were told there were a limited number of dresses available, forcing them to race to the closet and try to find one for them. One grabbed two, totally angering the others. "It was Darwin's dress theory!" one said. "The obnoxious will survive!" Not surprisingly, the women fought and scrambled for a hot dress, and perhaps for a shot at luring the millionaire. But what viewers weren't aware of when the show aired was that the women did not go to France looking for money. Some said afterward that they thought they were part of a different reality series altogether—not to date a wealthy bachelor. Bachelorette Sarah Kozar said after the show that she was led to believe it was 20 single and sophisticated women in France looking for love and adventure, not a dating show.

Still, *Joe Millionaire* became an instant hit, as viewers tuned in to see how the women reacted and schemed when faced with a hunky bachelor with a stuffed wallet. As viewers have come to expect, some of the women were ruthless in the way they played the game. Each week, viewers saw Marriott go on group outings with the women, and later one-on-one. And with most relationship reality series, there was plenty of alcohol to go around and the requisite hot tub.

The appeal for viewers, of course, was that somewhere along the line one of the women will be humiliated when finding out she played the game for a construction worker—and not a multimillionaire.

Adding to the emotional impact was early on the use of host Alex McLeod to tell the unlucky woman that it was time to leave. "We catered to every whim of these women," said McLeod. "That's why I don't feel guilty."

An average of 23 million people watched each week as Marriott whittled the bachelorettes down to just two—Andrich and Kozar. And in the finale, 40 million people tuned in, making it one of the largest single episode of a series that season.

"I'm a heavy-equipment operator for a construction company," Marriott told Andrich after revealing he wasn't a millionaire.

"I would like to continue the journey and see what happens," she said.

Producers then gave them each $500,000 for being part of the stunt. The journey ended soon after it started, or, more likely, after the Fox check cleared. They never were a couple. But that didn't matter. Viewers were tuned in to see how love blossomed, and more important, how the winner would react when learning of Marriott's lack of millions. The series worked because the entire show was filmed without any media exposure, thus preserving the unique twist involving Evan Marriott. Indeed, early on there was a small mention of Fox doing a relationship show, which may have kept reporters from digging any deeper, figuring it was another *Bachelor* rip-off.

Moreover, in the past Fox had been burned by the *Who Wants to Marry a Multimillionaire?* scandal, leaving most to believe that the network would produce something that resembled more of a traditional romance dating show.

"I'm not at all surprised with the success of ' *Joe Millionaire*," McLeod said. "I knew when they pitched me the concept I was excited. It's all in the concept. That's what sets it apart. It's hilarious. *Joe Millionaire* is funny and that is what people are responding to."

Producers and network executives noticed, too. They locked onto the twist aspect of reality television and immediately launched a wave of series where the main player was being duped in one way or another. While *Joe Millionaire* was racking up big, and surprising, ratings for Fox, producers were also quietly working on *Joe Schmo* and *Average Joe*, two series that would add a twist to the reality genre.

Joe Schmo was built around Gould, who thought he was going on a show called *Lap of Luxury*. Instead, the producers created a parody of the usual reality series, right down to the casting and host. Indeed, each of the cast around Gould could have come from a reality show casting template. For instance, like the first *Survivor, Lap of Luxury* had an older, stern former military man. There were also a couple of attractive women, some of them schemers. There was also someone playing a gay character, á la *Survivor* winner Richard Hatch.

"Reality TV was a bit stale," Wernick said. "You had the same sort of eviction scenes. We really thought this was ripe for parody. This was also before the twist was in vogue." What was ironic about the series, though, was *Lap of Luxury* could have been a real reality show. The game had the typical reality format. The contestants lived in a mansion, spent most of their time together, and were pitted against each other in challenges for prizes and immunity from being removed.

But even there, the producers cranked up the believability of the contests. In one, each of the contestants was required to place a body part on a nude porn star—with the goal being to be the player who could maintain contact with the porn star the longest.

Joe Schmo was interesting to viewers—and the producers—because Gould didn't always react the way they predicted, requiring the cast and crew to quickly ad-lib their way out. For instance, during the hands-on-a-porn-star stunt, Gould pulled his hand away first. By taking himself out of the game, it left the other cast members trying to figure out how long they had to play. Going in they all figured Gould would play to win, but when he didn't they were stuck with faking interest. Viewers watching at home got to see how Gould reacted, and how the producers dealt with his changes.

"We would sit in the trailer and say, 'Oh my God,'" Wernick said. "There was a fair amount of time where we were flying by the seat of our pants and had to throw out the script and the [show] bible."

Moreover, there was also a chance that one of the cast members could slip up and reveal the secret, which nearly occurred a handful of times. On one occasion, the older military guy, in discussing a previous contest, screwed up when answering Gould's question. Luckily, Gould didn't figure out he was being duped. "How many times did it come close?" said Wernick. "Often. Sitting in the control room it was one of the most fun, and the scariest times. We would sort of hang on every word."

Gould was the perfect contestant. He was emotional at times, seemed surprised when something went awry, and cried when fellow contestants were booted during a hilarious exit ceremony, which had the host toss a dish with the players face on it into a fireplace. In the last episode, scripted to have the jerk Hutch win, each of the cast members told Gould they were actors.

"The only real thing on this reality show is you," host Ralph Garman told Gould.

"We did this all for you, buddy," Garman added.

He wouldn't learn until later that the show was called *Joe Schmo*. But it didn't matter at that point; viewers were hooked, and the twist genre got yet another boost. "I was happy to be on a television show," Gould said. "And I wanted to be on a good one. I wasn't so sure I was on a good one, but when I found out [it was a spoof], it clicked in why it was so weird."

And it all worked because everyone played their part. "Actors and writers often talk about their work in the sense of passing the test of believability," said *Joe Schmo*'s Reese. "We had to sell it. We wanted it to be funny. But we needed to create a world where everything in this world was selling the deception, even down to the luggage tags. "If I were to just put this reality show on," he added. "I bet we could have fooled America into thinking all of these people were real."

Where *Joe Schmo* put one real person among a cast of actors, *Average Joe* took a beautiful woman and had her date a gaggle of not-so-handsome men. As with *Joe Schmo* the producers took advantage of the casting process, which left a lot of variables—and leeway—for contestants to be misled. Dating shows, for example, never state in applications that the bachelorettes will be presented with 20 hunky guys from which to choose. But, because *The Bachelor* had beautiful women dating an attractive man, and because *The Bachelorette* placed two dozen handsome men before a beautiful woman, most folks conclude that a given dating show paired up attractive people.

Not so with *Average Joe*. In fact, it was just the opposite. The producers found a beautiful woman, Melana Scantlin, a former NFL cheerleader, to be the center of the show. She assumed going in she'd have her pick of a bevy of studly men. She couldn't have been more wrong. "I think we're the anti-*Bachelor*," said executive producer Stuart Krasnow.

"We did the typical casting process," Krasnow told the *New York Daily News*. "But it was a little complicated. Part of our show was wanting to find guys who didn't look like, how do I say this politically correct[ly], who weren't hot guys." So, rather than let the average guys see who had also been cast they were kept apart. For all they knew going in, they were hot.

But, in casting, producers dismissed the really attractive men and found, well, average-looking guys. They found a mix of tall, short, fat, and scrawny men to vie for Scantlin's attention. Had they seen each other before the taping, it's possible some of the players could have figured the game out. More likely, though, some might have split, rather than being part of a show where they were presented as average guys.

"You never really have to lie about anything," Krasnow said. "We can't tell you exactly what's going to go on."

Playing along with the *Bachelor* concept, Scantlin stood out front of the mansion that would serve as home base for the taping, waiting for her potential mates to join her. In *The Bachelor* the women arrive one by one via limousine. At the start of *Average Joe,* a limo pulled up and a handsome guy walked over to Scantlin. But then he said he wasn't part of the game. Soon after, a busload of guys pulled up. One at a time they walked up to Scantlin and introduced themselves. Some were overweight. Others were blotchy from getting too much sun. Because they were pulling a ruse on Scantlin, the producers had another woman ready to step in if Scantlin decided to split. At first it was iffy. After the first few average guys got off the bus, Scantlin looked off to the side and questioned what was going on. She continued to play along, though.

"We really didn't know," Krasnow said. "Was she happy with us right after? No. I think she understood when you fill out an application and say you want to meet a guy who's funny and put looks fifth or sixth, that's what can happen."

Over the course of the six-week series, Scantlin dated each of the guys, and sent some packing. As a twist on the twist, the producers brought in a gaggle of handsome guys halfway through to tantalize Scantlin and torment the average Joes. Handsome ultimately won out, when in the end Scantlin chose one of the hunks brought in by the producers rather than one of the average guys. The finale came down to Jason Peoples, one of hunks, and Adam Mesh, a New Yorker from the average bunch. "I think I found a diamond in the rough," Scantlin said before selecting Jason.

A second episode of *Average Joe* was shot before the first one aired, also built around a beautiful woman dating average guys. And Mesh wasn't a loser after all. So many women wrote in saying they'd date him, that the producers shot *Average Joe: Adam Returns,* in which Mesh had his pick of the litter. Mesh, having perhaps felt duped the first time out, was extremely upset on camera when he was presented some model-quality women during the run of his show. During the episode, there was a long discussion, on camera, between Mesh and a producer. In the end, he won out.

Likewise, the producers of *Joe Schmo* immediately went into production with a second installment, but one that had a Joe and Jane Schmo in a twist on relationship series. The two believed they were in a new show called *Last*

Chance for Love, in which they would vie with other contestants for $100,000. They, too, were in a parody of the other relationship shows, and surrounded by stereotypical reality show contestants. And, they participated in hot tub dates, romantic dinners away from other competitors. Keeping with the parody, the producers also introduced revelations as "Falcon Twists," in which a falcon flew in to reveal the news, and Garmon, this time playing host Derek Newcastle, said "the Falcon has spoken."

Unlike the first *Joe Schmo,* the second version had the producers tweaking the format and concept during the taping. "All of these shows have new twists, the most shocking twist," Garman said. "The game is constantly shifting from one game to the next, so you don't know what it is. Initially it looks like *The Bachelor* or *The Bachelorette;* then, 'Are they playing for money or is this about true love or not?'"

However, where Gould made it through the first *Joe Schmo* without catching onto the twist, it wasn't long into the second version that one of the contestants figured out what was going on and forced the producers to change the game even further. Ingrid Wiese was cast in the second version as one of the real people among the actors. Trouble is, because she had a background battling booze and has a great sense of when someone was lying, figured out early on into production of *Joe Schmo 2* something was amiss. "My bull— factor is very high," she said. "I spend a lot of time sitting in meetings and listening to people, and have real reactions." Immediately, she knew something was wrong with the way people were reacting in the group meetings on *Joe Schmo 2.* Wiese went through a casting process to be on the show. But during the filming when a fellow player admitted his agent got him the job a day earlier, her suspicions were confirmed. Producers, faced with the revelation, then brought Weise in on the hoax and had her play along with the ruse.

Like Gould, Halling wasn't in on the joke at the start of *Superstars USA.* Produced by Mike Fleiss, the brains behind *The Bachelor* series as well as *Who Wants to Marry a Multimillionaire?* the show veered off of the concept of *American Idol.* Whereas *Idol* searched for the greatest singers, *Superstars USA* wanted the worst. But they never told those auditioning that that was the goal. Instead, thousands showed up for casting calls thinking they could be the next singing sensation. That should come as no surprise. Millions of wannabe singers watched folks such as Ruben Studdard, Clay Aiken, and Kelly Clarkson rocket to stardom after appearing on *American Idol* and figured fame was just an audition away. If the *Idol* winners could make it with the television exposure, so could they, many figured. And the format had proven successful in the Nielsen department as well. *American Idol* was the top rated show of the 2003–2004 television season, clearly indicating the genre had mass audience appeal.

"This is a genre ripe for parody," said then WB entertainment president Jordan Levin in announcing the show. "Back when we first introduced this type of show to an American audience with *Popstars,* we found that the most memorable and relatable contestants were the people who had perhaps more courage than talent," he added, referring to a previous WB talent show designed to find a new pop group.

"When I did *Who Wants to Marry a Multimillionaire?* ratings skyrocketed because people couldn't believe what they were seeing," Fleiss said in the announcement. "The fact that we are able to perpetrate a hoax of this magnitude with thousands of people for more than a moment is absolutely incredible." To keep the secret, contestants were never allowed to see other singers perform. Not taking too much of a risk, Fleiss stuck close to the proven *American Idol* model.

He cast three judges—rapper Tone-Loc, singer Vitamin C and producer Chris Briggs, who worked with Fleiss on *Who Wants to Marry a Multimillionaire?* They were, of course, to mimic the *American Idol* panel of Randy Jackson, Paula Abdul, and Simon Cowell. In this outing, Briggs was the cantankerous Cowell, willing to say anything to cut down a singer. But, here's where the game changed—big time. As each warbler wandered in, they heaped praise on those who stunk, and dismissed anyone who had a real singer's voice.

"Robert, Robert, superstardom begins with you," Vitamin C told one particularly bad singer. "You hit some notes, I don't know how you hit them. Do you still have both your testicles?" Briggs told another, equally awful contestant. But when a singer was good, they simply bowed their heads and dismissed them. With one attractive singer, Briggs said her voice was bad but that she was "hot" and asked for a date. "If they were bad, our panel showered them with praise," host Brian McFayden told viewers. "And if they were good, watch out." After each audition, McFayden—playing the role of Ryan Seacrest on *American Idol*—interviewed the contestants.

And to a player, each one was excited about the false praise they earned from the judges. "I'm on my way," said one joyously teary-eyed contestant. "This is the first step."

Growing up in Minnesota, Jamie Foss's singing abilities were always praised by those around her. She wanted to be an actress—or in the entertainment business in some way—and earned money singing at weddings and funerals. She, too, attended the Minneapolis auditions for *Superstar USA.* Foss found an audition call on a local Web site. "It said, 'Are you the next singing sensation?' And I thought, 'Yes, I am,'" Foss said. "I said, 'I'm going to audition for this." She never expected anything to come of the audition. And she never could have imagined simply going on an audition for a new television show would make her the brunt of on-air and off-air jokes. "I know I'm not a phenomenal singer," she said. "I still think I'm good."

She was selected for the show, but not because she was a good singer. She walked into the audition ready to sing four different songs. But then a producer said everyone was singing those tunes, and suggested "Like a Virgin" by Madonna. Foss didn't know the words, so she asked if she could write them on her hand. "They said, 'Oh we'll cut [the camera] out whenever you look at your hands,'" she said.

Of course they didn't. Having a buxom blonde looking at the words on her hand as she badly sang "Like a Virgin" was priceless. Producers also raved about her shapely figure. They encouraged her to play up being sexy. Foss and Halling were among a group of singers sent to California for the show's taping.

Among the group were a woman who could barely pronounce the words to the songs she sung—even producers couldn't figure out what she sang—and a flamboyant young man who modeled himself after Britney Spears. Yes, Britney Spears. Once in Los Angeles, the contestants were given complete makeovers, including new hair and makeup, wardrobes, put up in fancy hotels and treated like stars. They were in it for a $100,000 record deal. "Everything was so secret," Halling said. "Throughout the show they were great at keeping it a secret." As with most talent genre reality shows, a few singers were cut each week leading up to the live performances.

At the live performance end of the production, Fleiss had to work some magic on the audience as well. On *American Idol* the audience often reacts to the performances much the way the judges do, whether it is good or bad. But with *Superstar* Fleiss had to manage audience reactions as well. For some performances, the audience was padded with friends of his who were in on the joke, so they cheered the bad singers and booed the really good ones. At one taping he told the crowd the singers were sick and were from the "one wish foundation," and singing on stage was their wish. The thinking was that no one with a heart would boo a bad singer knowing going in that this was their dream and that the contestant was suffering from a terminal disease. (Fleiss's stunt did get some complaints from the Make a Wish organization.)

At another, the audience members were paid to sit there. The goal was to have an audience keep the mystery alive by wildly cheering the bad singers. It worked. "We lied, they believed," McFayden told viewers.

Oh, did they.

Halling, who survived the first round of cuts and had the stage name Jo-Jo, believed that was an indication of his singing prowess. "After I realized I was going to the next round, I think, I'm obviously a lot better than I think. Then I've got more attitude, that whole diva personality, which Jo-Jo's got."

The secret wasn't revealed to the players until the taping was over, but even then they couldn't spill the details to family and friends. For Floss, that meant getting an angry call from her mother after she heard a promotion for the new show on the radio. "Everybody in my family knows I'm a pretty decent singer," Foss said. "They took it a lot worse than I did."

Foss admits she was angry and frustrated for a short period of time, while Halling said he laughed hysterically when he found out. "We lied to you when we said you were a good singer," McFayden told Foss on air.

Trying to capitalize on the exposure, Foss vowed to move to California and spend a year pursuing acting. And she doesn't feel she has to prove to people she can sing. "People might think I'm just delusional," she said. "But it's not really what [they] think. I don't think I need to prove anything to anybody. That's just who I am. I'm a pretty decent singer. And singing is always subjective. My family thinks I'm good."

The twist in *Superstar USA* worked. Soon after it launched, the series became one talked about around the water cooler, perhaps one of the best tests of the success of a reality show. Also, radio stations around the country began talking about it and soon ratings were climbing. And because it worked so well, it hasn't been tried again—yet. Perhaps down the road, when the memory of the first show fades, the producers will be able to pull off another *Superstar USA*, but until then, Foss may be the one and only champion. It also extended the twist genre further, and added yet another dimension to the reality format.

After the success of *Joe Schmo*, Reese and Wernick took their twist format to a larger scale in *Invasion Iowa*. Riverside, a small town in Iowa, had billed itself as the future birthplace of Captain James Kirk of *Star Trek* fame, who was played by William Shatner. So, Wernick and Reese brought Shatner to Riverside under the guise of shooting a movie there, and using the residents in the town as part of the cast. The residents were told they would be in a big-screen film starring Shatner. The producers even allowed the media to report the film as fact.

"William Shatner, who played the cowboy commander of the starship USS Enterprise in the 1960s series *Star Trek*, was in Riverside to hold auditions for four small parts in a low-budget science fiction film he wrote with

Star Trek co-star Leonard Nimoy, who played Mr. Spock in the series and subsequent movies," the Associated Press wrote.

"Shatner told local residents that the working title of the film is Invasion Iowa," according to the Associated Press account. "He called the film 'his baby,' and said he's been dreaming of putting the story to film for the past 30 years."

But, when Shatner got there, he played the part of a stereotypical, egotistical big Hollywood star. "One of the dangers of shooting a show like this," Reese said, "is that you never know how it's going to end." The end of Invasion Iowa had Shatner telling the residents the entire process was a hoax, and rather than being a movie, they were in a week-long television series.

"Did we hurt their feelings, did we stun them with the truth?" Shatner told reporters before the show launched. "In fact, with the care and love that was engendered by everybody for everybody, the final result when we resolved it, was, amenable, equitable and in the end, which I believe we'll show, a thousand people showed up for last night's party cheering and crying." It also helped ease their pain that everyone in the film got paid, as did the town, which got $100,000 for being part of the hoax.

Shatner and the producers said they tried not to hurt anyone's feelings in the process. "And so we discarded many of the gags, many of the things that would have hurt feelings," Shatner said. "We tried our best to—when we did our jokes, to make them palatable. In the end, we tried to ameliorate as much as possible any hurt feelings."

Fox took the twist concept in a slightly different direction in 2004 with My Big Fat Obnoxious Fiancé," a series that had a woman trying to convince her parents she was marrying a fat obnoxious man. In this case, the man was played by an actor and the woman, school teacher Randi Coy, was charged with getting her family to believe she really loved the guy, no matter how poorly he treated her or them. Coy, a Catholic school teacher at the time, believed the person playing her fiancé was another regular person, when he was indeed, actor Steven Bailey. She ultimately convinced her family she was marrying the creep and won $1 million. At that point she learned Bailey was an actor.

"It was shock after shock after shock," she told the New York Daily News after it was over. During run of the show, Coy lost her teaching job when her school officials said the lying on television didn't fit in with the beliefs of the Arizona school. "Some felt it was a great opportunity for Ms. Coy, others felt the opposite, and they concluded from the show promos that it looked like something that wouldn't go hand-in-hand with Catholic values," Mary Jo West, a spokeswoman for the Roman Catholic Diocese of Phoenix said at the time.

Fox tried the concept again with *My Big Fat Obnoxious Boss,* a series spoofing shows like *The Apprentice,* in which real players are forced to compete for a job with a terrible boss being played by an actor. To get the job, or so they thought, the cast had to complete in ridiculous tasks like trying to sell reusable toilet paper. Fox, however, faced with low ratings was forced to flush the series early, proving again that the second version of a twist series rarely holds up.

Another take on the *Obnoxious* idea was NBC's short-lived *$25 Million Dollar Hoax,* which had Christine Sanford being handed a faux $5 million check from Ed McMahon. Sanford's goal, as set up by the producers, was to spend as much of it as she could while alienating her family. At every step along the way, actors were there to make the family feel worse as Sanford frittered the money away, without sharing any with them. "It's only going to get worse," a show narrator said after a Sanford shopping trip. Her family watches as she buys a Hummer and outrageous outfits. "It was only 20 minutes in," she said on the show, "and I was already feeling really crappy." Well, so were critics, who slammed the show's callous ways.

Sanford's efforts were all leading toward a bonus payoff scandal, in which she would spin a wheel rigged to land on $25 million. And, if she could convince all of her family to stick around for the big spin, she would earn $400,000 for the family. If they don't stand by her, she got nothing.

When the show ended, the family, which did stubbornly stuck near Sanford, they were told the truth and got the money and some other prizes. "You can have all the riches of this world," Sanford's father Guy said in the finale, "but if you don't have the love of a family, it's worthless." Considering the bad reviews and low ratings, *Hoax* was worthless, too.

A couple of other shows have also worked a twist into their general concepts, too. While not fully twists along the lines of *Joe Schmo* or *Average Joe,* the twists worked into a couple of shows changed the direction and fates of their players. Also, some of the twists caused serious distress to the people led to become part of a show only to find out along the way they were misled.

In 2003, Bravo aired a dating series called *Boy Meets Boy,* in which, much like in the *Bachelor* series, a gay man dated a group of supposedly gay men, in hopes of finding a mate. The twist: Some straight men were in the group of contestants, setting up the potential of a gay man falling for a heterosexual man. It was the first time a network had offered up a same-sex dating show, but by putting a straight contestant in the mix, it added a twist. "We have created a gay world where the straight guys are in the closet," producer Douglas Ross told the Associated Press at the time. If the straight man was selected, he won a prize.

In a similar twist, Fox launched a show in 2004 called *Playing It Straight*, where a female contestant named Jackie had to pick a mate out of 12 hunky guys. The twist? Some were gay. And if she ended up with a straight guy, she and he would share $1 million. If she fell for a gay guy, he got the cash. The trouble was that ratings for the show were so low, Fox never aired the finale.

Not all twist shows have been fun and pleasant, though. Once it was okay to dupe people on reality shows, producers used it as a tool to lure players in for one type of show and put them in another. In two cases—*Cold Turkey*, an anti-smoking show, and *Intervention*, a show in which families hold interventions to help addicted people get help, the subjects were lied to in order to get them on the show. And then, once the cameras were rolling, the twist was revealed.

The producers of *Cold Turkey*, which aired on PAX-TV, convinced 10 people to participate in a reality show by telling them they were playing for prizes such as driving a stock car or getting a chance to go into space with NASA. All 10 were also medium to heavy smokers addicted to nicotine. "This blows," Keith Jones said in the first episode after learning he was there to give up smoking rather than in for a chance to drive a race car.

The second season of *Cold Turkey*, as PAX TV publicity information stated, introduced 10 "unsuspecting chain smokers bamboozled into thinking they were joining the cast of a *Survivor*-style reality show called *Pushing the Limits* only to discover they've been brought together to quit smoking."

And the A&E Network launched a series called *Intervention*, in which people with a variety of mental issues, drug habits, or other problems were lured onto a show believing they would be part of a documentary covering their problem only to find out they would be part of an intervention.

The show, which got picked up for a second season, was slammed by critics, who attacked the duplicity of the process, especially with such risky subjects. Early episodes looked at a chronic gambler who relied on his family for money and an actress who suffered from agoraphobia and had a shopping addiction.

If anything, the notion of a twist has made it more difficult for the real people who get into reality shows to know exactly what the show is their on. Even for the actors getting into reality to gain exposure, the threat of a twist has created another level of anxiety. The real downside of a twist show, however, is that the short history has already proven that the concept can work well once, but when tried a second time it struggles. *Joe Millionaire* was a monster hit, but the second version didn't draw an audience even close. *Joe Schmo* drew ratings and generated water cooler buzz for Spike TV, but a second version didn't.

Joe Schmo was "well-intentioned and fun," Garman said; in contrast, shows such as *The WB's Superstar USA* and Fox's *The Swan* are hitting people in sensitive emotional areas. "We go to these people, we say, 'We're going to put you on a reality show,' and it is," Garman added. "And at the reveal, at the end, we hope they're going to have a good show, and you come out of the ride feeling strong."

CHAPTER 7

This Show Seems Awfully Familiar

The spring of 2004 marked a watershed moment for reality television in general, and specifically the people who create and telecast the genre. That's because during the late winter and early spring reality television faced reality: Producers and networks were copying ideas from each other and around the globe. They were producing shows similar to those planned by other networks at a rapid pace. In an odd twist, networks were duplicating reality show ideas after being pitched by the producers, who in turn took their shows elsewhere. And they got away with it.

In fairness, copying programs has been a staple of the television industry for decades. There's an old saw that says, "Success begets success." But in television, it's "Success begets copycats." Once a successful program hits the airwaves, rival networks seek to duplicate the success with similar, though not identical, concepts.

For example, when NBC found a monster hit with *Friends* rival networks sought a similar format. But doing so isn't that easy. Sure, anyone could try to mimic the basic format of six *Friends* hanging out together in an incredibly huge New York City apartment. But being successful in scripted entertainment is much more difficult. Besides the concept—six *Friends*, etc—an entertainment series needs a script and a cast. Legal issues aside, all of those factors combined make it difficult for another network to mimic the format of a hit show. And there are legal issues, specifically the copyrighted nature of the script itself.

Friends is just one example of a concept that ignited interest by other networks. In fall 2004, network television executives were contemplating how they would be able to capitalize off of the success of ABC's darkly comedic drama *Desperate Housewives*. Before that, networks looked for ways to copy HBO's hit *The Sopranos*. Yet long before the new schedules were announced, critics were warning network executives to take care in launching *Desperate Housewives* clones. The fact is that outright copying of a scripted entertainment show is difficult. Moreover, history has shown that the programs that come after tend to not fare well.

Friends ended its run in May 2004. Not one of the copycat shows that followed its launch in 1994 was around to say farewell. Come to think of it, few of the executives who launched duplicate shows were around, either.

Also, there has been a gentleman's agreement among network officials not to poach other networks' ideas. And if they did copy shows—the basic form of many shows are alike anyway—they rarely discussed such activities in public, let alone boasted about them. However, in spring 2004, the gentlemen's agreement went out the window when it came to reality television. The change launched a bevy of shows with similar titles, concepts and forms. So many, in fact, it was often hard for viewers to decide or decipher the differences between the shows: *Super Nanny* or *Nanny 911*; *Wife Swap* or *Trading Spouses*; *The Bachelor* or *For Love or Money*.

"It does seem strange to us to see that so many shows are copied," Stephen Lambert, producer of *Wife Swap* told television writers in July 2004. Lambert knows well the impact and experience of shows being copied. *Wife Swap*, a popular reality show in Britain, has the wives of two families switching homes for two weeks. The settings are often dramatically different. For example, a clean freak is put into a home best described as a dump. In the first week, the wives must abide by the rules of their new homes. If they eat steak, she does. If they're messy, she has no say. In the second week, she sets the rules, often resulting in massive changes in the host families.

ABC commissioned a U.S. version of the show from producer RDF Media, the same company that created and produced the British version, in December 2002, and it became public in January 2003, The deal wasn't unusual at all since many of the U.S. concepts for reality programming had been developed and tested elsewhere. For instance, CBS's *Big Brother* was a show that had aired in other parts of the world first. Network officials, after seeing shows like *Wife Swap* hit abroad, secured the U.S. rights to the concept. Somewhere along the way, though, networks and producers realized that it was easy enough to simply pluck the "idea" for a reality show, thereby getting around many of the copyright issues that halt full-fledged copies.

As with most other genres of television programming, there has been some level of idea plucking from the start. Yet, it was done without fanfare. Often, too, it was kept on a smaller basis, largely because some networks and producers had launched lawsuits when the copies got to close for comfort. For instance, CBS officials claimed ABC's critically lambasted series *I'm a Celebrity, Get Me Out of Here* was so similar to *Survivor* that they sought help from the courts.

CBS officials also sued to stop Fox's *Boot Camp* for the same reason. The lawsuit maintained the producers of *Boot Camp* copied specific elements from *Survivor* such as putting contestants in unfamiliar situations and kicking a player off in a ritualized ceremony. And radio star Howard Stern sued ABC and Telepictures over *Are You Hot?* a reality show he said was similar to his radio bit *The Evaluators*, in which women visited his show to get comments about their looks.

However, networks were hit with a blow—and producers perhaps emboldened—when CBS's suit to stop *I'm a Celebrity* was thrown out. Like *Survivor*, *I'm a Celebrity, Get Me Out of Here!* stranded a group of people in an unknown place, forced them to eat substandard meals, and compete in oddball challenges. And, every so often, one of the contestants would be kicked off the game. Unlike *Survivor*, *I'm a Celebrity* used low-level celebrities for their contestants. To the average viewer, it would be very easy to have described the ABC show as *Survivor* with celebrities. But the courts disagreed. In January 2003, a Manhattan U.S. District Court judge ruled for ABC and producer Granada that *I'm a Celebrity* was different from *Survivor*.

After hearing testimony and seeing five minutes of each show, Judge Loretta Preska maintained that the copyright law only protects the expression of ideas, not the ideas. She also claimed that *Survivor* had a serious tone, whereas *I'm a Celebrity* did not. *Survivor* also had better production qualities, she said.

CBS's lawsuit to stop *Boot Camp* was settled with the details never being released. *Boot Camp* didn't last beyond its first low-rated season. However, the decision against CBS emboldened producers and networks to go all out to pinch show concepts. And some of the copying was done blatantly. When ABC revealed it had picked up an U.S. version of *Wife Swap*, the plan was to launch the show in spring 2004. But then executives decided to hold it for the network's fall 2004 lineup. At the same time, Fox officials were working on a show about switching families in the first quarter of 2004, then Fox entertainment president Gail Berman told television writers in July

2004. "And when we learned they were putting it on in the fall, there was an opportunity in the marketplace," Berman said. So, Fox began developing and producing *Trading Spouses*, a *Wife Swap* look-alike and began airing it in July 2004.

"Clearly, *Wife Swap* isn't the first one that's been copied," Lambert said. "I mean, it's something that we were very upset about when we first heard about it.... We [have] a certain calm about it now." *Wife Swap* producer Jenny Crowther said British producers "were very shocked" about the copying going on. "So we were very disappointed," she said.

Trading Spouses launched on July 20, 2004. It started with strong viewership figures and was quickly labeled a summer ratings success in various media accounts. Those early ratings led to suggestions inside ABC and in media reports that the success of *Trading Spouses* could dilute the impact of *Wife Swap* once it finally launched. More serious, there was a concern that viewers could be confused between the two shows.

Concern on the part of ABC officials and *Wife Swap* producers were not misguided. History has shown that the first show in each of the genres—dating, adventure, and so on—have claimed the highest ratings and been considered the standard bearer. To that end, history has also shown that the second and third shows in those formats tended to not survive beyond their first cycles. "When you get the big one like an *American Idol* or a *Survivor*, one of those shows, the imitators pale in comparison, and that's what's healthy about the marketplace," said Fox's Berman.

But ABC's *Wife Swap* launched in 2004 and seemed to have bucked the second-show fails trend. *Wife Swap* started with began solid ratings in its own right. And, well into the fall of 2004 it was still a strong show for ABC. And it routinely generates good critical notices, whereas *Trading Spouses* has not. Even so, the calm that Lambert said existed in July 2004 was diminished in December 2004 when RDF Media filed a lawsuit against Fox and Rocket Science Laboratories, the producer of *Trading Spouses*, claiming Fox and Rocket Science stole the concept for *Wife Swap*.

In the suit, RDF claimed that *Trading Spouses* is too similar to *Wife Swap*, right down to the way they're edited and opening montages. RDF was seeking $18 million in damages, or $1 million for each episode of *Trading Spouses* that aired. "*Trading Spouses* more aptly might be entitled *Trading Copyrights* (or perhaps *Copyright Swap*) given that the defendants' series is nothing more than a blatant and wholesale copycat of RDF Media's original, innovative and highly successful *Wife Swap* series," the lawsuit stated.

Wife Swap was but one concept that appeared to be willingly copied by another network. When ABC hit big with the game show *Who Wants to Be a*

Millionaire? Fox launched *Greed,* a game show that didn't fare as well, though had many similar aspects in terms of style, tone, and look.

In a gross oversimplification of the process, it's just easier to rush a reality show into production. It's a much faster process than scripted series, which take months to ramp up to start production and then produce. A reality show can be cast, shot, and edited in a matter of weeks. Therein lies some of the reasons there have been so many copies. When a network says its developing a drama about a police precinct, rivals know there are copyright issues, casting, and production details involved to get a show on the air.

With reality, though, so much information can be pulled from a casting call sheet that even doing that publicly can offer rivals enough information to steal and idea. For example in early 2005, ABC posted on its Web site casting calls for 10 reality shows. Here's how some were described:

The Scholar

Set at a major university, *The Scholar* will be the first unscripted series ever to celebrate higher education as the ultimate American prize. Fifteen high school seniors, who might not otherwise have an opportunity to pursue a top-notch college education due to financial restraints, will be given the chance to compete for a full ride scholarship to the college of their choice. Applicants will have to demonstrate excellence in the areas of academics, leadership, school spirit and community service.

Or

Vacation Show

The makers of the new hit show *Wife Swap* are looking for families with big personalities for the pilot of their new show. Does your family vacation to fun, exotic or unique locations? Is your family entertaining, interesting or quirky? Are the kids in your family between the ages of 6 and 18? Would you like to show America what's great about your vacation? If so, get in touch, your family could be the stars of our show!

It's one thing for network officials to go out now and copy those ideas, once the concept has been revealed. It's quite another for network officials to have meetings with the producers of those shows and then go and produce their own versions of a similar show, without the involvement of the creating producers.

That's what happened in 2004, when Fox and NBC each developed reality shows built around a group of boxers fighting for the ultimate prize—a contract. But the real fight took place away from the ring, with sniping between producers and network executives. In early 2004, NBC went public with its plans to launch a series called *The Contender*. The show was developed at DreamWorks, a production studio created by Steven Spielberg, Jeffrey Katzenberg, and David Geffen. Katzenberg reached out to *Survivor* producer Mark Burnett to help develop *The Contender*, which would also include help from *Rocky* writer and star Sylvester Stallone and boxing great Sugar Ray Leonard. The concept was simple. Find a group of boxers of similar weight and skills, have them spend 13 weeks at a secret training camp, and have them fight for a chance at a championship bout in Las Vegas. Along the way, viewers would get a chance to see the personalities of the boxers, their lives, and loves.

"I think what we're looking to do is discover the next generation of fighters to create an opportunity for America to meet these kids, to fall in love with them, for them to become, you know, the kinds of stars that boxing enjoyed for many, many years," Katzenberg told reporters at a press conference announcing the show in March 2004. With Burnett on board, the star power of Stallone and Leonard, and big bucks—reportedly it was the most expensive reality show production to date—*The Contender* was on track to be a major show for NBC.

But then Fox stepped in with its own boxing show, *The Next Great Champ*, built around boxing great Oscar De La Hoya. Like *The Contender*, *The Next Great Champ* was designed to showcase unknown fighters and their families as they battled for a shot at a professional contract with De La Hoya's company. However, what made the boxing battle particularly messy is that Fox officials had met with representatives from both shows. And, when they couldn't get *The Contender*, they created their own. "It happens every day," Berman explained before either show launched. "Try to get a project, didn't get it, like the area, let's develop something in that area. This is the way it's done. Nothing unique about it." It was also a case in which the Fox show was able to get on the air much earlier than the NBC version, literally months earlier. Perhaps pouring salt into the wounds, Fox went out and got the rights to "Eye of the Tiger," which was the theme song for Stallone's *Rocky IV*.

References to the two boxing shows in the media could have done nothing but confuse viewers about the two shows. Burnett and DreamWorks tried to get the courts to stop the Fox show, but not on the grounds of copyright infringement. Instead, they attacked the validity of the actual fighting on Fox's show. They claimed the Fox fights weren't sanctioned properly. Fox then moved the launch date earlier. After several rounds with the judge, Burnett & Co. were rebuffed. The Fox show was allowed to go on.

"Quite frankly," NBC president Jeff Zucker said of the copying in July 2004, "I think it's bad for all of us." Zucker said if he were really concerned about Fox's boxing show, he would have rushed *The Contender* on. He didn't.

Fox's *The Next Great Champ* launched to lukewarm reviews and then weak ratings. In a matter of weeks the show was pulled from the Fox Broadcast Network and put on its sports cable networks. "Despite its local core audience, the underlying boxing theme of the series has proved too narrow for us," Berman said then. "In the end, it belongs on an outlet better suited to serve the boxing fan."

Besides the *Wife Swap* scenario, ABC has found itself in the middle of the copycat wars on many occasions. In fall 2004, Fox launched *Nanny 911*, a reality series in which a British nanny visits a home with unruly kids and tries to right the rebels. Fox beat to the air ABC, which has its own show called *Supernanny*, which, like the Fox show, is about a British nanny who attempts to tame a family's children.

Because Fox got on the air first with *Nanny 911*, there was again confusion among viewers over which show was which. There was also some suggestion that ABC copied the Fox show. Producers for *Supernanny* say they had the idea first and ABC bought their show long before the Fox program came along. Nick Powell, who created *Supernanny* in Britain, said he met with Fox and ABC officials, before selling the show to ABC. "I was disappointed Fox decided to do a very similar show," Powell said. "Part of me found it reasonably complimentary that some would recognize the strength of the idea." Powell said the difficult choice was not rushing his show on the air at ABC to compete with Fox.

The viewers, however, have no clue about whom did what to whom and when. Instead, they're hit with a barrage of promos for shows that look similar. Based on promos, it's hard to decipher between reality programs because unless there's a host as a constant, there are no regular cast members. For example, in the case of *Wife Swap* and *Trading Spouses*, there are no visible hosts. And, the families change each week, so viewers aren't accustomed to seeing the same faces, as on, say, *Survivor*, in which over the course of 13 weeks they know who the players are. So for a viewer flipping channels, perhaps unaware of which network their watching, a promo for *Nanny 911* looks just like *Supernanny*.

"I think what happens," ABC's entertainment president Stephen McPherson told writers in July 2004, "and it happens in comedy and drama as well, is that once there's a success, that people try to rip them off. It's one thing to do a direct rip-off. It's another thing to do something that is somewhat inspired by [that] movies in a new direction off an existing idea." McPherson noted that there are similarities between CBS's hit comedy *Everybody Loves Raymond* (which ended its run in 2005) and ABC's *According to Jim* because they are both family series with strong male points of view at the center.

ABC's *The Bachelor*, which launched on March 25, 2002, and became a water cooler show just like *Survivor*, may be the show that has "inspired" the most copycat programs. Indeed, by the time Alex Michel asked Amanda Marsh at the end of the first *Bachelor* to consider life with him—he didn't propose as the show was billed in the beginning—rival producers were hard at work with their own dating shows. The descendants, direct, and distant, of *The Bachelor* are many. *Joe Millionaire*, Fox's twist show that had women vying for a fake heir, was a near duplicate of *The Bachelor*, as was *For Love or Money* on NBC, the *Average Joe* twist shows also on NBC, and Fox's *The Littlest Groom* and *Mr. Personality*.

Each had minor changes in the format of the *Bachelor*, but the similarities were there. Take, for example, *The Littlest Groom*. The show was built around a male little person dating a group of little women. But then, as a twist, they tempted the bachelor with a group of regular height women.

Mike Fleiss, the producer of *The Bachelor*, thinks the fact that his show has been copied—repeatedly—"sucks." "There've been literally 18 copycat shows," he said. "There's been hundreds and hundreds of hours of pretty girls, and not so pretty girls, going on exciting dates, and then whittling down the field." Part of the problem, he said, is that no one tried to stop the *Bachelor* copies, the way that CBS attempted to stop the *Survivor* duplicates, which has led to the frequent use of the dating format. If there were a half-dozen *Survivor* rip-offs, Fleiss contends, CBS's show might not be as strong. "*The Littlest Groom*, *Married by America*, *The Player*, there've been countless shows," Fleiss said. "It makes [*The Bachelor*] less unique."

The fact is that in the fifth cycle of *The Bachelor* and *Bachelorette* franchise, the show started to lose some ratings strength, which could be attributed to a number of factors, including a less than spectacular cast and the competition. "It's a lot easier when you don't have a dozen copycat shows cluttering up the marketplace and making viewers seem they've seen a lot of it," Fleiss said. "Eighteen times that's happened, and 18 times the network bought things, and 18 times business affairs people bought shows, based on a sentence that said, 'It's *The Bachelor*, but with little people,' or with an Australian guy.' I've never seen a show so copied."

Fleiss is no stranger to the copying scenario, either. He was sued by Howard Stern for allegedly lifting the concept of a Stern radio segment for a failed ABC series *Are You Hot?* And his spoof *Superstar USA* was clearly based on the *American Idol* concept.

"Television, the creation of ideas, and being able to hold onto ideas is a very slippery slope," Powell said. "Nobody has yet been able to copyright their ideas. Where the frustration comes in is when you were there first." Adding to the struggle is that television is truly a global marketplace. Show producers have been selling the concepts for their shows—and sometimes their shows—around the world for decades. Indeed, it's not unusual for a producer and network to sell the idea, concept, and scripts to producers in another country to create their own version of a hit American show using local cast and the local language.

But with the concept copying, it's been difficult for producers to keep a handle on all of their shows. *Survivor*'s Mark Burnett, for instance, sold the concept of *The Apprentice* around the world, with countries finding their own versions of Donald Trump. "They're studying tapes, studying every move I make," Trump said. "I'm very honored by it." And, as with virtually every other reality show, there have been some countries where legally sanctioned versions have aired as well as other countries where producers have simply ripped off the idea. For instance, by early 2005 *Supernanny* was sold by Powell's company in 12 countries as a finished product and another 7 countries as a concept. Some other countries have simply lifted the idea with no credit to Powell. "I think these things go in cycles," Powell said. "TV is a hit business. It's always been a copycat business. Why is it happening right now? It's quicker to copy a reality idea."

Although there have certainly been a number of direct rip-offs, there also have been many shows that are similar in nature or concept to others. For example, in 2005, the A&E Network launched a series called *Inked*, which tracked the people working in and visiting a Las Vegas tattoo shop. At the same time, The Learning Channel launched *Miami Inked*, which did the same, just in Miami. The TLC show went to a second season, whereas A&E's version did not.

And in 2006, A&E launched *Dallas SWAT*, a reality show following an elite team of law enforcement officers on the job and off. And, at the same time, Court TV launched *Texas SWAT*, a show that followed SWAT team members from around Texas.

Likewise, some of the copying comes in just lifting little details of previous shows. That was the case in the summer of 2005 and later in early 2006. During the summer of 2005, ABC hit big with *Dancing with the Stars*, a ballroom dancing series that paired mid-level celebrities with real-life dancing professionals. Early on, viewers saw such stars as model Rachel Hunter and former New Kids on the Block group member Joey McIntyre struggling to learn the basic steps.

None of the stars of the show were huge by any measure. John O'Hurley, who was a supporting cast member on *Seinfeld*, hadn't been on a hit since that show ended in 1998. Kelly Monaco, a daytime soap star and one time Playboy Playmate, was known to a relatively small audience. And McIntyre, once one of the biggest pop groups around, had been struggling to get an acting career off the ground. At the time it was announced, the show was viewed as a goof and that the appeal would be based simply on viewers watching celebrities make fools of themselves. Yet, as often happens, *Dancing with the Stars* hit at the right time and became a ratings draw. Viewers tuned in, it seems, not to laugh at the stars—though some did, no doubt—but to root for them, too. Each week, judges in the studio offered their opinions of the dancing pairs, while voters at home cast their ballots. Then, each week one pair was sent home. "I think it's fun for the whole family," McIntyre told the *New York Daily News*. "Everyone can get around the TV and watch it together. It's old-fashioned live music and the modern elimination for good measure."

Whatever the reasons for the appeal, viewers turned out in large numbers each week, and in an unusual trend, the audience got larger every outing. It averaged 16.8 million viewers over the run, though peaked at 22 million for the finale, when Monaco and her partner outdanced O'Hurley and his partner. No surprise, ABC officials were so pleased with the ratings results, they commissioned a second cycle of the show and lined up such star as Tatum O'Neal, Lisa Rinna, Drew Lachey, Jerry Rice, Tia Carrere, and Giselle Fernandez. Drew Lachey, who in a radio interview admitted reality shows were not big in his house, eventually won the second edition of *Dancing with the Stars*, giving his career a significant boost.

The folks at Fox, looking to capitalize on the success of ABC's show, came back with their own version, though with a twist. Rather than duplicate *Dancing with the Stars*, they changed the concept a little and set it on ice. Rather than dancing, group of low-level celebrities tried figure skating. Producers lined up actor Dave Coulier (*Full House*), Olympic decathlon gold medalist and television personality Bruce Jenner, actor Todd Bridges (*Diff'rent Strokes*), actress Kristy Swanson (*Dude, Where's My Car?* and *Buffy the Vampire Slayer*), singer/actress Deborah Gibson, and weather forecaster Jillian Barberie. Swanson, who had been virtually out of the public eye for years, and who early on in the competition struggled to skate, ended up winning the competition and falling in love with her partner, Lloyd Eisler. The concept for *Skating with Celebrities* was the same as *Dancing with the Stars*, with the exception of the performing surface. In fact, early promos for the Fox show were very similar to those for ABC's show, and focused on the stars struggling to master the new sport.

"For most people, it's tough enough to learn these types of moves while on the dance floor or working out in the gym," Fox's executive vice president of alternative programming, Mike Darnell, said in a statement. "This competition will require our celebrity skaters to not only demonstrate rhythm, but also athleticism, grace and balance ... on ice, and before a team of unforgiving judges with both Olympic and world championship experience. No doubt there will be plenty of falls, bruises and scary moments." NBC then used The "Dancing" concept for *Celebrity Cooking Showdown,* a cooking competition that paired Celebrities with real chets.

And, as long as the reality genre continues to draw viewers, there will be more bruised egos and scary moments as producers see their concepts lifted by other networks and produce.

CHAPTER 8

Love Is in the Air

Television has been playing matchmaker for years. The concept of pairing singles began technically as a game show, though using real people. Today, of course, there are many dating shows built on reaching people of various stripes. *The Dating Game*, a television game show that launched in 1965, is the touchstone for all of today's reality dating shows. Host Jim Lange presided over the show, which had a fresh-faced bachelor or bachelorette questioning three unseen singles. Based on their answers to often goofy questions, the questioner picked one to go on an exotic, chaperoned trip. Whether there was a love connection or not between the couples didn't matter, nor was it ever known. The viewer's connection to the couples was cut off at the end of the episode, when Lange and the arranged couples blew the audience a big kiss. It was good clean fun, with a hint, albeit small, of a connection between the couple.

It wasn't until 35 years later that the television mating game got a significant push and became a lucrative, reality show staple. Interestingly, the first show to come out during the latest reality wave was not the biggest, nor the best known. In 1999, Universal Television—now NBC Universal Television—launched *Blind Date*, a quirky show that followed a supposedly real couple on a manufactured television date. On some occasions the couples got along well, very well, whereas on others they never connected. Every episode had a hint of sex or sexual tension. There were plenty of trips to hot tubs, and the occasional door closing on the cameraman to suggest an intimate moment between the participants. And in most episodes, as with many reality shows, alcohol flows freely, thereby enhancing the openness of the players.

A highlight, though, of *Blind Date* wasn't what happened on the date, but what was said in cartoon bubbles appearing on screen that supposedly expressed the inner thoughts of the daters. More often than not, those funny lines were more interesting than the couple on the screen. For the show's seventh season in 2005, producers added a few twists, such as having parents chose the dates, or a speed dating spin-off in which participants were under a time limit.

The key with *Blind Date* is that viewers aren't emotionally attached to the participants, no more than they were for *The Dating Game* decades earlier. Given that a 30-minute episode minus commercials leaves just 22 minutes of programming, there's not a lot of connection to be made with the love affair on the screen. In fact, it's safe to say that *Blind Date,* although it was the first dating reality show, is more of a comedy that just happens to be built around a date. "With all these new dating scenarios, the humorous zingers and pop-ups are funnier than ever," executive producer Tom Klein said at the start of the 2005 season. "Viewers can look forward to situations they can truly relate to whether they are a bride-to-be or just getting back on the market."

Therein lies the hook behind dating shows: relatability. Virtually everyone has been in a relationship of some sort and has been in the perilous world of dating at one point. So when Klein and his team show a clip of a guy staring at his date's breasts, and put a cartoon bubble with a comment over his head, most men can relate.

Still, it is largely female viewers who keep dating reality shows going strong. Women, young women, tend to tune into reality dating shows in larger numbers than any other demographic. If a show captures just a bit of that audience's attention—and becomes the proverbial water cooler show, where everyone the next day talks about what happened on air the night before—then it can be a hit.

Ironically, the guy most responsible for the current reality dating wave, Mike Fleiss, is almost the guy who killed it. In 2000, Fleiss, along with the folks at Fox, came up with the idea for a one-time show called *Who Wants to Marry a Multimillionaire?* Fleiss's idea was to hold a beauty pageant–like show in which one unseen guy, who was billed as a multimillionaire, would, by the end of the show, marry one of the contestants. Right there, on the spot, the groom would marry his television bride.

Who Wants to Marry a Multimillionaire? took part of its title from the ABC hit game show *Who Wants to Be a Millionaire* which had become an instant phenomenon a summer before. When that show became a hit, Fox offered its own show, *Greed*, which had taken the fun aspects of *Millionaire* and had people turn against each other in a nasty game.

Actor and radio personality Jay Thomas was the host of *Who Wants to Marry a Multimillionaire*, and started off the live, two-hour telecast by telling viewers, what would unfold on air was no joke. The show started with 50 women who wanted to get married that night to a really rich guy. Soon, the 50 contestants were whittled down to just 10, who then paraded on stage in swimsuits, like Miss America. When just five remained, the finalists were asked questions about their plans for the future, having children, and fidelity. "I'm embarrassed," Rockwell told the contestants. "It's not fair you didn't get to ask me all those questions."

The five finalists, to drive the point home, were wearing white wedding dresses. Before Rockwell made his choice, Darva Conger, a blonde who claimed to be a Gulf War veteran told him: "I'll be your friend, your lover and your partner.... You will never be bored." Rockwell fell for the line and proposed—and married—Conger on the spot.

In the days following, critics had a field day lambasting *Who Wants to Marry a Multimillionaire?* "Blending the dubious charms of the beauty pageant, the quiz show and an 18th-century Tortuga slave auction, the show was designed around a concept that's as degrading as it is cynical. Fox thought America could not survive without the spectacle of 50 young women crawling through rounds of competition, hoping to be the one chosen for a marriage proposal by an unseen millionaire," wrote Mark Dawidziak in the *Cleveland Plain Dealer*.

"Maybe television can sink lower than *Who Wants to Marry a Multimillionaire?*—a Fox network special that aired this week. Maybe someone can dream up something more degrading, disgusting and dehu-manizing. But it's hard to imagine how to do that without committing a felony," read an editorial in *The Commercial Appeal* in Memphis, Tennessee. The editorial went on to slam the show for making a mockery of marriage, stereotyping women, and attack Fox for trudging through sludge to get viewers. The editorial ended urging viewers to not watch if there was a sequel.

Critics notwithstanding, the show was a huge draw, averaging more than 16 million viewers for the two-hour telecast. More important, the show's audience built throughout, and more than 23 million tuned in during the last half hour when Rockwell made his choice. That show-ending audi-ence spike suggested people were telling others to watch during the show, making it an instant water cooler program.

Yet, before the made-on-television couple got back from their honeymoon, a major scandal erupted when it was revealed by the Web site www.thesmokinggun.com that an old girlfriend of Rockwell's had years earlier filed a restraining order against him. That information wasn't revealed during a preshow screening, and it led to critics charging Fleiss and Fox with putting Conger into a potentially dangerous situation.

Less than a month after the February 15, 2000, telecast, Conger filed for an annulment, claiming her television marriage to Rockwell was a fraud, and that he did not disclose his past issues. "Neither the contestants nor the show's producers seriously contemplated creating a proper marriage," Conger said in her documents. In those papers, filed in Las Vegas, where they were married, Conger said they never consummated the marriage. She also stated that they barely saw each other during the honeymoon. She also said the marriage was "a mutual mistake of fact and was entered into solely for an entertainment purpose."

This, of course, is what critics said about the show in the first place. For a period of time after the telecast, *Who Wants to Marry a Multimillionaire?* became a lightning rod for all that was wrong with reality television. Before *Marry a Multimillionaire*, reality programming was criticized as a genre because of Fox's reliance on cheesy video clip shows of car crashes or animal attacks. But, getting people to agree to and televising an instant marriage was a different game altogether.

As the drumbeat built against Fox, officials at the network used the moment to say they would get out of reality television business. "They're gone; They're over," Sandy Grushow, then head of the Fox network told the *New York Times* 10 days after *Who Wants to Marry a Multimillionaire?* aired.

"There was an internal investigation, an external investigation," Fleiss told *Vanity Fair* in 2003. "It was the lead story on the news every night, and in every tabloid. It was the darkest, most depressing thing I've ever been through."

However, playing off the old saw that there's a silver lining in every cloud, Fleiss, during his dark days in the aftermath of *Who Wants to Marry A Multimillionaire?* came up with the ideas for two more shows: *High School Reunion*, in which a group of friends were shipped off to Hawaii for a reunion, and *The Bachelor*, a contest in which one bachelor dated his way through 25 single women to come up with a mate.

"I like to take a topic that someone says, 'You can't put that on TV,' and then I put it on TV," Fleiss told *Vanity Fair*. "I want to feel a little bit dangerous, a tiny bit irresponsible probably, and that usually equals controversy, and that's sort of my stock-in-trade."

Before Fleiss could get *The Bachelor* on the air, several other reality dating shows came along, and pulled down the dating subset. Indeed, 2001 might be a watershed year for dating shows. It was also a time when network executives focused on calling the genre unscripted programming, rather than reality. The reason was simple: It was clear from anyone watching some of the shows that some of the scenes had been manipulated, some saying, perhaps scripted. Producers admitted stuff was contrived but never scripted.

As it turns out, Fox's push away from the genre wasn't long lasting, either. Citing smart business practices and an audience appetite for reality, Fox jumped back in with gusto—and, as history would show—would take more critical hits with shows that some said further pushed television content into the sewer. In January 2001, the network returned to the form with *Temptation Island*, a series that was a mix of *Survivor* and a dating show. Producers took four couples who claimed to be in "committed" relationships and shipped them off to an island near Belize. There, each member of the couples was tempted by very sexy members of the opposite sex. Among the singles set up for the men were a former Playboy model, a Miss Georgia, and a former Los Angles Lakers dancer. Once on the island, the partners were paired with singles on the island, and at the end of the six-week run the couples were to declare their vows, or not, for the partner they made the trip with. "I'm from South Miami Beach and I like it hot," said one of the hot female singles sent to tempt the men already in relationships. Even before the show launched, some watchdog groups were upset because promotions for *Temptation Island* suggested it would be a freewheeling sex romp.

"This is not a show, as you will see, about sex," Fox's Grushow told members of the Television Critics Association just days before the launch. "This is a show that is exploring the dynamics of serious relationships." It should be noted, however, that among the various background checks producers did on the cast for *Temptation Island* was a check for sexually transmitted diseases. Folks critical of the show also said the concept was designed to split the couples by making it nearly impossible for them to remain faithful to their mates. "I don't think this is a show that endeavors to pry apart couples," Grushow said.

At the end of the episodes, the group gathered around a bonfire at night in a scene reminiscent of *Survivor*'s tribal council, to discuss what happened on the island while the partners were separated. There were tears, or so it seemed, and perhaps a few broken hearts. On the first episode, the contestants were forced to watch videotape of their mates going on dates with others. "That turns my stomach," one woman said when she was told the producers wanted her to watch her boyfriend on a date. The couples were paid $5,000, and the singles were paid $1,500 apiece.

In the final episode, the couples were brought together around the bonfire to talk with host Mark L. Walberg. There were more tears, and all of the players said they still loved the people they went to the island with for the two-week television trip.

"I had an intimate moment with someone, and though it was nice and it was comforting and it was new, it wasn't my boyfriend," said Mandy Lauderdale to her boyfriend Billy Cleary. "I want us to be together for the rest of our lives. I never want to play this game again." Cleary, his girlfriend in tears, said he had a relationship with someone on the island but she didn't compare to Lauderdale. "If you'll have me," he said, "I promise to love you forever."

So it went, sort of. There was an epilogue at the end of the episode saying one couple was headed for the altar and that Cleary and Lauderdale shared a "passionate long-distance relationship."

Temptation Island was not without trouble, though. Despite the institution of new and improved background checks sparked by the *Who Wants to Marry a Multimillionaire?* scandal, the producers still missed a potential problem. Rules for the show stated the couples could not have children together. However, one couple, Ytossie Patterson and Taheed Watson, though not married, had a child together, which producers said they never disclosed during the screening process. Watson and Patterson were kicked off the show midway through the season. They later sued Fox and the show's production company, saying they all knew about the child. "We knew we were not going to be tempted," Patterson said at a press conference held to discuss the suit at the time. "We were actors going on the show for publicity." The couple also maintained that Fox officials knew of the child and carefully released the information during the show to generate more publicity, a tactic networks have been charged with ever since the reality genre took off.

In April 2001, the same month Watson and Patterson filed their suit against Fox, UPN launched *Chains of Love,* a goofy show about four women chained to a man, who released them one at a time. Each got a stipend, set by the man, based on how much her time was worth with him.

The first guy was named Andy, and he was chained to women who included a bisexual Australian bodybuilder and a woman who claimed to talk tougher than she really was. "Do you want me to touch your tomatoes?" one woman said during a segment where the chain gang created sandwiches.

"You can touch my tomatoes," Andy shot back.

The WB also aired a similar show called *Elimidate Deluxe*, which started out as a daytime series in syndication. Five contestants went on a date—one man and four women—and one by one the man kicked the females off, while also telling them why they were losers.

By the end of the year, Fox was offering *Love Cruise*, a seaside-set dating series in which eight women and eight men were sent on a Caribbean cruise, where the goal was to be the last couple standing. The winning couple, created from the contestants, got $250,000 and a trip.

"Ladies, when I blow my whistle, you're going to approach the man that you would most like to couple with for the next 48 hours," the host said at the start of the first episode. The contestants didn't rise much above that opening line.

Ralph, in the usual on-camera commentary offered up by most reality show participants, laid out his strategy: "Oh, you know, I'm not like, thinking about, like, you know, who I got to beat out or anything like that, because I'm the coolest guy on the ship, and that's what I've been saying ever since, you know, the beginning of this."

And then there was Lisa: "My impression, quite honestly, is that there are a lot of blondes with big boobs and not professional, and not that there's anything wrong with that, but I'm very different," she said, straight-faced. "I'm much more intellectual and so I think that the guys are going to have a choice between someone who might be a fun fling for two weeks versus someone who they could have a much more meaningful relationship with."

Love Cruise, though it lasted only one season, introduced viewers to Toni Ferrari, a surgically enhanced actress who later went on to play the busty bitch in *Paradise Island* and *Kill Reality*.

Also launched in 2001 as "Shipmates," sort of a sea-set version of *Blind Date*, which wasn't as successful.

No surprise, the 2001 crop of dating reality shows got lambasted by critics, who added shows like *Love Cruise*, *Chains of Love*, and *Temptation Island* to lists of series that would eventually bring down all of humankind. Over and over, critics of unscripted television used these programs as examples of what was wrong with the format and how in general they were bad programs. Interestingly, though, some critics, in writing about the finale of the first edition of *Temptation Island*—there were three cycles when the franchise was complete—said that the way the first show ended, with the couples staying together, was contrary to what anti-*Temptation Island* writers were saying before the show launched.

Despite the damage to the television dating game, Mike Fleiss got around to getting his idea of a televised courtship on the air at ABC in March 2002. Fleiss and his production team settled on Alex Michel, a handsome, Virginia-born, Harvard graduate with an MBA from Stanford. Michel said he was ready to settle down, if only he could find the right woman. The producers of *The Bachelor* lined up 25 single, attractive women who agreed to vie for Michel's attention during a six-week series. Among the women were a former Miami Heat dancer, a doctor, a Hooters waitress, and a pair of lawyers. "If you can't find a woman with all this, well?" host Chris Harrison told Michel as they walked through the Malibu mansion where the show was set.

The show started off with Michel standing outside a Malibu mansion greeting the women one by one as they pulled up in limousines. He then chatted with them at a cocktail party before conducting the first rose ceremony. The ceremony, as much a part of *The Bachelor* as the tribal council is to *Survivor*, is where the bachelor whittles down the field of bachelorettes. "You are totally empowered here," Harrison told the bachelorettes. "You don't have to accept."

In the first one, Michel handed out 15 roses, sending 10 packing and telling those remaining contestants that he'd like to know them just a little bit more before, perhaps, sending them home. Some of the losers took it well, others, having only met Michel a short time earlier, cried. By episode two, Michel took the women, five at a time, on luxury dates. In episode three, viewers saw chemistry develop between Michel and contestant Amanda Marsh, to where at one point, he gave her a steamy massage. During that same show, viewers saw Michel date Trista Rehn, the former Miami Heat dancer, though he wondered if she really liked him.

By the end of episode five, Michel was dolling out roses to Rehn and Marsh, setting up the April 25, 2002, finale. After visits with each woman's families, Michel told Rehn that if he had to choose right then, he'd choose her. He asked her to stay the night and she did. When it came to Marsh's chance for a final night with Michel before the decision day, they headed straight for the hot tub.

The show, as designed by Fleiss, was to end with a televised engagement. Not a marriage, like the Rockwell mess, but with one of the two women getting the final rose and a ring. Indeed, during the show viewers even saw Michel shopping for a ring at Harry Winston jewelers. At the end of the finale, Michel showed the ring to Marsh, but pulled it back. He told her he would keep it and said he would love it if she moved to California so they could see of the relationship flourished when the klieg lights were dimmed. "Before we walk down the aisle together, I want to make sure we feel the same way about each other outside the fancy world of mansions and limousines," Michel said.

Rehn, meanwhile, told Michel she didn't think they were meant to be together. She cried. "It's not that I a thousand percent wanted to be engaged today .... It's just that we had such a great talk the other night and he told me, 'it's you.' Those were his words," she said as a limo drove her away from the mansion.

The day after the final aired, Michel, Marsh and Rehn appeared on *Good Morning America*. "I'm definitely falling in love with Alex, yes," Marsh told Diane Sawyer.

"We're not engaged," Michel said. "We are dating and very excited and happy to kind of get on with our lives in a more normal way."

As it turned out, they never got engaged and split up soon after the show aired. However, the audience didn't split from ABC. The network immediately ordered more versions of *The Bachelor*, and Fleiss, once looked down upon the television world, was a star again. "It's a super relatable area," Fleiss said, explaining the appeal of dating on television. "That's why the show has become such a phenomenon. Everybody connects, they've pursued or been pursued at some point. That's the hallmark, the relatability."

And Fleiss has found a way to keep viewers connected to the show. When it came time to shift the focus to the women, and have a woman pick from 25 eligible bachelors, he returned to Rehn. The former Miami Heat dancer turned pediatric physical therapist was a fan favorite in the original *Bachelor* and had earned a following by being passed over by Michel. Rehn was given another shot at finding true love in *The Bachelorette*, which followed the model of the *Bachelor*.

Initially, there was some concern within ABC that having a woman be the hunter could leave some with the impression that the woman was easy. "If this show says anything to women, it should be: 'Do what you want and don't worry what people think of you.' I have great morals and I didn't do anything I'm embarrassed of or feel my parents wouldn't be proud of," Rehn told the *New York Daily News* before the show started airing.

Over the course of six episodes, Rehn worked her way through the crowd before settling on two finalists, Charlie Maher and Ryan Sutter. She chose Sutter, a firefighter from Colorado before an audience of 20.4 million viewers. "There was an unspoken chemistry that Ryan and I had that told me he was the one," Rehn told reporters after the show aired. "We complement each other very nicely." And did they. The two were married later that year in a televised blowout worth $1 million and aired on ABC as part of yet another *Bachelor* series.

Based on the success of reusing Rehn on the show, Fleiss has returned to past candidates and contestants a few times already. Bob Guiney, who made it to the final rounds with Rehn and also won a fan following along the way, became the centerpiece for an edition of *The Bachelor*. And Jen Schefft, who was selected by Andrew Firestone in the second version of *The Bachelor*, only to split with Firestone later on, also got a second try at love on *The Bachelorette*.

"Jen was such a popular character on 'The Bachelor' and long after the show was over," said Fleiss. The reason Schefft, or Rehn, or Guiney, or even Meredith Phillips, who was passed over by Guiney to become her own *Bachelorette*, were brought back is to capitalize off the goodwill they already have with viewers who may have seen them on a previous episode. And, in the case of Guiney or Rehn, they both earned strong followings because the outcome of their initial runs on *The Bachelor* didn't seem fair. "You're expecting," Fleiss said, "that a lot of the people who liked her will watch them again. It's the same thing with sitcoms, you don't replace the cast each season."

To spice up the show, one season Fleiss hired NFL quarterback Jesse Palmer to be *The Bachelor* and another season had actor Charlie O'Connell as the centerpiece.

Much to Fleiss's chagrin, *The Bachelor* has served as the model and inspiration for a legion of dating shows, some similar, others not as much, but all hoping the budding relation between two strangers is enough to get viewers drawn in. Fox did a blatant rip-off in *Joe Millionaire*, a similar series with a gaggle of women trying to be selected by a single bachelor. The hook there was the bachelor in question was a construction worker, who was described to the females as an heir to a fortune. Evan Marriott played the bachelor on the show who was coached by a real-life butler on how to act like he had millions.

TBS programmers tried their hand at the reality dating game with *Outback Jack*, a show in which 12 beautiful, high-maintenance women were shipped off to Australia to win the heart of the ruggedly handsome Vadim Dale. The twist was the women were told they'd live in a luxurious mansion, when instead they were forced to deal with the rough terrain of the outback. "Oh my God, I've never done my own nails in my life," one woman said.

In the end, Dale was to pick just one woman. No cash prizes were involved.

NBC took a stab at dating reality with a few shows. The first was *Average Joe*, a show in which a beautiful bachelorette was unknowingly faced with having to date average-looking guys. And, once she was settled in with the average guys, a gaggle of hunks were brought in to stir the pot. Adam Mesh, one of the average Joes from the first season, like those passed over on *The Bachelor*, got a second show when he was passed over for a hunk.

For Love or Money had a bachelorette dating a group of men, with a hidden cash prize available if she picked the right guy. NBC also had *Who Wants to Marry My Mom?* a five-episode series that was a spin-off of the dating show *Meet my Folks*.

Fox also returned with a dating show called *Married by America*, in which five singles were matched to strangers and immediately engaged. At the end of the five-week run of the show, the contestants decided whether to marry or not.

Even The Learning Channel is in the matchmaking game with *A Dating Story*, a much more sedate show than what the broadcast networks have aired, which follows one couple on a date and in the end gets each participant's reaction to the other. No hot tubs, no outrageous catfights, just two regular people out for a date and hoping for love.

Simon Cowell, the cantankerous judge on *American Idol*, tried his hand at producing a dating series for CBS with a show called *Cupid*. The series had advertising copywriter Lisa Shannon in the *Bachelorette* role in search of a perfect mate. But, unlike *The Bachelor* franchise, in which the singles are selected by the producers, *Cupid* put some of the audition decisions in the hands of Shannon and two friends. So, in the beginning *Cupid* was a lot like *American Idol*, in which in the early days the appeal for viewers comes from bad singers trying to win over, well, Cowell. Shannon also had at stake $1 million if she married the guy viewers picked in the end and stayed married for a year.

"I find it ridiculous on these shows that you have 20 guys selected by producers and you say to the girl, 'You will fall in love with one of these guys,'" Cowell told the Associated Press before the show launched. "I find that slightly absurd."

With the backing of CBS promotional push, and advertisements featuring Cowell, the show launched in July 2003 to good reviews, including a four-star notice in the *New York Daily News*.

"They say the age of romance is dead," Cowell said in the first episode. "And you know what? They're absolutely right." Despite Cowell's backing, though, the show never caught on with viewers.

Fox earned more critical barbs in February 2003 with *The Littlest Groom*, a *Bachelor* rip-off that had diminutive contestants in dating game. At the center of the show was four-foot-five Glen Foster, who was given a crop of 15 women, some his size, some not, to date. In a twist, the average-size women were sprung on Foster, leading to complaints from The Little People of America.

In 2005, the WB launched *Beauty and the Geek*, a show produced by Ashton Kutcher, with a group of very smart nerds being paired with beautiful but not-so-smart women. The couples were then put through a series of challenges to match their lack of skills. For instance, there was a spelling bee for the women and massage lessons for the men.

And in a celebrity twist, rapper Flavor Flav, who busted out on VH1's *Surreal Life* and moved into *Strange Love* with Brigitte Nielsen, in early 2006 starred in *Flavor of Love*. "In *Flavor of Love*, 20 single women from all walks of life, selected for their expressed love for Flav, will move into a 'phat crib' in Los Angeles and vie for his affection" is the way VH1's media information described the show. Producers promised the women would go through a cooking test, a sniff test, and dates at Red Lobster.

When the dating genre got underway, viewers and the media latched onto the notion that the couples, because all of what unfolded on air was supposed to be real, would end up either married or in serious relationships. However, that didn't happen in most cases. Even with *The Bachelor*, only Trista Rehn and Ryan Sutter made it to the altar. The fact that the couples never really stuck together, or all, didn't affect the ratings, either. As viewers began to realize that not everything on a reality show is real, but rather contrived or manipulated to meet a potential storyline, the pressure to create real-life couples became secondary to creating good drama.

Though ratings for *The Bachelor* fell during the end of the 2004–2005 season, perhaps because ABC was airing multiple versions each year, there's still no clear sign viewers are tired of watching others look for love.

Pay cable channel HBO also got in the dating business, sort of, with *Cathouse*, a show set in a Nevada brothel that showed clients meeting the women, and some of their "parties," which is the term for their dates. "Everybody does it; we're just smart enough to get paid for it," one of the women said at the beginning of the show."

"Yes I sell my body, yes I enjoy it," said another.

No surprise, HBO aired the show in late night, though it gave yet another view on the world of real-life dating.

"It's the vicarious thrill of Americans to watch the beginning stages of romance," said Alex McLeod, who was the host of the first *Joe Millionaire*.

"Viewers can't get enough.... American viewers will never get tired of celebrities, but they want to see real people. American television viewers can relate to real people."

Zora Andrich knows those feelings well. She ended up having the dubious distinction of being chosen by Evan Marriott on the finale of the first *Joe Millionaire*. They never had a relationship to speak of. Marriott later said he wasn't expecting to find love, whereas Andrich summed it up this way: "Nice guy—just no connection." Yet, lack of chemistry notwithstanding, viewers ate up the drama as the show unfolded on Fox. "There's a romantic in everybody," Andrich said. "So many people, strangers, said they cried, they cried when I won. It was such a fairytale they were moved to tears. Everybody wants that. Everybody wants a happy ending."

And as long as viewers are willing to understand that not all that they see is real, and to live in the fantasy of the adventure, then networks will continue to air unscripted dating shows.

CHAPTER 9

Singing for Fame, Fortune, or Just Attention

As a child and a budding singer Wayne Newton won a talent contest in Roanoke, Virginia. He was only nine at the time. After the win, Newton and his family traveled to New York to audition for *The Original Amateur Hour*. Ted Mack hosted the program, which began in 1948 on the Dumont network and in 1949 moved to NBC. The show actually began on radio, with Major Bowes as the host. A year and a half after Bowes died, it was revived on television.

Mack had been an assistant on Bowes radio show and the format for the television version was taken directly from the radio show. Mack played host to a variety of amateurs, real amateurs, ranging from mimes to comics to kazoo players and singers. Viewers voted for their favorite acts by calling the show or sending postcards. The winners were given scholarships. After he auditioned, Newton said he was told, "We'll call you. Don't call us."

Mack's staff never called. And Newton, who in 2005 would go on to be a part of E! Entertainment's reality show *The Entertainer* to find new talent to work in Las Vegas, is quick to note that Elvis Presley also didn't make the cut on *The Original Amateur Hour*.

Little did Newton know when he auditioned for *The Original Amateur Hour* that he would become part of the early influences for a genre of reality programming to find entertainers and people with other talents. One of the most famous finds during the *Amateur Hour*, though on the radio version, was Frank Sinatra. Gladys Knight and Pat Boone were also winners on the television version. For the most part, those appearing on the show never made it big in the entertainment world.

After *The Original Amateur Hour* several similar shows would pop up along the way giving amateurs in a variety of genres a chance at super stardom. Chuck Barris's *Gong Show* was one. By 1983, the syndicated *Star Search* was becoming a platform for future stars and also showcased regular people. Ed McMahon hosted the show, which allowed performers to compete in various categories, such as male or female singers, comics, and a television spokesmodel category. Unlike *The Original Amateur Hour, Star Search* did turn out many future stars, including such performers as Christina Aguilera, Tiffany, and Rosie O'Donnell.

As it was, after the talent show heydays of the 1950s, such shows were marginal hits at best and tended to operate around the fringes of the medium. The reality phase of music and competition began abroad in 1999, with the launch of *Popstars* in New Zealand. The reality show followed a pop group from its creation to hitting the road to fame. The show was a hit and was quickly made in several countries such as Denmark, Spain, Finland, Australia, and eventually Britain. *Popstars* launched in the United States on the WB and in Britain in 2001. Viewers watched along as potential group members were selected from auditions and then finally put together in a made-for-television band. The American version produced a girl group called Eden's Crush. In the British version, viewers were glued to the set to see who made the band and what happened after. The manufactured group's first single rocketed to the top of the charts.

Before *Popstars* aired in the United States, ABC had launched *Making the Band*, a series that tracked music mogul Lou Pearlman as he created a pop group. The series aired for three seasons on ABC and resulted in the creation of O-Town, a group that had a brief run in the pop world before disbanding. (Ashley Parker Angel, one of the members of O-Town was featured in his own comeback reality show on MTV in early 2006.)

While watching the undeniable success of *Popstars* in Britain, record producers Simon Cowell and Simon Fuller came up with a twist on the idea of *Popstars*. Rather than have a group result from the show, they wanted to have a contest where just one person won in the end of the show's run. Fuller and Cowell then took the show to the production firm Freemantle to see if they would make it. They immediately bought into the concept.

"We had both been auditioning artists in the music business for more than 15 years, and we instinctively knew what was being shown on *Popstars* was not representative of what really goes on in the audition room," Cowell wrote in his book *I Don't Mean to Be Rude, But....* "*Pop Idol* would expose what really happens in an audition. This was going to be the hook of the show and it was not going to be pleasant."

More than 10,000 people applied to audition for the show. Initially, Cowell wrote, the judges were too soft on those auditioning. Realizing it was not going to make for good television, they let loose with their real feelings. The next person who walked in the door was terrible and was told so, Cowell wrote. "We'd put the reality back in reality television," he said. When it launched, the show became a huge hit in Britain. *Pop Idol* yielded first season winner Will Young who went on to sell 2 million records with his first release.

Based on the performance in Britain, Cowell and Fuller decided to take the show to the United States, where reality television was just taking off. They pitched the show to a couple networks, which passed. Eventually, Fox officials said yes. *American Idol* launched on Fox in June 2002 with Cowell, Randy Jackson, and Paula Abdul as the judges. Cowell immediately stood out for providing frank assessments of the contestants' performances, which contrasted often with the softer approach from Abdul.

For instance, early on Cowell addressed Jim Verraros, a 19-year-old singer from Illinois by saying: "I hated your audition. I thought it was terrible. I don't know what that was all about."

His reaction immediately earned him the nickname "Mr. Nasty," and his sparring with fellow judge Paula Abdul over how he treated contestants made for excellent television. Early episodes of *American Idol* were centered on the audition process and included a steady stream of good and terrible singers. Viewers were hooked. Ratings soared for the show. By September, it was a hit. The finale, in which Kelly Clarkson beat out Justin Guarini to become the first *American Idol* champion, was watched by 22.8 million viewers.

"*American Idol* does not belong in the reality category," said Syracuse University Professor Robert Thompson, who runs the school's Center for Popular Television. "You never saw those people [outside of the competition] or if you did it was a short period of time outside the stage. Therefore, it was about all that stuff. What *American Idol* did was reintroduce the viability of the old-fashioned talent show," Thompson said. "Then it invited the marriage of the old-fashioned talent show with the new fashioned reality show." "*American Idol*" executive producer Ken Warwick, refers to the show as "Vareality", a mix of variety and reality.

If anything, *American Idol* had the spirit of a reality show and carried many reality show traits: real people trying out for television and then being voted off in a competition. The winner, like in *Survivor*, had a life-changing experience. *American Idol* worked with audiences for a couple of reasons. Early on, viewers were drawn to the auditioning process for the I-can't-believe-what-I'm-seeing factor when a really bad singer was on stage. Likewise, once the bad ones were cut from the show, then the tide turns toward rooting—and voting—for the ultimate winners. Then it becomes like watching a favorite team. "Without question, if it was done and everyone was fantastic, I don't think anyone would watch *American Idol*," Cowell said, "80 percent of them are terrible."

Cecile Frot-Coutaz, executive producer of *American Idol* said the show works because it's a pure format. "It's a very simple show," she said. "It's about, it's trying to find the next kind of next great singer, and it's about the American dream. It's about taking people who live a normal life in some remote part of the country, but have an amazing talent, discovering that talent and making the dream come true. I think there's something very powerful about that."

Not to be undervalued in the process is the role of the public, which votes on the outcome of *American Idol*. Although judges Cowell, Jackson, and Abdul can say someone is a great singer, it's up to the public to cast a vote for the singer they want to win.

Besides launching the careers of such talented singers as Clarkson, Clay Aiken, Bo Bice, and Carrie Underwood, *American Idol* has also been responsible for the career of William Hung, a very bad singer who turned his awful performance auditioning on *American Idol* into a very small recording career.

Hung wasn't the first bad singer to make it on *American Idol*, though he was the first to turn his appearance into a career of sorts. Otherwise, most really bad singers who go on the show know that going in and are just trying to get some airtime on the hit show. "In truth, with the bad singers, it depends where you come from," said executive producer Nigel Lythgoe. "I love the deluded. I don't love the university [student] and the graduate that comes along, makes himself look stupid because he is on a bet. We record everybody, so we've got it, and we'll normally drop that into a montage of stupidity, but not feature them as a soloist. It's the William Hungs that I love. It's the ones that believe you can be successful—and it's everybody's dream—you can be successful in this country by working hard. And he forgets that you need a modicum of talent as well, which he didn't have. But he believes like so many that come along to the auditions that if we invest our time as professionals in them, we can make them a star."

And that they have. As part of their deals to appear on *American Idol* the winner's first album is produced by and released by record companies associated with the producers. The show producers control what songs and the direction they'll take early on. Anyone making it into the top 10 of *American Idol* is signed to a deal for future work. Some have called the deals restrictive and unfair.

Not so, said Cowell, who points out the show helps propel a career that might never have happened. "None of them, when they win, are going to turn and give the money to charity," Cowell said. "This is a get rich quick scheme for somebody. If you don't like it, don't play."

Fox attempted to capture the *American Idol* magic in *American Juniors*, an *Idol* spin-off featuring singers between the ages of 6 and 13 in June 2003. The show was similar to the adult *American Idol*, although the judges were different, and as a result spared the juniors the wrath of Simon Cowell. However, many critics said because the show lacked the bite of a Cowell, it just wasn't interesting. Others said the children singers weren't as good as the adults and not worth watching. The first version struggled to get viewers, though Fox officials initially said there would be a second version. That edition was never produced and ultimately scrapped.

The producers of *American Idol* also staged one cycle of *World Idol* on Fox, which put the winners of the various international competitions in one big battle. It, too, lasted one season.

The arrival of *American Idol* also opened the door for even more music-based series, either direct competitions like *American Idol* or shows built around a theme, such as *Making the Band*, which once dropped by ABC in 2003 was picked up, altered, and continued at MTV.

Producers Ben Silverman and H. T. Owens, the team behind *The Restaurant* reality series, capitalized off the *American Idol* momentum in 2003 with their show, *Nashville Star* for the USA Network. Where *American Idol* looked for a pop star, *Nashville Star* searched for a country artist. A dozen contestants competed in the first cycle. They were judged by industry professionals and viewers at home. During the run of the show the finalists lived together in a house on Music Row in Nashville.

In addition to singing, *Nashville Star* also put contestants in what was called the "hot spot," a challenge where they had to act professional in a situation in which most stars routinely find themselves. One in the first season had the five finalists sing the National Anthem at a stock car race.

The first winner was Buddy Jewell, whose first CD hit the No.1 spot on the Billboard country charts. "I had been in Nashville for a decade writing songs," said Jewell. "*Nashville Star* landed me a record deal and gave me the opportunity to perform my own songs on the show in front of millions of Americans each week—with fan reactions via email and through my Web site. I would have taken me years to get that sort of dedicated fan base without the support of those people who followed the show."

The show was a hit for the USA Network, which launched its fourth season of *Nashville Star* in early 2006. *Nashville Star* works because it showcases the best untapped musical talent on television," said Jeff Wachtel, USA Network's executive vice president of original programming in announcing the new season. "One thing we've learned over the past three seasons is that there's an incredible pool of talented performers whose voices have yet to be heard." Even the runners up on *Nashville Star* have done well. Miranda Lambert, who finished third on the show, has since had a successful country singing career. *Nashville Star* has also proven to be a strong draw for celebrities. Singing star LeAnn Rimes was the host early on. Singer Sarah Evans stepped in at one point. And in 2006, Wynonna and Cowboy Troy were the hosts, with a series of big-named stars saving as judges.

American Idol is so good, it also has been spoofed. Mike Fleiss, the man behind *Who Wants to Marry a Multimillionaire?* and *The Bachelor,* took on *American Idol* in 2004 with *The WB's Superstar USA,* a riveting series that took the model of *American Idol* and turned it upside down. Rather than looking for good singers, *Superstar USA* looked for bad singers, truly bad singers, but the contestants were not told they were bad. Like *American Idol* there were three judges, including a former pop star and a cranky judge in the model of Simon Cowell. When a good singer performed they were told they were terrible. A bad singer, however, was showered with praise. It wasn't until the end of the show when the winner was told they were picked because they were really bad.

Because *Superstar USA* was built on a stunt, or more specifically a twist, it wasn't tried twice. In the past, the second cycle of some shows hasn't done as well as the first, especially with twist shows. *Joe Millionaire* didn't work a second time around, nor did *Joe Schmo,* largely because once the stunt is known—and viewers know what to expect—producers tend to shy away from the format.

American Idol served as the model for *So You Think You Can Dance,* a talent search show for dancers produced by *American Idol* backer Nigel Lythgoe in 2005 and again in 2006. It was also the model for *But Can They Sing?* a VH1 reality show with celebrities trying to belt out a tune. Among the performers were Joe Pantoliano, Morgan Fairchild, boxer Larry Holmes, and former model Kim Alexis. "I've embraced the fact that I can't sing," Pantoliano told the *New York Daily News* before the show launched. He couldn't, of course, but that was the idea behind the series in the first place.

The influence of *American Idol* and *Survivor* combined are found in a two reality shows that appeared during 2005 that were designed to find new members for real-life bands. Mark Burnett, the force behind *Survivor,* also produced *Rock Star* for CBS. The show was created to find a lead singer for the band INXS, which had been without a lead singer since Michael Hutchence killed himself in 1997. Unlike *American Idol, Rock Star* did not include any of the audition process as part of the show, and instead began with the field of contestants already picked. Brooke Burke and Dave Navarro served as hosts, and the surviving members of INXS were part of the judging process. Viewers were also shown some of the behind-the-scenes life of the contestants, such as rehearsals and living together in a house. "This was a band, it was going to take a singer, we weren't just going to crank out a pop star," Navarro said. "I thought it was an interesting twist."

"Yes, it's a music show, and somebody does win it," executive producer and former *Idol* producer, David Goffin said before the launch. "But some-body who wins becomes a member of an existing band. It's an incredible prize. I think we've got something that ends in a much bigger and better way [than *American Idol*]."

CBS banked on the show to be a big hit, but it wasn't. Three planned weekly telecasts were cut down, and eventually the show was moved to VH1 to finish out its run. Canadian J. D. Fortune won the show and imme-diately cut a record with INXS. Tommy Lee, who appeared in an NBC series following him going back to college, agreed to spearhead a new band that would search for a singer on CBS's *Rock Star,* set for summer 2006.

The R&B group TLC also went the reality show route to find a new singer. The group had three members, but one, Lisa Lopes was killed in a car crash. Like *Rock Star,* UPN's *R U the Girl* was about becoming the next member of the group, which members T-Boz and Chilli each said would not be a replacement for Lopes. Yet, it intentionally focused more on T-Boz and Chilli than the competitors. "We've all seen competition shows," executive pro-ducer Jay Blumenfield told reporters in July 2005, before the show launched. "I think there're good things and bad things about them. But we all wanted to try something new and really try to go on a journey with T-Boz and Chilli and see where it took us." Along the way viewers saw the contestants prove their singing and dancing skills, as well as their people skills in dealing with the two remaining members of TLC.

To some extent, NBC's *Last Comic Standing* owes something to *American Idol.* The series was a mix of *Idol*'s performance functions and *The Real World*'s living together strings. The show lasted a couple of seasons, though it has been hamstrung by controversy when it was clear some of the comics on the show were already professionals, and there were also questions about the judging process. Having worked out the kinks, *Last Comic Standing* was revived and slated to return on NBC in the summer of 2006, with 10 comics, male and female, living together in a house and vying for a talent contract with the network.

The common thread running through most of the performance and musical genre shows is that they tend to appeal to families and encourage family viewing. Families watch together because parents generally do not need to worry about salacious content on a show such as *American Idol or Nashville Star* because its not part of the mix. No one is forced to humiliate themselves to get to the next level. There isn't a lot of behind-the-scenes footage for parents to worry about kids seeing alcohol-fueled parties or dips in a hot tub. And, there is rarely any bad language.

During the 2004–2005 television season, *American Idol* was the most-watched show on television, averaging more than 27 million viewers an episode; that's up from more than 21 million the show earned in 2002–2003, according to Nielsen Media Research. *American Idol*'s audience levels stand in contrast to most aging shows, which tend to lose viewers in subsequent seasons, not gain them.

"I think unpredictability is the key to making great reality TV," Cowell told television writers in January 2005. "That is the definition of reality. It's real." Cowell is right. Amazingly, the fifth season of *American Idol* was drawing its largest audiences ever, routinely topping 30 million viewers for each edition. Typically, shows draw their largest audiences in the first season and fall from there. But *American Idol* increased audience with each season.

And it's that aspect of the performance shows that keeps viewers coming back and watching, waiting, and even hoping they'll be setside when a new star is born. Newton, who for decades has been one of Las Vegas's biggest stars, said giving people a shot at fame was one of the reason's he was willing to be part of *The Entertainer*. And if it existed when he was coming up, he would have tried out, too. "The truth of the matter is the thing that propelled me to want to be such an integral part of this show was the realization that what helped me in my embryonic stages of my career, don't exist for these people today, and it really is something that I absolutely would have done," Newton said. "I absolutely would have auditioned. I absolutely would have shown up."

He did in his day, on *The Original Amateur Hour*. Today, young singers are doing the same.

CHAPTER 10

Liars, Cheaters, and Scandals

Corey Clark was a contestant on the second season of *American Idol*. However, he made his biggest impact on *American Idol* well after his run on the show ended. He did so as part of a show scandal that almost cost judge Paula Abdul her job. Clark was one of the finalists culled from auditions around the country and shipped to Hollywood, where the show unfolded each week. Clark lasted through several rounds of eliminations on the show before a Web site disclosed that Clark had faced charges he had beaten his sister. The trouble was that Clark never told the producers of the pending charges, even though there are several steps along the way in becoming a contestant to disclose any legal troubles.

The producers of *American Idol*, the hottest reality show on the air at the time, had been image conscious about their contestants from the start of the show. Advertiser product placement is a big deal in reality shows. In the case of *American Idol*, there are commercials during the show tied to the contestants on the show. So, the producers were always on the look out for situations that could sully advertisers. Clark, with a pending charge, could be a problem, they conceded. So, Clark was cut from the show. He wasn't the first, and he certainly wouldn't be the last.

Little was heard from the budding singer until May 2005, when word leaked out that Clark was trying to sell a book proposal that contained major allegations of potential game manipulation and wrongdoing on the part of judge Paula Abdul. For the show, the allegations were a huge blow.

Throughout the series' history, Abdul had always played the part of the contestants' advocate. Whereas Simon Cowell was billed as "Mr. Nasty," and willing to cut down the weakest contestants, Abdul often cried when her favorites didn't win over the audience. When one of the other judges slammed a contestant, Abdul let them down with encouraging words.

Clark, however, maintained that advocacy went a step further and into sexual relations. He said he was slipped her phone number and invited to her house. While there, he told ABC, she began to show affection. "I liked it. I was like, Paula Abdul's hitting on me," Clark said. He also said Abdul gave him a special phone number so they could talk privately and gave him money to get better clothes for his performances on the show. He maintained Abdul was trying to help him win.

For her part, Abdul was silent, denying wrongdoing through spokespeople. In a statement, Abdul said she would not "dignify false statements" made by Clark, who was described as an "admitted liar and opportunist." Abdul's friends rallied behind her. "I just do not see Paula Abdul as a person who would try to sabotage *American Idol,*" said contestant Carmen Rasmusen, who benefited when Clark got booted by not getting kicked off herself because of low viewer votes. "I do not see Paula doing something that stupid that would hurt her image and hurt the show as well."

Rasmusen said she never saw Clark and Abdul alone. She also said she didn't believe Abdul showed favoritism. She did, however, recall a day when, after the men performed, Clark went up to Abdul at the judges table. "He went up and gave a rose to Paula," she said, "and said thanks. I am beginning to think, now, what if he was doing this because of [a relationship]."

The allegations were serious to show producers and Fox officials. The integrity of the show was on the line. Moreover, any damage to the franchise could cause legal problems, and, perhaps more important, declining ratings would wreak financial havoc for the network. A full-scale investigation was launched by Fox officials, though Abdul remained on the show and completed the season.

The *American Idol* trouble wasn't the first scandal to hit a reality show. But it may have been the largest, simply because at the time, *American Idol* was the top-rated reality show on television, and the only one to consistently maintain big Nielsen numbers week in and week out. During the 2004–2005 television season, the Tuesday edition of *American Idol* averaged 27.4 million viewers, according to Nielsen Media Research, making it the most-watched television show of any kind. It's no wonder Fox officials moved quickly to protect the franchise and the millions of dollars the show generated for the network each season.

On a larger scale, it exposed more of the risks of using non-actors on television shows. By the time Corey Clark began spilling his story of woe, the reality genre in general, and specifically producers of reality shows and the executives that air them, were well versed in scandals.

Just ask CBS officials.

In the early hours of a July 2001 morning, Justin Sebik and Krista Stegall were doing what many young adults do after a few drinks. They were flirting and kissing, as twentysomethings often do late at night. Their roommates were fast asleep. The only people aware of their actions at that moment were those at home watching a live feed on the Internet and a few producers alone in another room. While Sebik and Stegall were usual in the way they were carrying on like budding lovebirds that met at a bar, they were far from normal people. The two, he a bartender from New Jersey, she a waitress from Louisiana, were part of CBS's reality show *Big Brother 2*, in which a dozen disparate people are thrown together in a prefab home in Los Angeles and their every moment captured by cameras and microphones. Part of the show airs live on CBS, though other parts are taped.

When Sebik and Stegall were fooling around, the cameras were rolling, but not live on CBS. And only those who had subscribed to a live Internet feed were watching. But that's when things went wrong—way wrong. Stegall was lying on a counter, while Sebik hovered above. He suddenly broke off a kiss, and grabbed a kitchen knife. He held it to her neck. "Will you get mad if I killed you," Sebik said, as producers watched in horror. She laughed and he put the knife away.

The moment, estimated to have lasted less than a minute, instantly exposed the inherent dangers of putting so-called regular people, or nonactors, on television shows in what often results in a human experiment for the sake of entertainment. It wasn't the first time producers had a concern over Sebik, an outspoken player who often verbally jousted with other players. Earlier in the show's run, Sebik told a fellow contestant that he was "going to kick the s— out of you." He was warned then. Following the Stegall incident, he was immediately removed from the game.

Since the genre has created, scandals have erupted all around, ranging from potential violence to shady players to lawsuits. The incidents have raised questions about the genre altogether, and more so, the process producers use to find contestants for reality shows. Show producers and talent executives want dynamic personalities who can lure viewers to their shows. Wallflowers need not apply for reality programs. The trend has been to go for the more outspoken, outlandish, perhaps unsavory folks as contestants.

In defense of the producers, boring people won't draw a crowd. Boorish players, however, can make for interesting television. And scandal in reality television is not an American issue alone. A contestant who had past mental problems committed suicide after being voted out of the Swedish version of *Survivor* in 1997.

The earliest days of reality television in the United States were filled with bad people by design. Fox's groundbreaking series *Cops*, among the first reality shows, was built around police chasing bad guys. To that end, a large percentage of Fox's early reality—police chase videos, animals gone bad, and the like—were loaded with deplorable characters. The difference, though, was those people happened to end up on television because of their bad deeds, whereas the new wave of reality players was cast that way.

Concerns about potential problems developing from putting real people in reality programs were raised shortly after the word of the first *Survivor* hit the media.

How would people act, some wondered, when forced to survive in the wild and with a $1 million prize the goal? This, of course, was before any-one had a real sense of the extent of what "reality" in reality shows really was. If people really had to fight for food, eat bugs, and other odd delica-cies, would they go as far as killing or maiming each other for the sake of entertainment, and for a stake in a $1 million prize? At the time, reality shows were a new breed for television networks, producers, and ultimately the contestants. Until *Survivor* came along, the industry was familiar with working with celebrities—many of whom have their own legal and illicit problems—and scripts.

Yet, reality opened up a new horizon for all involved. For the networks, they exposed themselves to the risks of working with a pool of players—the contestants—who, for the most part, had no background in the industry. When an actor has problems off camera, everyone in the business finds out. But when casting a reality show—which generally covers any show without a script and using nonactors—the producers and networks must rely on background checks to weed out potential problems. Background checks, however, are only as good as those pursuing the information and the amount of money producers are willing to pay for the details. To that end, if the players start lying from the start of the process, it can be difficult to uncover inconsistencies or problems. If, for example, a contestant had posed for nude photographs using an alias, would background checks find them? Real life has already proven that to be a tough task. If players use other names and not had legal problems, would producers find out? Not usually.

Fox learned about hidden pasts the hard way in early 2000, in a mishap that nearly derailed the reality wave—albeit for a short time. In one of the earliest reality stunts, producers set out to find a multimillionaire who would agree to participate in a televised marriage. The idea was to have a gaggle of beauties try to win over the financially secure man and have him propose and marry the woman on the spot. The show was the brainchild of Fox's reality guru Mike Darnell, who said the idea came to him after watching ABC's *Who Wants to Be a Millionaire?* game show.

"This is no joke," show host Jay Thomas said at the start of the program.

Who Wants to Marry a Multimillionaire? aired the day after Valentine's Day, February 2000. It was part pageant, part *Dating Game,* and very similar in parts to *Who Wants to Be a Millionaire?* There were 50 women ranging in ages from 19 to the mid-40s at the start. The field was quickly cut to 10, who then walked on stage in bathing suits and wedding gowns.

Rockwell was kept in the shadows for most of the show, adding intrigue to the pageant. The women did not meet Rockwell until he emerged to pick and propose to Darva Conger, a nurse from California. "If you feel that I am the perfect woman for you, and you choose me to be your bride, I'll be your friend, your lover, and your partner throughout whatever life has to offer us," Conger said before the show ended. "We'll have joy, maybe a few tears, but more ups than downs. And you will never be bored."

"I know exactly what I'm looking for in love and in life and it's here tonight," Rockwell said before proposing to Conger. Before it aired, the program raised concerns about television producers having a hand in an arranged marriage.

The show was a hit in the ratings, and Fox officials immediately scheduled a repeat telecast of it a few days later. There was also talk of other marriage specials. But then the bottom fell out. While the couple were together on their chaperoned honeymoon, it became clear all was not clean on the show. Indeed, soon after the telecast aired, it became known that an old girlfriend of Rockwell's had filed a restraining order against him in 1991.

"Rick Rockwell threw me around and slapped and hit me in my face," ex-girlfriend Debby Goyne said in court papers exposed after the fiasco. "Recently, he said he would find me and kill me."

Critics carped that Fox had set up Conger with a potentially dangerous person. Rockwell repeatedly denied hitting any former girlfriends for any reasons. And said he didn't condone such action. There were also questions raised about Rockwell's true wealth. And Conger, who claimed she was a Gulf War veteran, was also challenged on her credibility. At the time of the 1991 war, Conger was a staff sergeant at the Scott Air Force Base in Illinois. Though she never went to the Gulf during the war, she claimed she was a "war" veteran as was anyone else in active duty at the time. It was a comment that didn't sit well with some veterans.

Red-faced Fox executives immediately launched an investigation into the Rockwell incident. Two months after the show aired, the network's investigation into how it was duped revealed there was nothing they could have done to have caught Rockwell's past. Investigators said the Fair Credit Reporting Act prohibited the disclosure of all but criminal records that occurred more than seven years earlier. And because of that law, producers had counted on Rockwell to be truthful. Rockwell, it turned out, had considered the restraining order "ancient" history.

By early April 2000, the Rockwell/Conger marriage, which never materialized in real life, was kaput legally. A Las Vegas judge annulled the nuptials. However, the reality television genre was changed dramatically—some might argue for the better. Television executives said they would take better care to check the backgrounds of their contestants. Fox officials immediately vowed to clean up its reality offerings, specifically any with aspects that were degrading or humiliating to contestants. To that end, the company hired PriceWaterhouseCoopers to monitor and conduct background checks of all contestants on reality shows.

As history has already proven, the stepped-up background checks have not stopped producers from being lied to about the backgrounds of contestants. In fact, it's only made players willing to do anything to get fame and, perhaps, fortune on television work harder to get on the shows.

Just months after the Rockwell incident, CBS executives were mired in a mess revolving around its series *Big Brother*. The American version of the a hit show abroad launched on CBS over the July 4 weekend in 2000 when 10 strangers were walked into a home built specifically for the show in the parking lot of the CBS studios in Los Angeles. Among them was an African-American man named William Collins, whose CBS biography said he was a youth counselor from Philadelphia. He liked cheese steaks, chess, and vacations in Harlem.

What he didn't tell producers—nor did he write it on his biography—was he was also known as Hiram Ashantee, a follower of the Khalid Abdul Muhammad, a former Nation of Islam leader who was dropped by that organization for calling Jews "bloodsuckers" and using other racial epithets. On the show, Collins called himself Will Mega, and often tangled verbally with other contestants. "I don't fit in here at all," Collins said at one point.

"Overall, there's a general idea by mainstream whites of what everyday life is like for African-Americans, and if you don't fit in with that, you're isolated."

CBS officials weren't aware of Collins's double life until it was revealed in a front-page story in the *New York Daily News*. Collins failed to mention his alias in CBS' *Big Brother* application, which clearly asks participants to "be honest." And the second question of what is a 13-page application asks: "Have you ever formally or otherwise changed your name? If so, what other names have you used and why?" Had Collins disclosed the name Hiram Ashantee, a simple Internet search would have turned up his connection with Muhammad's organization and likely sunk his chances at prime-time fame.

But faced with the reality that Collins was still a participant in the show, CBS chose to keep him on, rather than immediately dismiss him. "This series features a diversity of people, representing different voices and opinions. As long as they treat each other and our audience with respect, we will support each individual's rights to think and speak freely," a CBS spokesman said in a statement at the time. The statement did say the network would not tolerate or permit "hate speech" from being part of the show.

Privately, the network was furious that the system designed to stop such folks from getting on the air had failed. Making matters worse was that the revelation came just a day after it was publicly learned that another player on the show had shot and killed a friend in a hunting accident a dozen years earlier. The network reportedly spent more than $100,000 on background checks for *Big Brother*, which failed to turn up Collins's controversial past. After word of Collins's background got out, viewers voted him off the show.

"We double, we triple check, but once again, we're dealing with a lot of people out there who do have skeletons, and I don't know what we would do differently, but obviously we would examine the process," CBS head Leslie Moonves told reporters two weeks after the Collins scandal emerged.

Then Fox Entertainment chairman Sandy Grushow also told reporters that no one ever wants to go through what Fox did after the Rockwell mess. "But I think we learned some valuable lessons, and chief among them is that you've got to take a really hard look at these things. We are all playing with fire here and some one is going to get burned." Grushow, who has since left Fox, said there was "a danger attendant to doing these things" and that it was a "very challenging area."

But what they didn't know then was how many and how often reality show scandals would emerge. Unlike any other form of programming, sans sports, following the reality genre has become a cottage industry for some folks. Eagle-eyed fans scour each episode looking for clues on the outcome of the show and, more importantly, for tips and clues about the people involved.

Some of the attention given to the players on the shows was driven, in part, by the networks themselves. Typically, players on each show are not revealed until the show has run its course. For instance, CBS doesn't unveil the contestants of *Survivor* until after the entire show has been filmed. Likewise, the contestants on *Big Brother* aren't disclosed until they're actually in the CBS house and unable to be exposed to outside media interests. It holds true for virtually every other reality show that has been recorded before the show actually airs.

To that end, early in the growth curve of reality programming, networks only released a player's first name, perhaps with the initial of their last names, and some general background information about their careers and family life. From the networks' side, the secrecy was understandable. Before a show airs, they don't want the media digging into a contestant's past in search of finding out whether the player won or was sent home early. For example, finding a person of modest means driving a Bentley could suggest they've hit big on a reality show.

Moreover, in the early going, especially with *Survivor*, keeping the winner a secret was key to driving the appeal of the show. Rightly so, network officials were concerned that if viewers knew the outcome of the program they might not tune in for the run of the show.

So it is that the secrecy sent conspiracy theorists and diehard fans to the Internet in search of snippets about the contestants. Joining in the hunt have been the folks behind Thesmokinggun.com, who scan legal documents, court cases, and police reports in search of any potential wrongdoing on the part of celebrities and reality show contestants.

All of those factors, however, have led to the number of scandals being exposed while the shows are either airing or shortly after. For instance, during the course of the original *Survivor*, it was learned that contestant Kelly Wigglesworth was wanted in North Carolina for going on a $586 shopping spree using a stolen credit card.

Here are just some of the other dubious doings of reality show contestants along the way:

- *Big Brother 3* contestant Amy Crews had been arrested and charged with drunk driving in 1999 near her Arkansas home.
- Michael Carri, a contestant on CBS's *Big Brother 2*, was arrested in 1996 after he and two others were stopped by security guards at Warner Bros. Studios in what appeared to be a scheme to get on the set of the then-filming *Batman* movie.

- Taheed Watson and Ytossie Patterson appeared on Fox's *Temptation Island* in 2001, a show that was to test the relationships of unmarried couples by plopping them down on an island resort and tempting them with members of the opposite sex. In the end, they were to decide whether the relationship would go forward. Watson and Patterson never got that far because during the show it was discovered the couple had a child together, a clear violation of the show's rules. They were cut from the program. They later sued, claiming they were told to lie. The suit was eventually tossed out of court.

Even in 2006, reality shows were being hit with scandals. During auditions for the fifth cycle of *American Idol* twins Terrell and Derrell Brittenum wowed the judges with their singing. However, by the time the show began airing, the two had been in trouble with the police over their separate attempts to purchase cars.

Producers are the first to admit that dealing with nonactors opens them up to a great deal of risk on reality shows. It's a risk that caught talk show producers by surprise a decade earlier when that genre was thriving. In the mid to late 1980s, anyone with something to say—or a modest level of appeal—was given a daytime talk show. For a portion of the audience, it provided a platform for them to gain exposure to the masses, which they never would have gotten otherwise. Want to get on television? Easy. Call the number at the end of the show. What happened then, though, is some of the on-air guests were simply making up stories that matched the show's needs. And they did so, over and over, hopscotching from *Sally Jessy Raphael* to *Geraldo* to *Ricki Lake*, not stopping until they spilled the beans to the press, or some sharp viewer realized the guests looked familiar.

When talk shows faded, reality filled the gap, becoming a realistic shot for nobodies to become somebodies. Producers want outlandish characters. They want risk takers. Sometimes, as the past has proven, risk takers occasionally do not follow the letter of the law. Yet they do become dynamic characters on the small screen, drawing viewers and Nielsen Media Research ratings.

Those people are chosen after several rounds of interviews with a variety of show staffers, usually among them a psychologist who evaluates candidates to find out how they may react in tense, tight, or emotional situations. And despite their best efforts, people with troubled pasts continue to get on the air, embarrassing networks along the way.

Rob Campos is one of those people. In early 2003, he signed up for a new reality show called *For Love or Money*. Then 33 years old, Campos fit the needs of Nash Entertainment, which produced the show. He was handsome. As a lawyer, he presumably had money and a clean background. And he spent time in the military. In short, he would be a dream date for many women. The concept for the show called for 15 women to try to win Campos's heart. What he didn't know during the taping was that the woman he picked would get $1 million. What she didn't know was that she would be forced to choose between love and money. What no one in the production knew is that Campos was not as perfect as he initially seemed. Turned out he was forced to leave the Marine Corps after groping the breasts of a female Navy officer while drunk. No surprise—Campos never told that to the producers. It happened in 1999 and he was allowed to leave the military 20 months before his enlistment was to expire.

"NBC and Nash were not aware of the incident that occurred while Mr. Campos was in the military," NBC officials said in a statement. "The incident is not public record and this was not found in the public-record searches conducted by the investigator hired by the show. Nor did Mr. Campos inform the producers about the incident. Clearly, this would have been material information during the screening process."

For his part, Campos maintained he "believed it was a private matter that had been resolved. I received two commendations while in the military, as well as an honorable discharge, and did not believe that the incident was relevant to my potential participation in the show. In connection with the incident, I have acknowledged that I behaved inappropriately."

Yet, once again, it gave critics of the genre, and network executives, a chance to reevaluate their procedures. As in the Rockwell case, the Campos scenario raised questions about what sort of people were being thrown together for a television show and what were the potential downsides.

Critics have maintained from the start of the form that someone could end up getting killed on a reality show when a character flaw not exposed in the audition stage explodes during filming. There are, however, several levels of scandals that have come to light on reality shows. Rockwell and Campos are on the extreme end. The variety of drunk driving offenses collected by players on *Big Brother* and elsewhere along the way is in the middle. At the low end are some of the past experiences of players in porn, soft-core, or pure nude photography. Brian Heidik, the winner of CBS's *Survivor: Thailand* appeared nude in soft-core films before getting on the show. His CBS bio said he was a used car salesman.

Ami Cusak, a player on *Survivor: Vanuatu*, was listed as a barista and a model on the CBS Web site. What's not revealed is she had appeared nude in Playboy. Frenchie Davis, a dynamic singer on *American Idol*, made it to being one of the show's 30 finalists in 2003. But then she was dropped after word got out that she had posed topless for a Web site.

In Davis's case, she had identified her topless past in her *American Idol* application. However, that information wasn't exposed until she made the cut. Producers eliminated Davis from the show because they were concerned that advertisers on the show—many of which are incorporated into the series—would be tarnished by the connection. *American Idol*'s rules allow producers to cut players at any time for any reason.

Not all scandals are bad, however. More to the point, networks and show producers have used the questionable backgrounds of some players to gain attention for their programs along the way. Heidik's soft-porn background didn't come out until shortly before he was crowned the winner of that version of *Survivor,* which has been widely considered one of the weakest outings in the quality show.

Perhaps the best example of a show gaining attention because of a scandal was Fox's 2003 run of *Joe Millionaire*. The series, the first of the twist shows to have a player lie, had a gaggle of women trying to get a man to fall in love with them. The man was Evan Marriott, a construction worker, who was instructed to tell the women he had inherited $50 million. He then began whittling the field, eventually getting them down to two, Zora Andrich and Sara Kozar.

At the time, ratings for the show were red hot and soaring. Viewers were clearly taken by the lying aspect of the game, which portrayed the women as gold diggers only after Marriott's nonexistent fortune. The show became water cooler talk, and Fox officials took advantage of the frenzy. As the final episode of the series neared, Kozar's past was exposed. It turned out that, in addition to the sales and design work she listed as a career on her application, she also admitted to appearing in some racy bondage photos. The shocking images hit the Internet as viewers were waiting for Marriott to select between Kozar and Andrich.

Reality television had once again been slapped as bawdy, tawdry, and troubled, but Fox executives privately laughed. They knew about the images. Yet, in the days after the revelation, Kozar's image was plastered throughout the media as well as her tale. "I'll stand by anything I've ever done," Kozar told the *New York Daily News*. "My checkpoint living in L.A. as a young woman for the last few days has been... I would never do anything that I wouldn't call and tell my mother about." Kozar was not nude in the photos, just bound and gagged. It didn't matter. The deed was done and Fox benefited from the extra promotion when the finale drew more than 41 million viewers—a huge number.

Yet, appearing topless or bound before going on a reality show is much different than having run-ins with the law. There again, the level of scandal is in the eye of the beholder. Justin Sebik, who had been warned by producers of *Big Brother 2* for his verbal abuse of fellow housemates before holding a knife to the throat of Krista Stegall, didn't think his actions were dangerous. "If there's anyone that could perceive that as an act of violence, or a threat, then you're an idiot," Sebik told *Big Brother* host Julie Chen in a televised interview. "I don't know what kind of glasses you're looking through." When the incident occurred, Sebik spent an hour attempting to convince producers he would be fine for the rest of the show. He failed and was kicked off the program.

"I can't even fathom, if somebody's watchin' me kiss a girl first of all, if she felt threatened, I don't think she would have said 'Go for it.' And laughin' and kissin' me," told Chen. He also told Chen his actions during the show—he maintained he didn't threaten anyone—were just part of his strategy to get in the heads of fellow players. No matter what the strategy, Sebik's actions provided further fodder for reality naysayers who question the safety of contestants.

Before viewers voted her out, Stegall was portrayed as a victim in the affair. After she was dropped, she later told reporters she didn't feel threatened by Sebik's actions. In an unintended irony, Stegall admitted to another contestant—and captured by CBS's Internet feed—that her past wasn't perfect, either. Seems that she and a boyfriend were arrested for a simple battery after an argument. The district attorney later abandoned the case after the boyfriend asked the charges against Stegall be dropped. She later gave producers a letter from the district attorney saying he declined to prosecute.

"I've been through a lot in my life, and I thought I'd be mentally prepared for it," Stegall told Chen of her experiences inside the *Big Brother* house. "But it was a very stressful situation that I don't want to encounter again." However, as long as producers and network rely on nonactors as a form of entertainment, there will be similar incidents, and, perhaps one day, something terrible will happen.

Other scandals erupt because of the content, rather than the contestants. In late 2004, Fox officials revealed they had produced a series of specials called *Who's Your Daddy?* The shows revolved around a contestant who was faced with a group of men who could be his or her biological father. Through a series of meetings and interviews, the contestant was to decide who the father might be. Guess right, and the contestant got $100,000. Guess wrong and the faked dad got the cash. Before the first show aired, however, adoption officials were livid at Fox and the producers for making fun of real-life situations. They also slammed the producers for not taking into consideration the real emotional issues that occur when a child given up for adoption eventually meets his or her birth parents.

"To all our critics, I would just say watch the show," executive producer Scott Hallock told the *New York Daily News*. "People hear Fox. They hear money and they hear the title, and they think, this is terrible, this is salacious. If they watch the show they'll see that it really does have its heart in the right place." The initial episode focused on a woman named T.J. Myers, whose parents were high school sweethearts who gave her up when he was shipped off to Vietnam. Myers was no routine reality show contestant, either. Before *Who's Your Daddy?* she appeared in soft-core films, had worked as a model, and had a string of small parts in B-movies. And before *Who's Your Daddy?* aired she had already landed in another reality show for Court TV called *Impossible Heists,* in which she was part of a team of crooks trying to break into a building. And a few years earlier she had appeared in a USA Network reality show called *Combat Missions.*

Nevertheless, during the Fox show, Myers questioned the potential dads, spent time with them, and viewers at home cringed when it came time to make a decision. She decided correctly. "Thank you for having me!" she said, while crying at the end of the show.

A few days after the telecast she told a New York radio station she had no idea the show would cause such controversy. "You know, call me naïve," she told Scott Shannon and Todd Pettengill on WPLJ-FM, "but I really didn't realize it. Other than the adoption agencies, they were a little upset about the whole thing, and I don't understand why because I wanted to meet my birth father."

She did earn $100,000 for being on the Fox show. She claimed neither she nor the stand-in fathers knew about the potential windfall. "It was just absolutely amazing and full of love," Myers said. "I didn't understand why, when everybody wanted to meet each other, the adoption agencies were upset."

Nevertheless, adoption advocates were angered by the show. "As one of the 40 million Americans affected by adoption, I am writing to implore you not to air *Who's Your Daddy?*" author Deborah Capone wrote in an open letter released to the media. "By turning adoption reunions into a game show, *Who's Your Daddy?* takes an intensely personal and complex situation—and an increasingly commonplace one—and transforms it into a voyeuristic display."

Fox officials agreed. They didn't like the negative fallout and decided against airing the remaining six episodes of *Who's Your Daddy?* that were shot. "I don't think *Who's Your Daddy?* was a mistake," Fox Entertainment president Gail Berman said in January 2005 (she later left the network). "You put all kinds of programming on and you try things. I think the audience expects loud things from Fox. Sometimes they work and sometimes they don't. And in the case of this particular show, it just didn't work."

Some observers have compared the wave of reality scandals to the famed quiz show troubles of the 1950s. No matter what the origins, scandals remain a part of the reality landscape.

Fox, it seems, perhaps because of the nature of the shows officials attempt to air, has drawn the bulk of the reality scandals so far. Some of that may be attributed, in part, to the fact that in the early part of the 2004–2005 season, more than half of the Fox lineup was reality.

The Corey Clark/Paula Abdul controversy, though, was certainly the biggest and the worst. It took a team of investigators 600 hours of work over three and a half months, and interviews with 43 people, to come to the conclusion that Clark's claims could not be substantiated. "We have determined, based on the findings of this thorough and detailed inquiry, that there is insufficient evidence that the communications between Mr. Clark and Ms. Abdul in any way aided his performance," the network said in a statement released August 12, 2005. "Further, we are confident that none of these communications had any impact on the outcome of the competition."

The network and the producers said they would institute a nonfraternization program to ensure there could be no hanky panky between the judges and the contestants in the future. "I'm grateful this ordeal is over," Abdul said in a statement that day, "and I'm so looking forward to getting back to the job I love."

And reality show producers everywhere got back to trying to ferret out scandals before they're revealed publicly.

CHAPTER 11

Working for a Living

The explosion of *Survivor*-like clones—and the Nielsen ratings success of many of those shows—sent producers scurrying in all directions in search of a reality show concept. It was no surprise; the quest sent at least some of them into the workplace. If the key to reality success is ordinary people in extra ordinary circumstances, as Mark Burnett has often said, the draw for workplace reality might be just a bit different: Interesting people in ordinary situations.

Like competition programs, there has been a boom in workplace reality show as well. From motorcycle building shops to hair salons, restaurants, mortuaries, shows to find models, starlets, an airline, casinos and even working with the master of business himself, Donald Trump, the workplace has proven to be an interesting landscape from which producers can create reality programs. There has even been one show designed to help business owners run better companies.

Like other reality shows, the casting with workplace and business reality shows is as important as the show concept itself. Donald Trump and Mark Burnett, the executive producers of Trump's NBC series *The Apprentice* are the first to admit casting can affect the creative and ratings success of the show.

In *The Apprentice*, a group of 16 contestants compete for a one-year job with Trump worth $250,000. Contestants for the show are culled from open auditions, and all of those making it onto the how have had some level of success in the business already. For example, the fall 2005 *Apprentice* winner

Randal Pinkett had been the founder, president, and chief executive officer of BCT Partners, a multimillion dollar management, technology, and policy consulting firm based in Newark, New Jersey. And he had five degrees, including a stint at Oxford.

"You get a pretty good idea," Trump said of the casting process. "Every once in a while you'll see someone who's a star. You'll see somebody that just works."

The casting process for the apprentice helped find Omarosa Manigault-Stallworth, the headstrong female player from the first season who landed several other deals after appearing on the show. And it also yielded investment banker Raj Bhakta, who used his time on *The Apprentice* to launch a congressional campaign in Pennsylvania. "I am running for Congress because America is at a crossroads," Bhakta said in a campaign statement on his Web site. "Our government cannot continue spending more than it makes. We have to make tough fiscal decisions to eliminate our gaping trade and budget deficits, and keep the American Dream alive for future generations."

The Apprentice may be the ultimate business show because it mixes real business tasks with intense product placement by sponsors. For example, each week, the teams of contestants compete to create a product, or a jingle, or to market something for a major national brand such as Burger King or Bally Fitness. Then, the success of each team is weighted against the other. The losing team must face Trump and his sidekicks Carolyn Kepcher and George Ross. There, the trio picks the performance apart and ultimately fires one of the players. In some cases, more than one player got the boot.

But, no matter what the task, the success of *The Apprentice* comes with the players. The third cycle of *The Apprentice* was considered to be a weaker version largely because of the makeup of the cast, something Trump acknowledged early on.

Not all cast members are outsiders, either. With A&E's *Family Plots*, an intriguing series built around a mortuary, the cast were all family. Also on A&E, the employees, managers, and passengers make up the cast of *Airline*, a series that follows the daily doings and misdoings of Southwest Airlines.

And there are the Teutels, Paul Sr, Paul Jr., and Mikey, the family focused on by Discovery's cameras for *American Chopper*, a captivating reality drama about a trio of motorcycle builders and their families. The show is set in their upstate New York chopper building facility, and much of the series is devoted to watching the Teutels build their one-of-a-kind motorcycles.

But at the heart of the series is the family. Father Paul is a tough, rough-around-the edges guy with bulging biceps. He's taken to wearing sunglasses inside, and often bickers with his son.

The family was found by producer Craig Piligen, who worked on *Survivor* and is also behind *American Casino* and *American Hot Rod,* two other workplace reality shows. Piligen had lined up another East Coast company to serve as the backdrop for the show, but then near the start of production, something went wrong, according to Paul Sr.

Within three days, the Teutels and their then three-year-old company Orange County Choppers were being filmed daily for the new series. Since it launched, *American Chopper* has changed the image of motorcycle enthusiasts and made the Teutel family household names. "It's quite an exciting time," Paul Sr. said of the attention he's gotten since the show took off.

Indeed, that's a prime motivator for anyone to get involved in a reality show. Face it, once agreeing to do a show, the subject matter must get used to having camera crews tracking their every move for weeks, or months, on end. In the case of *American Chopper,* it takes three weeks of shooting to create each episode—and motorcycle. The cameras, too, can be a major burden, capturing every conversation, argument, and deal.

"Some people think the show's hilarious," said Paul Sr. "I think the real deal is the combination of the interaction and the end product. Though there's some dysfunction going on, it's fascinating enough that some people who don't understand mechanics can see something from start to finish."

"I am most surprised by how quickly you forget that the cameras are around," said Lorenzo Fertita, who with his brother Frank is a chief officer at the Green Valley Ranch Resort, Casino and Spa featured on the Discovery Channel's *American Casino.* "They just become part of your daily environment and you go about your daily routine."

The Discovery Channel found an audience with an unlikely topic—Alaskan crab fishermen. *The Deadliest Catch* followed a group of fishermen living on the high seas in search of a big payday. Along the way, boats sank, people were killed, and viewers were exposed to one of the toughest, riskiest jobs on the planet. At its heart, though, *Deadliest Catch* wasn't about the crabs but the men who risk their lives in that line of work.

The reasons for becoming part of a reality show are many. Money, though not a lot, certainly comes into play. Increased recognition comes along with being on the show, which can generate more income down the road. When HBO signed a deal with All City Bail Bonds, a family-owned bail bond business run by Tom Evangelista and his family, the deal called for the company's phone number to appear on *Family Bonds.* So, in every episode is a shot of the exterior of the company's office with a close-up on the sign that has the businesses phone number.

Family Bonds, which lasted just one season, was not the only show to delve into the bail bonds business, either. A&E had a hit with *Dog the Bounty Hunter,* a series built around Duane "Dog" Chapman, who with his wife Beth, run a bail bonds business in Hawaii. Chapman, who sports a blonde mullet, spent time in Texas jail where he vowed to clean up his act. He now spreads the word of clean living to those he chases down for money.

Some reality show participants just want their lives to unfold on television. "What we hope to do here is to—through the graciousness of A&E [Networks] and [producers] Hybrid Films is to open up what we do on a daily basis," Rick Sadler, who runs the funeral home at the center of *Family Plots,* said before the show launched. "It's part of American life that I think has always been shrouded—no pun intended—from everyday view. And there really isn't any reason for that to be. And I think we want to give you an insight into what it is that we do care for these families and make this funeral happen in the way they want it to happen."

There's more to making a good reality show out of a workplace, though. And it takes more than a good cast. Like any television series, there's got to be a reason for people to watch, especially if it's on a topic that is out of their area of interest. Few people, for example, would say out of the blue that they wanted to learn more about how a funeral home works. In fact, most people avoid even talking about a funeral home. But, with the right cast, and the right scenarios—dramas, real-life dramas—then the subject matter becomes secondary to the people being presented.

Ben Silverman, producer of *The Restaurant* on NBC, said the notion of following the opening of a new restaurant would be filled with potential drama. "I felt that the restaurant was an environment that had tons of dramatic tension and was a place where many people played out dramatic incidents that happened within their lives, whether they were getting with a girlfriend, breaking up with a girlfriend, telling their parents that they were pregnant for the first time," Silverman said.

"And I thought that the table had a lot of interesting aspects," he added. "But I also thought that a chef and his staff, was like an interesting ensemble drama of any of the televisions shows that are out there right now."

Jonathan Tisch, chairman of Loews Hotels, said he agreed to participate in The Learning Channel's *Who's the Boss,* a series that put the chief executive officer in low-level jobs, because it was a chance for him to connect with the people who work for him. "So this was a way for me, now as the CEO, to re-engage myself with the people, with the employees, with our front lines who are vital to our success," Tisch said. "And I wouldn't have traded this experience for any other show. This maybe reality TV but in my mind, this is real TV."

Unlike reality series such as *Survivor, Fear Factor,* or *American Idol,* with few exceptions, there are no prizes involved with workplace shows. There was no winner with *The Restaurant.*

NBC's *Apprentice,* in contrast, though set in the business world, is more of a competition program, closer in roots and execution to *Survivor* than to, say, *Airline.* So it is that the drama and tension is created through so-called real-life situations and by the people.

Take *Family Plots,* for example. Most of the staffers at the Poway Bernardo Mortuary outside San Diego are related in some manner. Shonna Smith, the head mortician; Emily Vigney, the office manager; and Melissa Wissmiller, the assistant funeral director, are all sisters. Rick Sadler, who runs the place, is dating Wissmiller. The sisters' father, Chuck, a boxing coach, works as a driver for the firm. Although the life of a family in the business is interesting, no doubt, the show really hinges on their relationships.

For instance, Shonna Smith often reacted emotionally when dealing with the families setting up funeral arrangements. Wissmiller and Sadler's relationship exploded on one episode, creating problems for Smith and Vigney, because Sadler suddenly turned frosty. And Chuck, the father, is a character in his own right, losing a paycheck needed to buy a car in one show, and setting up a punching bag in the garage of the funeral home in another. The actual funeral-home work—while there—is secondary to how these people get along together.

The same holds true for *Airline.* The program hinged on how the company's employees interact with the customers. In two seasons, viewers saw counter workers deal with extensive overbooking, disorderly customers, and a few drunks here and there. Also, viewers saw employees stage a singing contest and one couple get engaged—in the air.

Generally, though, there are lots of scenes of stranded customers struggling with long delays, overbooked flights, and missed trips. The first season wasn't a public relations home run for the company, however. So much so that the company's President, Colleen Barrett told staffers in an internal memo to let the Southwest Airlines public relations arm know of any "special interest" stories to highlight on the show.

"It was a very scary decision to make," Barrett told a group of business leaders in Kansas City in May 2004. "They came to me three times before

I said yes." And before agreeing to a second season, she also asked the producers to add more balance by depicting positive stories as well as the conflicts with passengers. "Our goal in letting the world in for a glimpse behind the scenes is to show how hard we work to connect people for really important events in their lives—closing the big business deal, reuniting with loved ones, and seeing the joy in a child's first flight," Barrett said in a press release announcing the second season.

After the success of first season of *The Restaurant* on NBC, Ben Silverman returned with *Blow Out*, a similar work-place reality series, though this time focusing on the opening of a new Beverly Hills hair salon owned by Jonathan Antin. Antin, the handsome owner, oversaw a group of stylists and proved to be a tough taskmaster. He's said he was inspired by Warren Beatty's womanizing character in the 1975 film *Shampoo*. "For me, it was a great opportunity to put hairstylists on the map, but on a different map, sort of on the upper echelon-of-professionals-map," Antin told *Entertainment Weekly*. "I think of my hairstylists as doctors and lawyers—really important people that make great money and have securities and investments. I wanted to show all of that." Antin said his business was doing well before *Blow Out* launched, but that the reality show enhanced what he's done. During the run of the show, viewers saw Antin launch his own hair-care product line and open more salons. "My salons were slammed prior to *Blow Out*," he said. "The opening of the salon in Beverly Hills was going to be busy either way. Yeah, the product definitely became more easily recognized faster than other products."

Silverman also produced a short-run series called *The Club*, which followed the opening of a new nightclub in Las Vegas. The show revolved around a Los Angeles party planner/public relations expert Allison Melnick, whose job it was to get attention for the club, and the people who worked there. No surprise—the waitstaff was beautiful, as were the club-goers. "I always thought a nightclub was a wonderful place to tell stories about business," Silverman said.

"To say, 'Let's do a show about a nightclub is nothing,'" he added. "But to find people at a specific moment of their lives, and capture that moment, their dreams and their goals, is very compelling television."

That was the case with *Forty Deuce*, a reality show Bravo aired in 2005, following club owner Ivan Kane, who with his wife and former dancer, Champagne Suzy, allowed their efforts to open an old-time burlesque club in Las Vegas to be filmed. "*Forty Deuce* is something I know I can take anywhere," Kane said at one point during the show. "I can open another club in Vegas."

The drama in *Forty Deuce* came in watching Kane convince the owners of the Mandalay Bay hotel in Las Vegas to let him open the club and then the actual opening. Kane struggled with trying to get his top dancers on time to the new club, one of which is a beautiful woman who likes to have fun. Surprise! She was out late the night before and fails to show. *Forty Deuce* was notable only because one of the producers was Zalman King, who is best known for steamy films and the Showtime series *Red Shoe Diaries*. Kane may have been able to make *Forty Deuce* work in Vegas, but it didn't work on television.

Subject matter for workplace shows has been as wide and varied as the reality genre itself. During the 2005 television season, the ABC Family Channel aired *Las Vegas Garden of Love*, a show set in one of Las Vegas's storied wedding chapels and built around the family that runs the chapel. Stephen Hopkins, one of the executive producers of *Las Vegas Garden of Love* said initial footage shot at the place was "extraordinary" and reminded him of great character dramas. "They didn't have to editorialize or be clever about this stuff," Hopkins said of his fellow producers. "Just the very footage they showed me was such an exciting dynamic different thing that I'd ever seen and something that's unique to Nevada, unique to America. There's nowhere in else in the world it exists."

Though it's not specifically classified as a reality show, HBO's ongoing series *Taxicab Confessions*, which has specially wired cabs driving around in major cities and capturing the antics of the passengers, is very much in the current vein of reality shows. There's no competition, but it clearly shows what its like to be a cab driver and how people will act when not aware they're being filmed. Those antics have included heartfelt conversations about troubled lives, sexual activities, and occasional nudity. Some of the activities are sparked by conversations with the drivers, too. "It's not hard at all," said driver Brenda Roman. "People generally talk to me. They get in and they say, 'Oh God, a female. They start talking right away."

In one episode of *Taxicab Confessions*, Roman carried a group of women who started singing and eventually bared their breasts. Roman sang along with them. "I don't care about their boobs," Roman said, "if they want to sing, sing."

Some of the fun of *Taxicab Confessions* comes at the end of the show when producers show the riders signing releases allowing them to use the footage. What happens is the cabdrivers drive around, encouraging the conversation. When it's over, they then reveal they've been filmed and ask participants to sign a release. "Have you heard about *Taxicab Confessions*?" Roman was seen asking a couple that just got intimate in her cab in one episode. "You're too hot to be a real taxicab driver," the woman says. "Oh f—, I'm in my underwear." And, apparently, because the clip did air, the woman must have agreed to sign the release.

Cable's SoapNet has aired a couple of versions *of I Wanna Be a Soap Star,* in which contestants battle for a shot at a 12-week run on a real daytime soap opera. "They experienced everything you would experience on a regular soap," said executive producer Eric Schotz.

UPN has had good success with *America's Next Top Model,* a reality show hosted by supermodel Tyra Banks that gives the winner a modeling contract, while exposing viewers to the business world of modeling. Contestants must compete in challenges such as posing for photos in a swimsuit; in the very first season, viewers saw them endure getting bikini waxes on camera.

Bravo's *Project Runway,* a competition series for budding fashion designers, and MTV's *8th & Ocean,* also fall into the workplace genre. *Project Runway* is a *Survivor*-like series designed to find a new designer. Each week the contestants go through challenges geared toward someone in the fashion business—and in the end, a winner gets a deal. The show *8th & Ocean* was a reality drama set in a Miami modeling agency, where viewers got a glimpse at life inside, as well as the lives of a group of incredibly attractive people living in a great place.

To that end, Bravo also tried the modeling genre in *Manhunt: The Search for America's Most Gorgeous Male Model,* a series that launched in October 2004 with Carmen Electra as host. The show started with 30 models, 10 of whom were dumped early in the first episode. In keeping with the *Survivor* theme, the remaining models were put through a sort of modeling boot camp. The show was roundly panned as cheesy, and for good reason. Early on, model and judge Bruce Hulse had all the men undress to their underwear so he could rate them. The men were asked to switch to Calvin Klein boxers and then were forced to jump out of an airplane and parachute to the ground with an instructor. After that trying moment, they had to pose for the camera. "Gimme seductive," Hulse shouted. "Your dog just died," he yelled at another.

The Travel Channel gave viewers a peek inside the world of travel attendants with *Flight Attendant Training,* which followed 40 students as they went through a six week program. During the show, viewers saw them go from serving drinks to running emergency evacuation drills.

Spike TV also dabbled in the sports business world with *Super Agent,* a series that tailed football star Shawn Cody, who played Donald Trump to a group of agent wannabes vying to represent him.

MTV took viewers inside the public relations world in *PoweR Girls*, a show that followed the happenings at a public relations firm in New York run by Lizzie Grubman, best known for backing her SUV over club-goers on Long Island's trendy Hamptons area one summer evening. "I'm looking forward to MTV viewers seeing the hard work and long hours it takes to run your own business," Grubman said in MTV's press release announcing the show. "It's difficult, but it's also a ton of fun and there's nothing I would rather do."

Viewers of the first episode of *PoweR Girls* saw Grubman drop a nasty item about Lindsay Lohan to a New York newspaper, and they saw her put down an employee's boyfriend, on camera, but behind the staffer's back. "PR is a tough business," Grubman said on air, "and life is not always glamorous behind the velvet ropes." At another point, Grubman told viewers: "We're in the ego business. All we do is kiss ass. We're professional ass kissers. We make everyone feel like they're the best."

Wayne Newton tried to show potential stars what being a Hollywood headliner was like on E! Entertainment's *The Entertainer*. Model Fabio led a group of hunky men through a contest to become a romance novel cover model for the Oxygen Network's *Mr. Romance*. NBC offered wannabe stunt workers a shot at becoming the *Next Action Star* in a series designed to find a new action actor. And billionaires Richard Branson and Mark Cuban each tried to host Trump-like shows in which they gave potential business leaders a shot at sharing their wisdom.

Music mogul Damon Dash served as a Trump-like character on BET's *Ultimate Hustler*, a show to find a new entrepreneur that aired in 2005. "People always try to pretend they're smarter than they are, tougher than they are, richer than they are, more of a hustler than they are," Dash said in the opening episode. "I'm going to break them down one by one."

And the Reverend Al Sharpton, a one-time presidential candidate, hosted *I Hate My Job*, a show for Spike TV, in which he oversaw a group of people ranging from a card dealer in Vegas to an animator who want to change jobs. Sharpton, like Trump, arrived in a black limousine to impart his wisdom, and he had an attractive life coach and cohost, Stephanie Raye. During *I Hate My Job*, contestants were put through a series of challenges such as finding new outfits without having any money, credit cards, or outside help. In the end, one of the players got his or her dream job. "I wanted to be the workingman's Trump," Sharpton said before the show launched. "Trump fires people, I hire people." Few people watched, however.

A&E and The Learning Channel each aired shows set in tattoo shops. TLC's *Miami Ink* followed a group of tattoo artists in a Miami shop and showed how they went about creating and applying their designs on the bodies of customers. In one episode, a man got a tattoo of his twin sons to honor his wife, who died in the World Trade Center. In another episode, a young woman had a star tattooed on her foot to honor a friend who died way too young.

Besides *The Restaurant,* cooking and working in kitchens has been the subject of several reality shows. The Food Network held an on-air competition to find a new show host. PBS had a show called *Cooking under Fire,* which was described as an intensive 12-week competition designed to find a first-rate chef. Bravo has a show called *Top Chef,* which, like the others, is geared to find a new cook. And Fox aired *Hell's Kitchen,* a reality show in which chef Gordon Ramsay shouts, pushes, and drives a group of contestants through a competition to find a new chef.

"I think what Fox managed to do was bring the dynamics and the real nitty-gritty crux of what it takes to run a restaurant," Ramsay told reporters in January 2005. "And it's not just the cooking. It's the detail in the dining room, the amount of work that goes into prepping that food, what it's like to lose money and buy ingredients and mishandle them, what it's like to have an air conditioning unit break down in the middle of service, what it's like to have customers waiting 25 minutes for their starters." Ramsay said *Hell's Kitchen* was a real-life drama. "It's just something that's incredibly natural," he said. "And it shows every aspect of the dynamics, and the failures, of what it's like in a real live restaurant."

Producers for The Learning Channel also tried to show viewers what it was like atop a real live bull on *Beyond the Bull,* a reality show following members of the Professional Bull Rider tour.

For those who couldn't make a go of their own business, TLC aired *Taking Care of Business,* a show with a team of professional business gurus who would go into a small, struggling business and give them a financial and sales makeover.

The Learning Channel also brought viewers into the world of hairstyling and real estate in Texas in a series called *Sheer Dallas,* which used a salon as a touchpoint to show a variety of characters from the area. "I believe one thing about *Sheer Dallas* is that it's something that's going to make you feel good," said Dee Simmons, who appeared on the show. "It's going to make you happy because you're looking into the lives—they're very real. These are true stories." Viewers didn't buy in, nor did critics, and the show lasted just one season.

The list of potential benefits of being on a successful workplace reality show is endless. A highly viewed program can cause viewers to buy a product or visit a store. Good attention can drive viewers to a restaurant or, say, a hair salon. And, being the subject of a successful reality show can have a significant effect on the sales of related merchandise.

The Teutels' Orange County Choppers company, the subject of *American Choppers* on Discovery, generates significant revenue from the sales of T-shirts and other company license items. And, a lot of those sales can be attributed to their appearance on the reality show, which has also boosted their draw at motorcycle trade shows.

Since *The Apprentice* launched on NBC, Trump's media and licensing career was reenergized. A game company re-released a 10-year-old board game, and Trump signed deals to sell everything from T-shirts to bottled water. And in one strange deal, Trump, an avid nondrinker, agreed to help market a brand of vodka, the profits of which were turned over to Mothers Against Drunk Driving.

But not everything involving a reality show can be positive. Acting badly on television can cause viewers to avoid a business. For example, based on what got on the screen, it would be understandable if viewers wanted to avoid Southwest Airlines. And why not? they saw passengers stranded or kicked off flights. They also saw overweight folks being forced to buy two seats or face not flying at all. As the Southwest folks were quick to point out, though, the company, highly ranked by passengers outside of the show, flies more than 65 million people a year. That means that what got on were just a few of the transactions. But that's the conundrum for business owners. Reality show producers are looking for drama. And in the business place, that drama often comes from customers who are unhappy with the service they've received. There is no inherent drama in happy customer who moves through the transaction with ease. But give a show producer a diner upset with his or her food at a restaurant, or a passenger bumped from a flight, and, well, let the cameras roll.

The other aspect, though, for anyone being on television is that stuff ultimately gets on the air they've forgotten about or was ignored at the time. "I'd be dishonest with you if I said I wish, of course, there were things that happened that I wish they didn't capture," chef Rocco DiSpirito, the focus of *The Restaurant* said. "I curse too much, for example. But any other day, I'm a good guy. I hope I get most of the decisions right in *The Restaurant*, and I hope that comes through by the sixth episode."

However, there's a lot that got on the show that DiSpirito might have preferred not hit the small screen. He was portrayed as being aloof to the troubles of the venue, such as a staff revolt. And in the second season, his battle with business partner Jeffrey Chodrow took center stage. Moreover, the last thing any restaurant owner wants to see hit television is his building's landlord discussing the possibility of rats going from the restaurant into the building. "I cringed when I saw that, yeah," DiSpirito said. "I didn't realize that was on TV, but it is a realistic part of what we face as restaurateurs in New York City."

To that end, what people in all reality shows find out is that things are said about them they may not know about until the show airs. In DiSpirito's case, staffers were badmouthing him and the way he ran the company. Antin, who faced a near revolt from his staffers, who were upset with his hard-driving ways, had a similar experience. "I don't love watching people bitch and rag on me," he told *Entertainment Weekly*. "It kind of makes me look a little more mean than I actually am. But you know what? I'm human and I have my moments. I hope I look like a nice guy, because I think I am."

Jesse James, the host of *Monster Garage*, agreed to a series of three biographical reality shows, built around his motorcycle business. A component of the third special was his relationship, marriage, and the eventual divorce from porn star Janine Lindemulder. As with many reality shows, some footage and information makes it on the air that James would have preferred never been seen. But, as he said, it was part of his life and crossed over with his work life, so it belonged on the show.

"It was painful to do the editing, to watch it 300 times, to go through a rough time in my life," he said of the show. "A lot of the stuff Janine was forthcoming about, I didn't know what she said. A few times, man, I said, 'Forget it, I gotta pull the plug on this.'" He didn't and the show did very well for him.

"We're like everybody else," said Paul Teutel Sr. "Other than us displaying it on a national network. The reason we're so popular is people identify with us, because their relationship [with their family] is basically the same. But they do it behind closed doors."

Some of the same dynamic played out on HBO, which aired *Family Bonds*, a reality series built around a family-run bail bonds business. At the heart of the series were the Evangelistas, Tom, Flo, their daughter, sons, and extended family. By day, they were a typical, though rough around the edges, family. By night, the male family members chased bail bond jumpers. Like any other reality program, the success or failure of the program hinged on the characters, rather than what they were doing. And with the Evangelistas, they had a bounty of drama and characters. The patriarch, a cigarette-smoking tough guy, led the pack. His wife, a chesty woman with flowing blonde hair and heavy makeup, bragged to friends of their sexual exploits while getting her nails done at the Classy Lady salon. "Tom came home at 3 o'clock in the morning," Flo Evangelista told her friends, "and we had sex four times before I got up at 7 o'clock." It was a family show at heart. At one point, Tom took his son Sal out for his first job in the bail bondsman business. Tom told the kid to stay safely behind him. "I don't need to bring you home with a bullet in your head to your mother," Tom said. "She's gonna be very upset."

When not chasing crooks, Evangelista talked about chasing them to school groups on career day and bragged about his sexual life to his pals. Evangelista said he agreed to do the show so he could promote his own business. He saw each half-hour show as a commercial for his bondsman business, giving him more promotional muscle than he could ever get from the usual phone book ads. And, in fact, every episode included a close up of his company sign, along with the phone number.

Evangelista hasn't been the only bail bondsman to go on television as the star of a reality show. Duane ("Dog") Chapman, a bail bondsman best known as the guy who tracked down murderer Andrew Luster in Mexico, starred in a show for A&E that followed him and his wife as they did their business. The show, like *Family Bonds*, drew a few million curious viewers each week, giving new exposure to a business that hadn't gotten much attention—certainly not in a positive light—on the small screen.

Another business sector considered along the same vein as bail bondsmen is car dealers, and they, too will get their day in the television soon. Cable's FX has developed a show built around a father-son team of used car dealers in the hardscrabble town of Bethlehem, Pennsylvania, for a series called *Or Best Offer*. "We wanted to do something in this world [of used car salesman], something that had meaning to it, something more than showing used car salesman selling cars," Eric Schrier, vice president of current programming and alternative series said when the show was in development. Producers searched the country for the right salesman to highlight, looking, again, for the right characters, the right talent for which to hang a show on. Find a boring salesman with a pocket protector and the show goes nowhere. Find a character, a real character, and anything can work. "These were the best characters we found," Schrier said.

"It's an interesting world," he said. "Car dealers have this rap for them, that they're pretty sleazy people. We wanted to delve deeper; it's something all people deal with." That said, without the 'character' of the stars, the business reality genre falls apart. "It isn't really centered on their dealing as car salesmen, as they trick people," Schrier said. "That's what I like to call the set dressing. It's what they are. It's how they bring food to the table. But this is how they're trying to make a life for themselves in this profession. It's more centered on the characters than the profession."

It's that kind of thinking that will keep reality show producers scrounging around for interesting characters in other workplace scenarios. The list of possible businesses to highlight is endless. *Or Best Offer* never made it to air in the end. Officials at FX passed on the final pilot. However, that wasn't the last anyone has heard of a reality show set around a car dealer. In early 2006, A&E aired *King of Cars,* a reality show following the staff of a real dealership in Nevada. "It's good TV, because there's always something going on," dealer Josh Towbin told the *Las Vegas Review-Journal.* Towbin, it turns out, is not a reality-show rookie. He first appeared on The Learning Channel four years earlier on *It's a Living.*

Bravo, which has been a reality haven in recent years, is also at the head of the pack when it comes to reality programs set in the workplace. The network had already shown viewers what life was like for the owners of show dogs in *Showdog Moms & Dads,* for the parents of kids in entertainment in *Showbiz Moms & Dads,* and for those who had kids who were good in sports.

In 2006, the network was set to air *Million Dollar Listing: Hollywood,* a six-episode series looking at the world of high-stakes real estate in California. "This series is representative of the type of programming that Bravo is committed to providing," said Lauren Zalaznick, president of Bravo. "It reveals the drama behind a the familiar world of real estate in the most affluent neighborhoods of Los Angeles, and delves into the lives of agents who will do just about anything to make the sale happen—focusing on these 'characters,' the sellers, the buyers, and their intertwining lives," Zalaznick said.

Also in 2006, the network was scheduled to air *Tabloid Wars,* a series set in the newsroom of the *New York Daily News.*

There may be no end to the workplace genre because every job, good or bad, is populated with interesting people, the kind of people reality show producers tend to seek out. The workplace, of course, is just the backdrop. It's the people, the cranky designers, the brave fishermen, that make or break a show.

CHAPTER 12

There Is a Life after Reality

Bob Guiney realized the true impact of being on a reality show about a year after he turned up in not one, but two versions of ABC's *The Bachelor*. Guiney hadn't intended to be a reality television star. He was selling mortgages when two of his assistants sent his name into the producers of *The Bachelor*. At the time, he had just gone through a divorce and struggled with an ailing knee.

The first time out, he was one of the bachelors vying for the attention of Trista Rehn on *The Bachelorette*. Though he was passed over, Guiney had developed a following among *Bachelorette* fans, so the producers made him the next *Bachelor*. After eight episodes he selected Estella Gardiner. They broke up two months later. Yet, just by being on the show, Guiney had been able to meet daytime star Rebecca Budig. They eventually married. It was after being married to Budig, and being invited to Oprah Winfrey's 50th birthday party, that the impact of being on the show really hit home. "I'm looking around all these people," Guiney recalled. "Stevie Wonder is playing 10 feet away from me and I'm sitting there dancing with Tom Hanks." He also realized that had he not been on *The Bachelor*, he never would have met his wife, nor would he have a budding television career. "Had it not been for that show…," he said. "Rebecca wasn't going to walk into my mortgage office."

Guiney is just one of hundreds of former reality show stars dealing with life after appearing on a hit show. Since *Survivor* hit big in 2000, reality show producers have been giving hundreds of supposedly regular people a shot at prime-time infamy every year. If there are at least 20 reality shows on a season, with roughly a dozen players each, that's potentially 240 new stars every year. Life for a lot of them will never ever be the same once the show stars airing. For some, adapting to regular life after the show ends can be extremely difficult. For others, the experience can be a springboard to a new career, a new life. And for others, it will be a highlight in their life; yet, they'll go back to doing exactly what they did before the show.

"There's a whole reality subculture," said Lisa Montgomery Kennedy, the former MTV veejay, who hosts Reality Central's *Reality Remix* show "A lot of them, after being on television, become infamous, they become like a character. They've been exposed. Their life has been on television. It's a strange thing for people to come up to you and recite details of the show. It gives them a sense of importance."

"And if you have people coming up to you on the streets, why do you want to go back to your home town and be a box cutter or a hairstylist?" she added. No doubt, coming back to regular life can be a traumatic experience for some. A lot of how people react to reality show stars after the show is over depends on how the people were portrayed on the show itself. Most reality show contestants claim they were inaccurately portrayed on air. They may have been made to look weak, or strong, or a loudmouth. Depending on how they were portrayed, though, may have something to do with what people say on the streets.

For example, viewers, and critics, were shocked at some of the stuff that came out of the mouths of a group of women appearing on Bravo's *The Real Housewives of Orange County*. The women lived in a gated community, and one admitted in the opening episode that 85 percent of them had breast implants. "It's kind of hard to wake up at 6:30 in the morning and do nothing," one of the women, Jo De La Rosa said in the first episode. But Jeana Keough, a former Playboy model, and one of the women on the show, said the show wasn't accurate. "We've collapsed their reality down from the 800 hours of footage that we shot," producer Scott Dunlop told the *Daily News*. "Do you end up type-casting them or do they type-cast themselves? I think a camera can draw the extremes of personalities out."

Victoria Fuller and her husband Jonathan Baker appeared on CBS's *Amazing Race*. They were the perfect reality show couple: she a former Playboy model and he a hard-driving husband. They fought each other and their competitors on the show. At one point, Fuller was pushed by her husband, which angered some viewers. "When the show was going, people were in a state of shock," Fuller said. "Because we were portrayed so negatively. We got a million e-mails on our Web site, hate mail. And then it started to turn. We walked a bunch of red carpets and people stopped writing."

Despite the negative fallout, being on the show, and sticking out in a large cast also helped. In fact, it's been the standouts, either those with the loudest mouths, the baddest attitudes, or the most outlandish behavior that have been able to extend their media life beyond a reality show experience. Fuller and Baker have landed radio gigs and were considered for a VH1 reality show in the wake of their *Amazing Race* experience. "Our relationship is closer," Fuller said. "We set goals and maintain them and achieve as much as possible. We're very passionate and we're looking to reach for the stars." Outside of Playboy, Fuller is an artist. "It was all worth it anyway, even if this didn't happen, Fuller continued. "I'm still pushing forward as a pop artist. We're still intact. It's all about having fun. I'm having the time of my life."

Omarosa Manigault-Stallworth, one of the characters to come out of the first *Apprentice,* has become a fixture on red carpet premieres and has dovetailed the *Apprentice* exposure into appearances on *Fear Factor, The Surreal Life,* and *Battle of the Network Reality Stars.*

Guiney, besides marrying a soap star, has worked several shows on a part-time basis and served as one of the hosts of *Battle of the Network Reality Stars* and appeared in a series of spots on daytime soaps for ABC.

Elisabeth Hasselbeck, before marrying football star Tim Hasselbeck, burst on the reality scene as Elisabeth Filarski—one of the final four contestants on CBS's *Survivor: The Australian Outback.* The perky blonde won the hearts of millions as the easygoing yet determined competitor on the show. When she left *Survivor* Hasselbeck landed a job as the host of the Style Network's shopping series *The Look for Less.* But in November 2003, Hasselbeck landed a cohosting job on *The View,* the daily talk show produced by Barbara Walters. Ironically, one of the people Hasselbeck beat out for the job was Rachel Campos, herself a reality show veteran, having appeared on MTV's *The Real World.* From that November day on, every morning Hasselbeck shared tales of her life, her thoughts, and of being a mother with Walters, Star Jones, Meredith Vieira, and Joy Behar. "It was important to us that we'd have somebody who would argue with us and talk about social issues," Walters said in announcing the hire.

Hasselbeck sticks out among *Survivor* contestants, though. After 12 seasons, most players return to their regular lives, or what's left of them, back home, where oftentimes they've been held up as local heroes in area newspapers and radio and television shows.

Speaking engagements, which can be extremely lucrative, can generate income and keep a reality-show contestant active for years to come. Rodger

Bingham, who appeared on *Survivor: The Australian Outback* and befriended Hasselbeck on the show, commands $3,500 a speech, according to the Premiere Speakers Bureau, which books his appearances. And Bingham is on the low side. Many of the top *Survivor* contestants are signed with speaker's agencies. Others can be found working appearances at shopping malls all over the country. Even *Survivor* producer Mark Burnett commands more than $50,000 per event.

The All American Talent & Celebrity Network speakers bureau has a list of reality stars on its roster, including *Bachelor* franchise stars Bob Guiney, Jen Schefft, and Alex Michel; *The Apprentice* players Heidi Bressler, Katrina Campins, and Jennifer Crisafulli; and stars of many other reality shows. Schefft, who failed to find true love on two editions of *The Bachelor,* said she has no plans to make much more of her exposure. "I have a normal life, I don't have plans to move to Los Angeles or New York," she said. "It's a life experience.... I can't believe I was lucky enough to do that and meet these people. I think for me it's been an exciting life experience."

If they want, though, many can milk the exposure on television for a while after the show ends. If a player finishes on top of the show, then there are usually some commercial endeavors available, should they want to be part of them. "I think the coolest thing that's in front of me is I'm the spokesperson for NutriSystem," said DeLisa Stiles after being crowned *The Swan.* "After that, I just have to see where life takes me. I'm not scared for the first time in my life. I've never pursued something risky. I don't need to have to have a fallback." Zora Andrich, who was selected by Evan Marriott at the end of the first *Joe Millionaire,* also landed a deal with NutriSystem. She also appeared on the cover of a book touting the NutriSystem weight-loss program.

The impact of being on a reality show can also pay off in terms of sales of products as well. Joey McIntyre, the former New Kids on the Block group member, admitted that it didn't hurt with his acting and music ambitions to have been on the top-rated *Dancing with the Stars.* McIntyre's dance partner, Ashly DelGrosso, a professional dancer, also hoped to benefit from the national attention. Ballroom dancing, she said, doesn't get much prime-time exposure. "This has been a once in a lifetime experience," she said. "I finally get to be on national television and do what I love."

Rob Mariano and Amber Brkich appeared on separate versions of *Survivor* and later on *Survivor: All-Stars,* where they fell in love. From there they got a television special about their wedding on CBS, and then starred in a version of *The Amazing Race.* Mariano and Brkich have built a career around their appearances on *Survivor.* Mariano joined CBS's *The Early Show* in early 2006 as a regular contributor with a segment called "Rob to the Rescue," a series in which he helps viewers deal with real-life problems. And Brkich wrote *Amber's Guide For Girls—Advice On Fame, Family, Fashion And More.*

What the participants do after a series ends also hinges on what kind of contract the show has with contestants. Most include a clause that locks the contestants to the network for a period of time after the show. And in some cases, the producers and the network have a hand in what the players do next. In virtually every case, the players can't do anything without the network's permission while the show is on the air.

With a show such as *American Idol,* the connection between the winner's career and the show is measured in years. The reason for the ties between the shows and the networks is to, in some ways, protect the network's investment in the contestant. No doubt, without the show, the one-time regular person wouldn't be a star. Likewise, the networks, more so in the beginning of the reality wave than now, wanted to protect their franchise by limiting player involvement with only approved products or appearances.

Melana Scantlin, who was the first female star to appear on *Average Joe,* told reporters in early 2004 that NBC had exercised a "talent hold option to where they have first right of refusal. So, they're pretty—I mean, they were so good to me." Scantlin, a former Miss Missouri, was able to parlay her exposure on *Average Joe* into a cohosting gig on the Game Show Network's *World Series of Blackjack.*

Long Island native Kimmi Kappenburg, who appeared on *Survivor: The Australian Outback* blamed the contestant contract she signed for keeping her from getting extra work after the show ended. "It ended up working to my disadvantage," Kappenburg said in a September 2003 press release from the New York Institute of Technology. "After *Survivor* aired my contract with CBS did not allow me to work for any competing network for 2 1/2 years. So when I was offered a job somewhere else, I couldn't take it without CBS's approval." Kappenburg said the limitations of the contract were not something she thought about when signing up for *Survivor* and the shot at $1 million.

That shot at $1 million and instant fame, like all television exposure, comes with some downside, too. There are Web sites dedicated to tracking the on-screen events of every show and the players. The folks behind thesmokinggun.com Web site also delve into the legal backgrounds of every player as well, oftentimes exposing hidden secrets of long past run-ins with the law or unsavory histories.

"Once people started knowing your life, if your privacy was never an issue for you, suddenly it becomes one," Kappenburg said. "I had people following me, people knowing my address, people knowing my phone number. People were presumptuous about different things. Every once and a while you get a crank call or somebody is standing outside your front door."

Wendy Pepper, one of the participants in the first season of *Project Runway*, parlayed that experience into appearances on Bravo's *Celebrity Poker Showdown* and *Battle of the Network Reality Stars*. But, she also admitted on another Bravo reality show, *Project Jay*, that the exposure cost her her marriage. She disclosed the break up in the show that followed *Project Runway* winner Jay McCarroll. "So poker and I...happy marriage. Which is good, because I don't have a marriage anymore," Pepper told McCarroll.

"Oh, really? What happened?" McCarroll said.

"Fame," Pepper responded.

Conversely, ABC aired a special edition of *Wife Swap* focusing on how being on the show actually helped marriages.

It also means, at least in the beginning of the fame cycle, a routine trip to the grocery store, something that happened without fanfare before the show, becomes a chore in itself. Before appearing on *Survivor: Pulau*, Stephenie LaGrossa was a pharmaceutical sales representative visiting doctors' offices in New Jersey. She stood out on that version because early on she was the last surviving member of her tribe. She finished fifth. Then, producer Mark Burnett liked her so much, she was invited back for *Survivor: Guatemala*, where she finished second.

Gone was the ability to go to the mall without trouble. "I can't and it's so weird," LaGrossa said. "I'm just a regular person, too. It's fun, it's so much fun. But sometimes you just want to get in and out of Target." She's wasn't complaining; just stating a fact about how life changed after the game. She also said one of the best things to come out of the *Survivor* experience was partnering with some friends for a beachwear company and signing with an agent for speaking engagements.

Jenna Lewis, the single mother of two who stood out on the first *Survivor*, turned that into experiences hosting on VH1 and had a small role on along with a couple of other Survivors on CBS's *Nash Bridges*. She also landed a small part on a UPN series called *Freedom*.

"It was an idea I had based on the popularity of the show," *Nash Bridges* executive producer Carlton Cuse said at the time. "Within the world of *Nash Bridges*, we can take advantage of the hype and 15 minutes of fame of the Survivors."

But that same level of fame can backfire, too. Shortly after Lewis married model Travis Wolfe, the two decided to film their sexual adventures in a Los Angeles hotel room. Somehow the tape got in the wrong hands, and it was being sold on the Internet. Lewis denied she and Wolfe did it on purpose to generate revenue. "The biggest fear is that somebody is now looking at them and you're like 'oh, my God.' And that's a sickening feeling," Lewis told ABC News' Chris Connelly. "I mean, I'm a mom. It's just so hard that now someday I'm going to have to look my daughters in the eye and try to explain this away," she added. "And then to hear people tell me that I did it really makes me a little bit angry."

First *Survivor* winner Richard Hatch battled with the IRS over income for years after the win, keeping him in the media eye.

Randi Coy, a Catholic schoolteacher in Arizona before agreeing to appear on *My Big Fat Obnoxious Fiancé* ended up losing her teaching job after her bosses thought the concept didn't mix with teaching.

Brooke Thompson also found out the hard way that appearing on a reality show isn't the best route for career success. Thompson appeared on VH1's series *Flavor of Love,* a dating show where a gaggle of seemingly desperate women attempted to land a relationship with wacky rapper Flavor Flav. Thompson appeared on the show as Pumkin, and ended up being the runner-up. Like any good reality show character, Thompson stood out among the rest for her actions, of which included spitting in the face of a rival. It was such a good performance, though, that when it was over she lost her job as a substitute teacher in the Bakersfield, California school district because officials there thought she might be a distraction. "She is a victim of her own celebrity," district spokesman John Teves told the Associated Press at the time.

The struggle really is for reality show contestants trying to survive in the entertainment world after being on an unscripted show. Generally speaking, reality show contestants aren't viewed in the same light as trained actors. They're seen by casting directors of entertainment shows as, well, a level below full-fledged actors. Yet many of those actually getting cast on reality programs tend to be budding actors, or people who have some desire to act down the road. Ironically, many of the contestants on reality shows are actually acting. Rather than being themselves, they're playing a part of a stereotypical reality show character they've seen before.

Therein lies the rub. Getting respect from the creative community has been difficult for many of those who have tried to break into acting after being on a reality show. Colleen Haskel from the first *Survivor* starred in Rob Schneider's 2001 film flop *The Animal* and hasn't done a thing since. Jerri Manthey, who was on *Survivor: Africa,* has had a few film parts since *Survivor* ended and has appeared on stage in Los Angeles. And, as a treat, the producers of *Blind Date* reaired an episode that featured a pre-*Survivor* Manthey.

Playboy has been a frequent stop for post reality show stars. Manthey was on the cover of the September 2001 issue. Fellow Survivors Jenna Moresca and Heidi Strobel have appeared in *Playboy,* as has *The Real World*'s Trishelle Canatella. *Who Wants to Marry a Multimillionaire*'s Darva Conger and *Joe Millionaire*'s Sara Kozar also took advantage of their fame to grace the pages of *Playboy*.

"When you make a mistake of that magnitude, you can't do anything but say, 'I made a mistake,' learn from it and move on," Conger told the Associated Press during a promo stop for the *Playboy* appearance. "I just wanted to be on television for 10 minutes. I never expected all of this would happen." Conger said she wouldn't have thought about appearing in *Playboy*, but she needed the money because she was fired from her job as a nurse after the *Multimillionaire* fiasco. "They made the offer when I had no other options open to me," she said. Conger also appeared in Fox's *Celebrity Boxing*.

Besides *Playboy* Canatella has appeared on *The Surreal Life* and on E!'s *Kill Reality*. "I really didn't know what I wanted to do when I came out to Los Angeles," Canatella told reporters while promoting *The Surreal Life*. "My major in college was broadcast journalism. I've always wanted to do sports broadcasting and get into hosting. And that's kind of the route I'm going in right now.... It wasn't like I'm going to go in here and I'm going to make a career or whatever of reality television."

Alison Irwin first broke into reality television as a much-loathed player on CBS's *Big Brother* before she landed a spot on *The Amazing Race*, where she was partnered with her boyfriend. "I went back to my old job," she told reporters in July 2004. "I had told them before I went on *Big Brother* that I wanted to go back to work for Abercrombie. They welcomed me back with a promotion, so that wasn't really a big deal for me. But other than that, nothing—nobody really came out of the woodwork and said, 'Oh, we want you do that, this or that, or anything like that. It's more like recognition, I think, from reality shows."

To others, just being on a reality show has been a downside. For instance, some participants on ABC's *Extreme Makeover* said they've had trouble adapting to life after getting massive physical overhauls because some of those around them can't deal with the changes. Fellow workers have been jealous, and spouses have had difficulty with their newly made-over partners.

As for Bob Guiney, often referred to as "Bachelor Bob" by show fans, he's thankful for the experience of being on a reality show. "Some people are famous just for being famous," he said. "I'm trying to do things that warrant attention. Ad the same time, it's not like I can do anything about it. There are times when I don't want to be Bob the 'Bachelor.'

"I used to run from it," Guiney explained. "I'd almost get mad when people would say, 'Hey, it's 'Bachelor Bob.' Now, I can't run from it. I'm thankful people know me at all."

CHAPTER 13

Real or Not, It Doesn't Matter

When *Survivor* hit the airwaves in the summer of 2000, part of the appeal was the notion that the people were real, regular folks from the street, and that everything that happened on screen were as it really happened before the cameras. These weren't actors. They were people. They were everyday people from all walks of life who were willing to do seemingly anything to win $1 million, even agreeing to be stranded on a small island without basic necessities.

In that first reality show outing most viewers were willing to ignore the facts that the people were on the island for 39 days and just an hour of footage aired every week, suggesting that lots more happened than was shown. "Real" would be seeing every hour, even the extremely boring ones the contestants spent on the island. And, viewers also overlooked the fact that the contestants, "castaways" as they were called on the show and by the media, were not alone but surrounded by camera crews, medical teams, and producers.

It was real, or so everyone thought. What viewers learned later on, and by 2006 seemed to accept just fine was that reality programming isn't real. In many cases, it's not even close. Such talk when *Survivor* launched would have been blasphemous. The notion that everything was real was largely driven by the media, which pumped up—and played into CBS's media campaign—the idea of real people struggling for food on an island. It was sexy. It sold papers and magazines. If only it was real.

Incidentally, it was *Survivor* that gave viewers their first notion that the reality was unreal. That's because a number of the players coming off the game mentioned what got on the air wasn't exactly who they were. Through editing characters were created or, more realistically, enhanced. A producer can't make a bitchy character out of someone who is sweet all of the time. But those cantankerous players who gave producers enough similar footage to piece together saw the editing booth results of reality.

And in reality, viewers should have realized it wasn't all real early on when *Survivor* producer Mark Burnett was the first to admit that *Survivor* was a contrived drama and referred to it as an "unscripted drama," rather than using the term "reality" for the genre. "This new type of television, which is not so really reality, it's more like an unscripted, nonacted drama," Burnett said on NBC's *Today* show. "I mean, that's what I do, at least. A reality show is more like *Cops,* I think."

Cops, of course, was one of the first programs built completely on footage of real people. The Fox staple follows police officers as they deal with every day crimes. *Survivor* was different, though. The crimes and scenarios are real; camera crews simply capture the moments. It's shot more like a documentary, with producers getting the action as it happens. The difference is that shows such as *Survivor, The Biggest Loser, American Candidate,* and *The Next Action Star* are built around people being put into various situations and cameras filming them.

As it turns out, Burnett was also part of the first reality show pseudoscandal when in 2001 it was revealed that Burnett staged or reenacted some scenes of *Survivor* so he would have better camera angles. For one scene, Burnett hired stand-in actors to duplicate a scene of contestants swimming across a river. The reason for the stand-ins was to reshoot a scene from overhead without capturing images of the ground-level film team used during the actual competition. "I'm not embarrassed about it," Burnett told a panel at the Museum of Television & Radio. He added that the footage "didn't change the outcome of the race."

The scenes were shot from high over head looking down at a group of people swimming. No faces were clearly visible, and if Burnett hadn't mentioned the reshoots, no one would have ever noticed or care. To that end, no one ever questioned the fact that the shots of alligators, bugs, and other critters that inhabit the areas where *Survivor* was set weren't actually in the same place as the contestants at the time.

What Burnett's admission did that May 2001 night, though, was change the way people viewed reality television in general, and specifically with the media. Until then, Burnett had always stressed that what happened on the show was real. Yet, apparently not all of it was. At the time, CBS issued a statement saying: "What Mark is talking about is nothing more than window dressing. It doesn't involve the contestants and doesn't in any way influence the outcome of any challenge, tribal council, or change the view of reality as it occurred. The series is exactly what it appears to be—16 people battling the elements and each other."

Likewise, first-season contestant Stacey Stillman sued Burnett and CBS, claiming Burnett met with two contestants during the filming to influence their decision and get her rather than Rudy Boesch voted off the show. "And I'm saying a product was sold to the American public as a reality show, in order to lure viewers in, in order to raise ad rates, and that what was sold to them as being pure reality was not pure reality," Stillman said on MSNBC after filing the suit. CBS and Burnett denied the charges, as did other contestants who were said to have been involved in the scheme.

"It was real as it could possibly be—for such an unreal situation of putting people on an island," Sean Kenniff, one of the original contestants told the *New York Daily News* at the time.

Dragged into the discussion over what was real in *Survivor* was the issue of whether it was a game show, which would require certain things to occur by law (specifically, producers not altering the outcome) or if it was an unscripted drama, not covered by those laws. Eventually, the flap died down, however, and the show moved on.

Nevertheless, the suit raised questions about what was "real" in reality. Yet, at the same time, it also opened up people to the realization that it wasn't real. "I remember the journalists were absolutely breathless in their outrage," said Professor Robert Thompson, who heads up Syracuse University's Center for Popular Television. "But consistently, when you talked to viewers, there was a sense, in many ways, that viewers understood the esthetics of reality TV long before the professionals."

Some of the problems, perhaps confusion, stemmed from the use of the term *reality* as a way to describe the new form of programming Burnett brought to viewers with *Survivor*. Television writers and network executives could easily describe sitcoms and dramas, but this new form of television had no clear-cut description. Despite repeated claims from Burnett that *Survivor* was unscripted drama rather than reality, the reality moniker stuck.

The not-so-real reality of reality programming actually began in the days of MTV's *The Real World*, the first reality show of note. For starters, the people were brought together to live in a specially wired apartment with camera crews living in another room. That wasn't real simply because those people were there for the show and not because they came together on their own. Also, despite the impression left by the show—an impression that continues to this day—the housemates are not confined to being together or even spending all their time in the house. They leave. Some go home from time to time during filming.

One of the staples of reality shows, the confessional segments, may be one of the most tweaked segments in all of reality. The segments are usually brief interviews with the contestants talking about some aspect of the show viewers either saw or will see unfold. Oftentimes, the segments appear too clean, too perfect. That's because producers will ask for reshoots it the speaking wasn't right the first time.

NBC's *The Apprentice* has a couple of scenarios in each episode that stretch the meaning of reality. Every episode ends with a scene of the "fired" player heading out of Trump Tower and into a waiting cab. Those cab shot are shot at the beginning of the season, long before anyone knows when they'll be kicked off the show. When players are summoned to the boardroom to meet star Donald Trump, they're only allowed to bring in one carry-on bag. After they're booted from the show they return for the rest of their belongings.

ABC's *Wife Swap* is built on the notion that the program unfolds over a two-week period. Filming, however, often is done in less time, a fact never reflected on-screen.

Moreover, as reality programming has become a launching pad for future actors—and out-of-work actors—then the idea that anything that happens on the screen is real is up for question. Many of them have had acting jobs before landing on the reality shows, yet they're described on-screen as being in some other business. Ytossie Patterson and Taheed Watson from Fox's first edition of *Temptation Island,* said afterward that producers knew they were actors, yet they were identified as an executive administrator and a production assistant, respectively. On Fox's *Joe Millionaire,* the bachelorettes were culled from acting and modeling agencies. Zora Andrich and Sarah Kozar, the final two bachelorettes who were vying for Evan Marriott's affection at the end of the show, had acted professionally, albeit on a small scale, before landing the reality show job. Neither, of course, was identified as an actress. Mandy Lauderdale, who appeared on the first *Temptation Island* in postshow interviews said she was an actress, yet appeared in *Road Trip* as an extra a year before *Temptation Island*. Lauderdale was described as a singer-waitress in Fox's bio.

And Andrea Langi, who appeared in two editions of NBC's *For Love or Money,* was in a film and an episode of *Law & Order: Special Victims Unit* before landing on the reality show. When she appeared on *For Love or Money*, Langi was billed as "party planner from New Jersey." "The reality of my life, is, yes, I am somewhat of a struggling actor," Langi said.

Being an actor actually comes in handy on reality shows when it comes to the contestants. After the first *Survivor* contestants realized they could launch acting careers on reality shows, so the genre became a haven for wannabe actors who might have had trouble going the traditional route. Beyond straight acting, the appearances also led to endorsement contracts and speaking engagements, oftentimes putting the players on a path of an entertainment career that may have not been considered before the show. Those cases were rare, though. Most players going on reality shows in this era are looking for something more than just a shot at a prize.

The influence of *Survivor* and MTV's *The Real World* much earlier on how much was real in reality was profound. Before either show, no one knew what to expect from the programs or the genre. But after once cycle of each, future contestants saw how to play the game or gain air time. Now, virtually every show has an outspoken female, who gets labeled a bitch. There's often an African-American player standing up for equality. Frequently, there's a gay player, modeled after Richard Hatch's brilliant performance in the first *Survivor*. Players now go into reality shows with agents, and knowing that the loudest, brashest contestant gets the most air time. Oftentimes they'll alter their performance on the shows just to gain air time.

"People that go to MTV talent searches are essentially going to try out for certain roles," said Thompson. "Everyone who comes on is absolutely savvy to how they work. You don't have to tell the obnoxious woman, or whatever, to be obnoxious, because she knows. They're completely aware of how it works and in most cases it doesn't matter."

To that end, really bad singers show up for *American Idol* auditions just so they can get air time, and, maybe, a shot at fame for being terrible.

Victoria Fuller, who with her husband Jonathan Baker appeared on CBS's *The Amazing Race*, said they went in knowing they would play the role of the villain. "We always thought we would be the team people loved to hate, but not really hate," Fuller said. "All of our favorite characters were villains— Richard Hatch, Omarosa, Johnny Fairplay," Fuller said. "Once everything is said and done, you don't remember what they've done, but you remember them."

Just having cameras on all the time can lead to a change in the way a person behaves. "With any reality show that's a real challenge," said Tony DiSanto, the producer of MTV's *Laguna Beach* and *Run's House*. "It's always a concern when you go into a reality show; are people going to put a wall up, is reality going to be altered? Yes, reality is altered. Our job as producers is to reduce the alteration of reality." In the first couple of days on any shoot, the alteration is dramatic, according to DiSanto. Over time some of that diminishes. But not always.

During the first edition of *The Simple Life,* a show that had rich girls Paris Hilton and Nicole Richie live with an Arkansas family, Hilton generated laughs when she asked the family what Wal-Mart was. The line played right into the fish-out-of-water aspect of the show the producers wanted. Hilton, however, admitted later she added some flavor to her ditzy blonde attitude because she was on a television show. "I'm doing a TV show," Hilton told reporters before the launch of *The Simple Life 2.* "Obviously I wouldn't act like that in real life. The things I do on the show, I know I'm being filmed. But I don't really mind [looking dumb or spoiled]. I know it's a funny show. It makes people laugh. That's all I care about. I'm just entertaining people." She and Richie also admitted they messed up on the jobs they were given on the farm to enhance the humor in the show. If they didn't, they said, the show would be boring.

"On reality shows you're made more of a persona, a personality," said Tara Scotti, who with her brother Charles, appeared on an episode of *Fear Factor.* Scotti said at one point a producer prodded her to be a little more competitive and aggressive toward other contestants. "I was loving everyone," she said. "The way they say it, is, 'So and so is talking smack about you' in a way to get you pissed off."

"Pissed off" can lead to controversy, and conflict, which anyone who has watched two minutes of a reality show know its part of the mix. "There are so many things you said, they edit it," she said. "They clip it in a way to make you look different than you are."

Editing, heavy editing, is also part of the process that drains some of the real out of reality. Many players complain about the editing of reality shows, though they know going in they're susceptible to what may happen in the editing bay with what they said along the way. A report in *Radar* magazine, citing five veteran production staffers of reality shows, said editors routinely clip together bits of dialog to have people saying something on air they never said. It's a process that's been dubbed "frankenbyting" by people in the business.

"I think on *The Bachelorette,* everything was real," said Bob Guiney, who appeared on *The Bachelorette* and later *The Bachelor.* "Those are exactly how I remember them. From *The Bachelor* I really wanted to have fun. They sort of edited, and packaged it, and I was a little bummed that there were some funny moments that ended up on the cutting room floor."

Guiney said during a rose ceremony on *The Bachelor*, in which he selected the women who would continue on in the show, he accidentally knocked the rose off the stem. So, when a woman walked up, rather than say, "Debby, will you take this rose?" he said, "Debby, will you take this stem?"

"They actually shot around it," Guiney recalled.

Victoria Fuller, who with her husband Jonathan Baker, made waves on *Amazing Race* when Baker shoved Fuller and seemed to dominate and berate his wife, said the show was edited so to only show the bad stuff between the couple. "I felt that, really, out of 500 hours, they only really use an hour of footage, six to eight, tops," Fuller said. "And they're taking the most sensational, most raw moments." In the end, Fuller said, "It's not really an accurate portrayal of your real self; it's you on a heightened level. In my real life I'm never running around with a back pack, or never washing my hair."

Having appeared on two editions of *The Bachelor*, Jen Schefft is well aware of how the show can be altered in the editing bays after the filming has stopped, yet she understands the process well enough to understand why and how it happens. "It's very realistic," she said. "They can't make people say something they didn't say. We were there for five weeks pretty much filming the show every single day, all day. You can't show everything that happens. You're just seeing the highlights. It's true, but it's condensed." Everyone has more sides to them, but not all of that makes it on the air, Schefft said, adding she didn't feel misrepresented during her run on *The Bachelor* and *The Bachelorette*.

Following her win on *The Swan* DeLisa Stiles felt her portrayal was fairly balanced with the exception of how her ex-husband was portrayed on the show. During the show viewers saw the moment when she was served divorce papers from him. "He's not so bad a guy," she said. "He has a lot of good qualities. But the show is so limited in its scope."

Beyond editing, the entire idea of reality or unscripted programming—especially in 2006—is up for debate. Hollywood writers have frequently challenged the notion that reality shows are unscripted. The hosts, they argue, don't just whip off their introductions and instructions without some writing help. Challenges, which are choreographed, tested, and directed, also have some written instructions. Others have suggested there were larger shooting scripts that outlined the show step by step. "We have to take all the little bits and give it a clear story arc, give it structure, out of what in reality might be a big mess. That, to me, is writing," Todd Sharp, a Hollywood writer who worked on several reality shows told the *New York Times*.

"In a show like *The Bachelor* there probably is a little more scripting than *Survivor* or *Amazing Race*," Guiney said.

Scripting in reality may actually be a misnomer. There are shooting scripts, which tell producers where to be and when, and all involved the genre admit some situations are staged for maximum drama. Producers will stick a contestant with a height fear on a top bunk or send them on an airplane ride to stir their emotions. They'll also pair unlikely partners in bunk situations, hoping the emotions will bubble up while the cameras are on.

"We create situations," *Survivor*'s Burnett told the *Hollywood Reporter* in May 2004. "This is clearly contrived situations creating genuine emotions. Because, were I to wait for 16 people to happen to be shipwrecked, I'd be waiting a long time to do a show."

Laguna Beach's DiSanto said that producers go in with a plan based on the events going on in the subject's lives, though that plan often changes along the way. For instance, on *Run's House*, which followed Run DMC's Rev. Run (Joseph Simmons), the producers knew Simmons's daughter was going to graduate from high school and that there would be a party, so an episode storyline, per se, was set up to plot an episode around that event. "They'd ask me what's going on, what we're going to do, and we'd say such and such, and that's how the show would get named," Simmons said.

Producers will frequently reshoot moments if they've missed the dialog or want the subjects to say something more clearly, or more directly, or to get a better angle. "There was a little bit, but it was only if they didn't catch it," said Elaine Bramhall, who appeared on ABC's *Wife Swap*.

"They really try to capture the essence of what you may have said before," Stiles said of her experience on *The Swan*. "They may say, 'In this interview we need to get this in a concise statement.' They try to take what you were feeling."

"None of the dialog is scripted," DiSanto said. "But just like any reality show, you may miss something. You may ask them to do it again."

On a larger scale, just like throwing a group of people together who might not normally be together just to film a show, producers tend to steer the situations for the best dramatic effect. On a show like *Survivor* or *The Amazing Race*, those situations come in challenges. On *The Real World*, those situations develop by having hot tubs and lots of alcohol available, which could lead to sexual shenanigans before the cameras. Likewise, *Real World* contestants usually have a job or a project to work on, which, of course, leads to the creation of tension for the cameras.

On a more exaggerated scale, sending Hilton Hotel heiress Hilton and her friend into the Midwest to live with a farm family creates an entirely con-trived situation for the benefit of the cameras. "It's not their lives," executive producer Jonathan Murray told reporters before the launch of *The Simple Life 2*. "But it's taking them as real people and throwing them into situations where they're out of their element.... And out of that comes humor."

Those are all scenarios that would be unlikely if the people were thrown together and left to their own devices, but for a reality show the situations are there to make good television. "When you're on *Survivor*, when you're on *Amazing Race*, they put you in situations where you're not yourself," Fuller said.

"They didn't direct us, but the certainly arranged for situations that they thought might lead the story where it would go," said Bramhall. In Bramhall's case, the most direct involvement came midway through the taping of her edition of *Wife Swap*. On the show, Bramhall, a highly organized married mother from New Jersey was sent to the home of a single mother with unruly kids and a messy house. Under the guidelines for *Wife Swap*, during the first half of the swap, the visiting wives are to live by the existing rules in the house. After that period, which is supposedly a week, the visiting wives create a new set of rules for the home, which are usually marked by dramatic changes that go totally against what the wife who lives there demands. In some episodes, where kids were denied television, the visiting wife equipped the home with televisions. In more than one, unhelpful husbands were called on to clean the house and handle some chores. In others, if the kids were not allowed junk food, the visiting wives ordered junk food for the second week of filming.

Early on in her stay at the new home, Bramhall had difficulty meshing with host family. So much so, when it came time to create new rules, she soft-pedaled them, figuring it would be better to ease them into new situations rather than make dramatic demands. However, dramatic demands are what make for good drama.

"They consult you for the rule changes," Bramhall said. "The production crew has to make arrangements, arranging for [the other woman's job].They also wanted me to come down much harder than I would have. I said, 'Let's see if we can make some improvements.' They said, 'no, no you've got to change all the rules.' What happened, I was not surprised. I said they're all going to walk out."

And, when it came time for the show to air, the rules Bramhall read were not the ones she originally conceived. Instead, they were juiced for her to create tension in the home. "I just didn't think it would be effective," she said. "If we went a little softer we could meet half way."

DiSanto said the involvement of the producers may redirect locations based on the ability of the producers to actually shoot the show. If, for instance, the group of young men and women on *Laguna Beach* say they're heading out for dinner and the restaurant they've chosen will not allow his camera crews in, he'll suggest they go to a different location where they can film.

How much altering happens, either through editing, reshoots, or adding elements after the fact has a lot to do with the program in question. By all accounts, lower-quality shows tend to have the most alterations. "I think it depends on the show," Murray, the producer of *The Real World* and *The Simple Life* told reporters. "In the case of *The Real World*, we had an episode about [housemate] Frankie [in 2004], who cuts herself.... That was played very straight and just as it happened. With Paris and Nicole, we might put a funny sound effect, we might have some fun with it. I think the audience doesn't have a problem because of the context of that show."

Ultimately, more than five years after *Survivor* opened the door for reality or unscripted programming to become a full-fledged staple of the prime-time landscape, and covering topics from hair salons to teens dating (the N network's *Best Friend's Date*), issues about what's real or not have fallen to the background. No longer does it matter if the shows are all real or not; rather it's whether they're good and entertaining. "This is not *CBS Reports*," Thompson said of the reality genre in general. "People are not watching it for the same sort of accuracy."

CHAPTER 14

The Gift That Keeps Giving

In the short time since reality programming has become an accepted, and embraced, form of television, it's undeniable it has had a dramatic impact on popular culture. The genre has made stars out of nobodies; given viewers a glimpse into a variety of worlds, ranging from life on a golf course (*Big Break*) to battling animal experts for a shot at hosting a show on Animal Planet (*King of the Jungle*) to life as very rich people (*Rich Girls* and *My Super Sweet 16*).

With the exception of a few prime-time dramas and comedies in the past decade, reality television has dominated the media and the office talk in recent years. No wonder, the medium has shown viewers parts of the world and people they never imagined seeing before. They've also heard things they never imagined. "I don't think I need to be rich, but I think it makes life a lot easier," Brittny Gastineau said in the first episode of E! Entertainment's *The Gastineau Girls*, about Brittny and her mother Lisa. And there were friends Ally Hilfiger (daughter of the fashion designer Tommy) and Jamie Gleicher, the teenage stars of MTV's *Rich Girls*. "We just prance around this damn city like it's, like, our shopping haven," Hilfiger said in the first episode. But she went on to add that, "Just because we're rich doesn't mean that we're not good people." Any viewer without a million bucks was immediately transported into the world of those who have money.

There have been plenty of moments like those as reality show producers use people and places to tell stories. And there have been more than enough people to populate those shows and provide moments of humor, sadness, fear, and zaniness, all in the name of entertainment. "I'm not even putting on underwear," said one of the contestants on *The Bachelor* in 2005 as she prepared for a date with Charlie O'Connell. Or there was the time on NBC's *Who Wants to Marry My Dad?*, a show where the three daughters of Marty Oakland searched through a handful of women for one good enough to marry their father. One of those contestants vying for Oakland's hand took a lie detector test in a bikini. Viewers have watched along as a group of Amish teens were introduced to mainstream life while living in Los Angeles on UPN's *Amish in the City*. And for a while FX brought the world *Todd TV*, a show in which a guy lived his life in front of the cameras, without knowing viewers at home had some input into what kinds of tasks he faced. The show failed, but it was yet another experiment along the way in the go-go years of reality television.

For all the silliness, and shocking moments like Verne Troyer urinating in front of the cameras on *The Surreal Life*, there are touching, even heartbreaking times, too. "My family, if I die today or tomorrow, they have nothing," boxer Najai Turpin said in an episode of Mark Burnett's *The Contender*. "But now, this give me the opportunity to go out there and give them something. Give them something to look forward to in life." Shortly after the show ended, Turpin killed himself, making the on-air statement, which aired after the suicide, one of those touching moments reality television has been able to deliver.

There have also been touching times on NBC's *Starting Over*, a show with direct roots to *The Real World*, but with a self-help twist. It's built around a group of women, each trying to fix some area of their lives, while also living together and being visited by councilors. There are plenty of tears, lots of smiles, and a few hugs. There have been similar moments on *Celebrity Fit Club* and *The Biggest Loser*, two weight loss shows where the end results are often positive for the players.

Sure, viewers know by now that some of the moments are manipulated or concocted by producers and tweaked in the editing bays. But that doesn't matter. What does matter is whether it's good television or not.

The jury of viewers has already ruled that the genre is here to stay. Just take a look at the ratings for shows such as *American Idol*, *Survivor*, or *Amazing Race*. Reality television is here to stay. The big question, though, is where does it go from here and what new arena can producers explore and exploit? As 2006 began, among the shows producers were seeking contestants for included a competition show on MTV for budding journalists to work at s The A&E Network was seeing couples were spending out of control to the point it hurt their relationships. The Oxygen network was searching for a couple to appear in a new show in which each partner's ex-lovers gave insight to the current partners. And TBS and NASH Entertainment were searching for feuding neighbors to appear in a show.

Will any of them work? That's the great unknown. Some really good ideas have failed, and others have never made it on the air. But midway through 2006, it's clear producers are willing to try just about anything, and anything touching on the human existence such as money, sex, and shelter.

What is clear is that people talk about reality shows in ways they rarely talk about prime-time scripted entertainment. If someone does something wacky on a sitcom, it's part of the show. If someone does something equally wacky on a reality series, it's the talk of offices around the country.

Reality has captured viewers in a way that no one could have expected when CBS launched *Survivor* or even when MTV started *The Real World* in 1992. As long as it does, expect the genre to continue. It's clear producers have just touched the surface with what they can do with reality programming. Someday, if producers keep pushing, a camera will go with a guy to the moon as easily as it'll go on a date in Paris. Throw in a little alcohol, a hot tub, and attractive people, and there's no doubt the viewers will follow along.

Further Reading

Benza, Jack. *So You Want to Be on Reality TV*. New York: Allworth Press, 2005.

Bianculli, David. *Dictionary of Teleliteracy*. New York: Continuum Publishing, 1996.

Burnett, Mark. *Jump In! Even If You Don't Know How to Swim*. New York: Ballantine Books, 2005.

Burnett, Mark. *Survivor II: The Official Companion Book to the CBS Television Show*. New York: TV Books, 2001.

Burnett, Mark, and Martin Dugard. *Survivor: The Ultimate Game, the Official Companion Book*. New York: TV Books, 2000.

Cowell, Simon. *I Don't Mean to Be Rude, But...* New York: Broadway Books, 2003.

Robinson, Matthew. *How to Get on Reality TV*. New York: Random House Reference, 2005.

Index

About the Author

RICHARD M. HUFF has been a working journalist and author at both trade and consumer publications for the past 22 years. He is currently the television editor and writer for the *New York Daily News*. His breaking news reports, celebrity interviews, and analytical features on the television business appear daily and are syndicated to newspapers around the country. He is also a journalism instructor at the New School in Manhattan, where he teachers courses on basic journalism and sports reporting.